The Correct Use of Colour Around the Home

A Collection of Classic Articles on Interior Design

By

Various Authors

Copyright © 2011 Read Books Ltd.
This book is copyright and may not be
reproduced or copied in any way without
the express permission of the publisher in writing

British Library Cataloguing-in-Publication Data
A catalogue record for this book is available from
the British Library

Contents

Elements of Interior Design and Decoration.
Sherrill Whiton..*Page* 1

Modern French Decoration.
Katharine Morrison Kahle...............................*Page* 24

How to Work Wonders with Your Home..........*Page* 35

Fashions in Furnishing - A Guide Post to Decorating.
Ruth W. Lee..*Page* 43

Creative Home Decorating. Hazel Kory Rockow and
Julius Rockow..*Page* 63

Popular Home Decoration.
Mary Davis Gillies..*Page* 111

How to be Your Own Decorator.
Helen Koues..*Page* 127

The Ross Crane Book of Home Furnishing and
Decoration. Ross Crane..*Page* 139

The Modern Painter and Decorator.
Arthur Seymour Jennings..*Page* 163

The Complete Home Decorator.
Catharine Klock..*Page* 177

Decoration for the Small Home.
Derek Patmore..*Page* 180

The Practical Painter and Decorator................*Page* 189

Furnishing Your Home. C. G. Tomrley............*Page* 212

Decorating Your Home.
Kay Peterson Parker..*Page* 224

Painting and Decorating - A Comprehensive Manual
for the Crasftsman. John P. Parry......................*Page* 230

Decorating for and with Antiques.
Ethel Hall Bjerkoe...*Page* 234

Home Decoration.
Dorothy Tuke Priestman.......................................*Page* 248

I Decorate My Home. Derek Patmore..............*Page* 263

Painting and Decorating. A. E. Hurst.................*Page* 273

Practical Home Making.
D. D. Cottington Taylor..*Page* 295

Decorating for You. Florence B. Terhune.........*Page* 309

COLOR AND COLOR SCHEMES

The source of color. Science has proved that all color comes from rays of light. The white rays of sunlight may be separated as they are in the rainbow or mechanically subdivided by a prismatic lens giving a colored band called a spectrum. (The dominant *spectral colors* in the rainbow are usually called violet, indigo, blue, green, yellow, orange, and red; but there are many intermediate hues.) Conversely, a combination of all spectral colors produces white. This does not hold true for paint colors; when paint colors corresponding to the spectral colors are mixed, the result is a dark gray.

Each material in nature has the capacity of absorbing one or more of the subdivisions of a ray of white light. The rays that are not absorbed are reflected to the human eye, and the object then is said to be the color of the nonabsorbed rays. A leaf, for example, absorbs the red rays and reflects only the blue and yellow rays, making it appear green. An exception is seen in the chemical compounds known as *white lead,* zinc white, and titanium, which absorb no rays and therefore reflect all the rays of light causing them to appear white to the human eye. Carbon or soot from a wick flame absorbs all the rays and therefore appears black. If in a dark room, a red light is thrown on a green leaf, the leaf will absorb the red light. Since there are no blue or yellow rays thrown upon it, the leaf will reflect no rays but will appear black, even though the surrounding areas may appear red. If a white light is thrown on the leaf it will appear green, reflecting the blue and yellow rays contained in the light.

Rays coming from artificial light have the same general characteristics as those coming from the sun, except that they are but an infinitesimal fraction of the sun's rays in strength.

The sun's rays have other characteristics besides those of color. The most important of these are the heat-rays, which increase toward the red end of the spectrum. Fortunately, the atmosphere absorbs and tempers many of these rays; otherwise, habitation on the earth would be unbearable. The sun's rays are hottest when the atmosphere is of least depth. Since the sun is directly above us in summer, its rays then reach us through the shortest distance of atmospheric depth; but in winter the sun is at a low angle, and its rays penetrate a greater atmospheric depth, giving us a lower temperature. Red and yellow light rays are stimulating and promote life and growth in nature. The sun's rays also contain an actinic property that causes chemical changes. The blue, violet, and green rays affect the photographic plate, cause skin to tan and textiles and paint to fade. They are the destructive rays of sunlight, preventing growth and causing disintegration. The peculiar distribution of these rays explains the apparent inconsistencies in the values and effects of various colors in the photograph. A shade of yellow or red will photograph much darker in appearance than a blue of similar strength. Other properties in light rays are brought to practical use in motion picture sound films, in the X ray, in electronics, and in the mechanics of radio activity.

The color problem in interior decoration. A knowledge of the original source of color is useful to the colorist in helping him realize the importance and influence of light upon any color scheme he may develop for a particular purpose.

The decorator produces his color scheme by using objects or surfaces in natural color, such as woodwork and marble; or materials, the colors of which have been selected by the manufacturer and are limited in range, such as in porcelains, textiles, and wallpapers; or surfaces that are to be colored by paint, stains, or dyes for which the decorator has an unlimited range of selection. The problem is to select colors to develop a harmony that will be pleasing in appearance and produce a desired psychological and emotional reaction upon those who observe it, and one that will be suitable for the purposes of the room and co-related to the amount and quality of the natural or artificial light that is available. Many attempts have been made to reduce the principles of color harmony to a formula by means of charts. These have been found to be of limited value to the decorator. Charts are not used by experienced artists, and their use by the beginner has the danger of preventing development of ability in color selection by methods of reasoning and visual reactions. Designers of textiles, wallpapers, and posters may sometimes use charts for preliminary tests of color combinations because in such designs colors are used in comparatively small areas and are visualized in the same light. The decorator has a more complicated problem, inasmuch as colors used in a room are on surfaces that stand at a variety of angles, vary in texture, and receive different degrees and character of light. There are too many considerations that a decorator has to meet to permit the use of a limited mechanical chart in the selection of a color scheme. Interior decorators must use a set of guiding principles that will enable them to accentuate the desired character of the room, and contribute to its functions and the psychological satisfaction of its occupants.

Color characteristics. Pigment colors have four characteristics. These are known as *hue, chroma, tonal value,* and *finish*. *Hue* refers to the color itself, such as red, blue, yellow, green, etc. The hue is the same whether it is a light or dark variation or a dull or brilliant one; pink is a red hue; lavender is a purple hue. Chroma or *chromatic value* refers to the relative degree of intensity, brilliancy, or saturation that exists in a color. A ripe tomato is a red hue of a brilliant chroma; the majority of flowers are in colors of brilliant chromatic values. A brilliant pigment may be dulled or neutralized until it becomes almost a gray by adding to it a pigment of the color that is directly opposite to it on a standard color wheel. If this is done in specific amounts, one obtains definite steps or degrees of neutralization of that color. The most neutral step is very close to a gray that has been slightly tinged by the original color, and it is possible to arrange a row of samples of any hue, each of which is slightly more or less brilliant in chroma than its adjoining one.* If a color sample chart of this type is made, showing stepped or graded examples of a hue between gray and its most brilliant state, the steps can be numbered or lettered in an arbitrary but consecutive manner for purposes of convenience, and the series shows the degrees of neutrality of that particular hue. The various pigment colors cannot all be divided in exactly the same number of chromatic values or degrees of neutrality because some are lighter than others. The most brilliant yellow is very light compared to the most brilliant blue or red, and the former neutralizes very rapidly so that the same number of steps of neutralization is not possible. *Tonal value,* sometimes merely called *tone* or *value,* is the relative degree of lightness between an *off-white* and an *off-black* of any hue. A pink is a light tonal value of red, an ivory is a light tonal value of yellow or orange, and a brown is a dark tonal value of orange. Light tonal values are often called *tints* and dark values are often called *shades*. Tonal values of any hue may be graded arbitrarily in relatively even steps between the extremes of white and black. *Finish* is a quality of pigment colors and refers to the presence or absence of a luster, gloss, sheen, glaze, or other light reflection of a surface. In the absence of a glossy surface, the finish is called *mat*. Metals such as gold and silver, silk textiles, enamel paints, and glazed ceramics reflect light rays, and the portion of the surface upon which the ray shines appears a different color from the portion that does not come directly within the reflection of the light ray.

* This is an arrangement resembling the notes of a piano scale, which are sounds that have been standardized for convenience. Intervening sounds exist, but cannot be played on a piano and are considered unnecessary for most types of music. The stringed instruments such as the violin can produce the so-called quarter tones.

The *complement* of any hue is the hue or combination of hues that is lacking in the original color to produce the complete range of colors in the spectrum. In a Color Wheel, complements are always shown in sectors directly opposite to each other. A simplified example is as follows:

Hue	Hue(s) forming complement	Complement
Red	Blue and yellow	Green
Orange	Blue	Blue
Yellow	Red and blue	Violet
Green	Red	Red
Blue	Red and yellow	Orange
Violet	Yellow	Yellow

Colors also have certain commonly accepted qualities, the origin of which may have a scientific basis, or may be due solely to mental association. Orange and its adjacent colors are known as *warm,* and their use in decoration contributes to the warmth, gaiety, and cheerfulness of a room. These colors may be used in rooms with northern exposures to give the effect of sunshine. Blue and its adjacent colors are *cool* and are supposed to be advantageous in counteracting excess warmth or sunshine, although this would seem to be only a psychological condition. Certain colors are called *distant* or *receding;* these are the light tonal values in general and the variations of greens, blues, and violets, colors that are recommended for small rooms to give the effect of larger space. Other colors are considered *near* or *approaching;* these include those of dark tonal values and particularly the derivations of red and orange. As green is the middle color of the spectrum, it is considered to have the most restful effect of any hue. This quality has caused its use in hospital rooms.

The term *subtle* is often used in describing a color; it is applied to grayed variations of mixed primary hues that sometimes appear to change color under different lighting or conditions. One is not always sure of their ingredients. The word, as applied to color, is in popular use, but has no scientific application.

The strong chromatic values of all hues are more exciting and fatiguing in their effect than those that are neutralized. A restful effect is obtained best by the use of grayed values on large plain areas and mild tonal contrasts in patterned surfaces. In general more satisfactory results in decoration are obtained by using mixed colors rather than the pure primary pigments: red, yellow, and blue.

Classification of colors. An infinite number of colors can be produced with pigments by combining red, blue, yellow, black, and white in varying proportions; but, there are, in practice, only 24 basic hues of full chromatic value with a sufficient variation to be perceptible to the eye. When hues are neutralized the adjoining colors often cannot be differentiated.

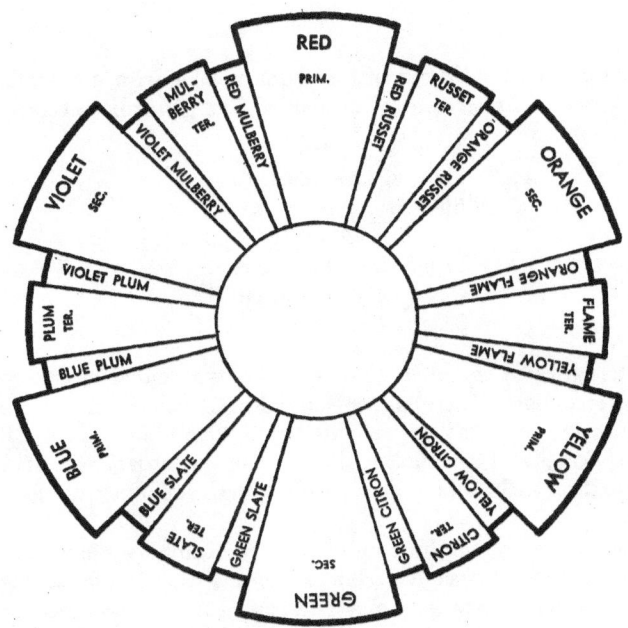

Color wheel showing the 24 basic colors in their proper relationship. Colors that are complementary are opposite each other. This arrangement is for the mixture of pigment colors only. Colors from light-rays vary in their complements from those shown above. The arrangement is for hues of full chroma or equal tonal value. Each hue is subject to an infinite number of neutralized gradations toward both white and black. The wide segments indicate the primaries and secondaries; the medium sized segments indicate the tertiaries and the smallest segments indicate the quaternaries.

Since each of the basic hues can be neutralized to at least 40 noticeable and different tints or shades, there are about 1,000 different and easily distinguishable colors available to the decorator.

The 24 basic hues may be divided into what are termed *primaries, secondaries, tertiaries,* and *quaternaries.* These divisions, indicated on the color wheel above, are as follows:

3 Primaries: Blue, red, and yellow.

3 Secondaries: A combination of any two primaries:

>Violet, a combination of blue and red
>Orange, a combination of red and yellow
>Green, a combination of yellow and blue

6 Tertiaries: A combination of a secondary color with any additional quantity of one of its constituent primaries. The generally accepted designations are:

> Plum or blue violet
> Mulberry or red violet
> Russet or red orange
> Flame or yellow orange
> Citron or yellow green
> Slate or blue green

12 Quaternaries: A combination of a tertiary with either its constituent primary or secondary. There are no standardized names for these intermediate hues and they vary only slightly from their adjoining hues. They may best be designated by coupling the name of the tertiary with its additional admixture, such as blue plum, violet plum, yellow citron, greenish citron, etc.

One may, in theory, continue indefinitely the combinations in varying proportions of these 24 basic hues, but the results would differ so slightly that for practical purposes they may be disregarded. It should be noted, however, that it is only possible to combine colors that are close to each other on the color wheel to produce another color of strong chromatic value. If opposite colors are combined, they neutralize each other and the result will approach a gray.

Other colors with which a decorator has to deal are the grays. These can be produced either by mixing the three primary pigments in approximately equal quantity, or by combining black and white in various amounts to produce different tonal values of gray. In mixing the three primaries with white, it will be found almost impossible to prevent one of the colors from dominating, and this is particularly noticeable in the lighter tints, so that each gray will differ slightly in hue. White is of course extensively used by decorators, but usually in an off-white tint. Pure white is rather glaring. White harmonizes with almost any combination of stronger hues. Black should be used with discretion. It is best employed in generally dark color schemes where its strongly contrasting value does not make it too striking. It can be used in small areas, such as trimmings, edgings, weltings, and ornaments, to accentuate the adjoining hues.

Discrepancies between theory and practice. The three pigments red, blue, and yellow, when combined in paint colors will produce a dark gray. Two of them mixed in approximately equal quantities will produce other definite colors (orange, green, or violet). But if the third is added, the original combination will become neutralized or approach a gray. This is what is termed neutralization by a complement, and each step toward gray is called a degree of neutrality of the color. Neutralization by means of a complement will tend to darken the tonal value so that it is almost always necessary to add some white if the same tonal value is required. This method of neutralization tends to maintain the chromatic strength of a color to a greater extent than by adding a gray or black pigment as described below. It is for this reason often preferred by artists. Since practically all house paints are pigments added to white lead as a base, this causes them to become tints, and, as a general rule, tints are used for the great majority of interior color schemes.

Pigment colors may also be neutralized by the addition of gray, black, or white. Black pigment should be used sparingly in neutralizing pigment colors, since it has the darkest chroma of all and tends to submerge the chromatic value of the other hues very rapidly. Some gray and black pigments contain a small amount of blue. When they are mixed with yellow they have a tendency to produce a greenish hue. To counteract this, a small amount of orange—the complement of blue—must be added to the mixture. When gray or black is mixed with red, the red will sometimes turn purplish. Yellow or orange must then be added. Browns, which are made most simply by mixing orange with black, may turn yellowish or reddish, depending upon which color dominates in the particular orange pigment used. A small amount of blue may be added to a brown mixture, but too much will cause the warmth of the brown to disappear.

Because the chemical constituents of pigments differ, the mixing of paint colors does not always work out in practice as the theory would indicate. There are, for instance, many different blue pigments, some having a slight tinge of green and others having a slight tinge of red. The mixture of these tinges with a second color would give a slightly different result. The only accurate method of obtaining desired hues by mixing different colored pigments is by trial and error and the correction of unwanted tinges by adding their complements.

As colors are increasingly neutralized they become more harmonious with each other, because they gradually approach the same color, i.e., white, black, or gray. The degree of neutralization in colors that are to be used in close proximity is a matter for the judgment of the artist, who must take into account the color effect he wishes to produce. He must avoid monotony, but introduce relief and variety only to a point where they do not begin to fatigue. *There is no more important point for the decorator to keep in mind in planning color schemes for rooms than the analysis of the degree of neutralization of the colors that he intends to use.* The combination of large areas of colors having strong chromatic values in interior color schemes invariably become offensive and tiresome.

Color terminology. The most confusing detail in the study and use of color is in finding a method for naming the hues and their variations of chroma and tone, by which one can intelligently convey in words a reasonably accurate idea of what color the speaker has in mind. The number of colors that can be produced by mixing pigments is unlimited and no complete standardization of names is possible, and one cannot carry an exact color in one's mind. The names of colors convey slightly different impressions to every one and even manufacturers' pigments using the similar designations vary greatly in hue.

There are several common systems for naming colors, but all are arbitrary, and, in spite of the fact that an infinite number of colors exists in nature, the colors used in commerce and art probably do not exceed several hundred. In addition to the popular systems of color designation, there have been several organized for standardizing names, and these, though not official, are practical and have been accepted by many of the largest business organizations in the United States. The popular systems are three in number and are as follows:

1. Using the names of the common hues such as red, blue, yellow, orange, green, purple, etc., and designating a dominant tinge if necessary (reddish or grayish purple) or associating an adjective or the word tint or shade. (Light tint of green, pale green, shade of dark bluish green, etc.)

2. Using a romantic name for sales purposes or popular appeal, by using the names of flowers, fruits, gems, and other natural objects, or using French names. (Plum, orange, rose, amber, emerald, cerise, beige, taupe, etc.)

3. Using the name of a painter's pigment. (Ultramarine, Sienna, Ochre, Vermilion, Van Dyck Brown, etc.) See Chapter XV on Paints and Painting.

There are two major commercial systems of color identification, the promoters of which publish color charts that organize the spectrum into a fixed number of hues, and show a reasonable number of the chromatic and tonal values of each. The systems are known by the names of their creators, Munsell and Ostwald. The color charts have become standardized and are extensively used throughout Europe and America. Instead of a name, there is an identification number or letter applied to each color, which if learned conveys reasonably well a mental image of each hue and its tone and chroma. These systems have nothing to do with methods of harmonizing colors, but are only for establishing specific color designations.

The most frequent romantic terms used by decorators for color designations are given below:

Absinthe	Amber gray	Apple green	Ashes of roses
Adam green	American beauty	Apricot	Aquamarine
Amber	Amethyst	Ash gray	Aubergine

Bay	Cucumber	Moss green	Rose pink
Beige	Delft blue	Mulberry	Rose pompadour
Blue	Dusty pink	Navy blue	Royal purple
Bottle green	Ecru	Nile green	Ruby
Brick red	Eggplant	Nutmeg	Russet
Brown	Eggshell	Ochre	Salmon
Buff	Fawn	Off-white	Sapphire
Burgundy	Flame	Olive green	Scarlet
Café-au-lait	Flesh pink	Oyster white	Shell pink
Canary	French gray	Parchment	Silver gray
Candy pink	Garnet	Pea soup	Sky blue
Celadon	Havana	Peach	Slate
Cerise	Heliotrope	Pearl gray	Smoke gray
Chartreuse	Henna	Periwinkle	Stone gray
Chestnut	Indigo	Pink	Tan
Chinese red	Jade green	Plum	Tangerine
Chocolate	Juniper	Pomegranate	Taupe
Citron	Lavender	Pompeian red	Tête-de-negre
Colonial blue	Lettuce	Powder blue	Tobacco
Colonial yellow	Lilac	Primrose	Turquoise
Copper	Lime	Pure gray	Verdigris
Coral	Maroon	Putty	Verdure
Cream	Mauve	Red-pepper	Violet
Crimson	Mimosa	Robin's-egg blue	Wedgwood blue

The Munsell system of color designation. The Munsell system is perhaps most practical for decorators' use and is described herewith:

The various hues of spectrum colors are arranged in a Color Wheel, each hue being indicated in its most brilliant chroma near the outside circumference of the wheel. The hues are then neutralized in graded steps toward the center of the wheel, until they all approach a neutral gray circle at the center. There are ten superimposed wheels, arranged according to 10 steps of tonal values, the darkest at the bottom (black), and the lightest at the top (white). Each wheel limits its colors to those of a single tonal value.

The regular editions of the *Munsell Book of Color** contain 40 hues, each showing tonal values from 2 to 8 with their corresponding chroma scales. These are not subdivided into primaries, secondaries, tertiaries, etc., as described in this text, so that it becomes necessary to make an arbitrary selection to correlate them with the triangular subdivision of red,

* Published by the Munsell Color Co., Baltimore, Md. Student charts are also available and will be found extremely useful for all students of decoration. In ordering ask for N.Y.S.I.D. Standard Charts of primaries, secondaries, and tertiaries. These are furnished with unmounted chips, but instructors should have a mounted set which the students may use as a model. Mounted sets are available, but are considerably more expensive.

blue, and yellow, and their combinations in creating a 12- or 24-hue colorwheel. To do this it is necessary to use the following Munsell hue designations to create the 12-hue wheel as shown in the frontispiece of this book.

Common color name (N.Y.S.I.D. Standard)	Munsell color number	Munsell hue name	Munsell initial indication
Red	5	Red	R
Russet	10	Red Yellow-Red	RY-R
Orange	15	Yellow Red	YR
Flame	20	Yellow-Red Yellow	Y-RY
Yellow	25	Yellow	Y
Citron	35	Green-Yellow	GY
Green	45	Green	G
Slate	60	Blue-Green Blue	B-GB
Blue	70	Blue Purple-Blue	BP-B
Plum	80	Purple-Blue Purple	P-BP
Violet	85	Purple	P
Mulberry	92.5	purplish Red-Purple	pR-P

Student charts are obtainable for each of the above hues. There are spaces for seven of the tonal values on each hue chart. Black is 1, off-black 2, off-white 9, and white 10, the intervening tones being numbered from 3 to 8 inclusive. The chromatic values are shown for each hue at each tonal value; the second chromatic value is an off-gray, and the brilliancy increases in even steps as far as available pigments will permit. The brilliant chroma colors are indicated by the high numbers 10, 12, 14, etc. The indication for each sample chip is marked in the manner of a fraction, such as 2/6, which indicates the 2nd tonal value and 6th chromatic value of a particular hue. The light tones are placed at the top of each chart, the dark tones at the bottom. The grayed chromas are placed at the left side in a vertical line and those of increasing brilliance toward the right.

There are many advantages in using an orderly system of color samples. Other colors can be easily recorded by comparing them to the chips. The graded chips are also useful in classifying colors under any illumination as light or dark, neutral or strong, or as light and neutral, dark and neutral, light and strong, dark and strong, etc. With these color samples as reference chips it is easy to visualize or describe color harmonies that are developed by applying certain rules in an orderly system of color identification and nomenclature.

Principles of color harmony. The methods used for selecting colors for room interiors differ from those that apply to other branches of art and industry. The painter and illustrator select colors that are to be used within a small area and their purpose is to delineate and accentuate subject matter. The advertising artist wishes to call attention to what he has to say and uses brilliant colors for this purpose. The industrial designer thinks of the suitability of his color selection for his product and its potency in sales appeal. The decorator, however, wishes to create a mood or atmosphere that is suitable for the use of a room. He deals mainly in backgrounds for human beings and his selections cannot be protruding elements in a decorative scheme. While certain hues must be used according to requirements and taste, the consideration of these is less important than the chromatic or tonal values that are to be decided upon. While the painter's colors cover a small area of canvas, the decorator's problem is complicated by the fact that he is confronted with a great number of surfaces that vary in size, texture, material, and lighting.

There are some persons who have a better "color sense" than others. They react emotionally to colors and are able by instinct to select agreeable color combinations for decorative use. Emotional judgments are often uncertain and it is always advisable to have a logical reason for any selection and to compare such a selection with established principles. Empirical formulas have been evolved for use in developing color schemes for rooms. Such formulas are not limited by exact boundaries and must be considered only as a general guide to a safe result, if not one that shows evidence of virtuosity.

In planning the color scheme for any room a preliminary consideration must be given as to its degree of vitality, or chromatic key. Whether the use and purpose of a room requires neutral or semibrilliant chromatic values, and whether its lighting requires a tonal key of light, medium, or dark values. Interest in a color composition is attainable by contrast and variety of color areas, hues, chromatic and tonal values, and the use or elimination of patterns. It is advisable to make a tentative plan as to what and where these contrasts are to be introduced. The unity of a color scheme is more easily attained by few colors. The use of one color only would produce a monotonous effect, and many colors create confusion. The artist therefore must make his decision as to how many colors may be used to create interest and variety and yet avoid chaos. There should always be a dominant color in a room. Two colors should not be used in equal areas. White, gray, and black may be used in small areas and need not be counted as extra colors in a scheme; their tendency is to give greater unity to divergent hues.

It is usual for planning purposes to subdivide a room into its component areas of color distribution as follows:

Dominant areas—Wall, floor, and ceiling.
Medium areas—Draperies, large upholstered furniture, bed covers, etc.

Small areas—Small upholstered furniture, chair seats, pillows, table covers.
Accents—Welting, fringes, small accessories, small pattern motifs in wallpapers and textiles, flowers.

The general rule that is applied in reference to the chromatic value of these areas is called the "Law of Chromatic Distribution." This is as follows: *The larger areas should be covered in the most neutralized colors of the scheme. As the areas reduce in size, the chromatic intensity may be proportionately increased.*

A color scheme is usually created by the treatment of the dominant and medium areas of a room. The smaller areas and accents are less important to the general effect of the scheme, although greater unity is attained by several repetitions of the same hue accents in various parts of the room. For example, a bright color used as welting for a sofa could be repeated in a wallpaper pattern or in a porcelain ornament.

There are various combinations that are possible in color schemes, as follows:

One hue scheme—One hue used throughout with contrast obtained by suitable variations in tone and chroma.

Neutral and one hue scheme—Where dominant and medium areas are gray or white and one contrasting hue is introduced in small and accent areas.

Analogous scheme—When a complete scheme is limited to any three adjoining hues on a 12-color wheel, and distributed according to the law of chromatic distribution.

Complementary scheme—Where complementary hues are used for the dominant and medium areas and are generally repeated in higher chromas in the smaller areas. In schemes of this type, practice has proved that the use of exact complements is less agreeable than the use of complements that are tinged with the same hue (i.e., in a red and green scheme, it is better to have both hues slightly tinged with either yellow or blue. A red-russet harmonizes more agreeably with a green-citron, or a red-mulberry with a green-slate).

The use of the color wheel. The frontispiece of this book shows a color wheel of 12 hues in a chromatic and tonal value that has proved to be average usage in colors for the background areas of a room. The hues have been identified by their common names and by their Munsell chart designation. All are 7th tonal value and 2nd chromatic value by Munsell standards. This means they are medium light colors and strongly neutralized. They may be conveniently used as wall colors for any room. By adding white to a paint matched to any of these colors, an 8th or 9th tonal value may be obtained. The 3rd, 5th, 7th, and 8th tonal values of gray are shown on the lower line of chips and a tonal identification may be made with any color sample by comparison with any of these chips. Rooms that are poorly lighted should have backgrounds in the 8th or 9th tonal value. No wall should be pure white. The 9th tonal value of any hue may be considered as an off-white. If a dark wall is desired for a room, it is inadvisable to use one that is no darker than the 5th tonal value as shown in the line of grays, and a semigloss finish is necessary. The 2nd chromatic value of any hue has been found to be the strongest that is suitable for large areas such as walls and ceilings. More brilliant chromas for such areas are too definite in hue to be agreeable. If the Munsell charts are available, it will be found that 4th and 6th chromatic values are the most brilliant that may be used for the secondary color areas of a room. Accents may of course be in the most brilliant chromatic values. Ceilings are usually painted in an off-white of the wall hue, although this tonal value is not essential. Plain floor coverings may be in 4th or 6th chromatic values, as dust and usage tend to neutralize them.

In addition to their use in selecting wall paint, the frontispiece colors and values may also be used in the selection of the backgrounds of wallpapers and textiles. For textiles intended for draperies, slightly brighter colors may be used than for wallpapers, as the shadows caused by folds tend to neutralize the colors of the fabric.

In mixing pigments for light tones, it is advisable to start with white paint and slowly add the colored pigments until the proper tone and chroma is obtained.

Symbolism and psychology of colors. Colors unquestionably have a psychological effect and produce certain thoughts or emotions. Whether this is due to some inborn element in the human mind or whether it has merely developed through long association is not known. Theatrical producers have studied the association of colors with emotional reactions to a greater extent than other artists, but decorators have, though to a less extent, used the generally accepted associated thoughts. Light, cool colors, such as turquoise, robin's-egg blue, lavender, and light foliage-greens suggest quiet, freshness, and repose. The light, warm colors, such as tan, cream, ivory, pale yellows, and apricot, suggest cheer. Pleasure and excitement are created by brightly lighted areas, and depression is aroused where visibility is low. Mystery and romance are stimulated by meagre illumination, and vulgarity by strong lights. The bright warm colors, such as orange and red, suggest excitement and exhilaration. The darker colors are more dignified, richer, and more vigorous in appearance. A room may be cheerful or gloomy, friendly or cold, according to its predominating hues, and a very definite "mood" may be produced by color treatment. Colors also have different appeals to persons of opposite sex. Men as a rule prefer darker tones than women.

The symbolism of certain colors is frequently called the "language of color," and a knowledge of the ideas associated with certain colors is useful to any decorator.

White—Purity, peace, faith, joy, cleanliness.
Red—Passion, anger, warmth, gaiety, martyrdom, revolution.
Blue—Restfulness, coolness, sky, constancy, truth.
Black—Darkness, despair, sorrow, mourning.
Green—Spring, hope, restfulness, coolness.
Yellow—Warmth, cheerfulness, fruitfulness, jealously.
Gray—Humility and penance.
Purple—Justice, royalty, depression, suffering, church color.
Gold—Royalty, luxury, power.
Pale blue—Male child.
Pink—Female child.

Effect of distance and area upon color. In considering a surface that is to be colored, it is necessary to consider the distance from which it is to be viewed, as a colored surface that is near by will appear more brilliant in tonal value than the same surface when placed further away. The neutralization of the more distant surface is due to the interposition of the atmosphere, and while this is of minor importance in a small room, it should be seriously considered in rooms of large size.

Colors appear stronger in their chromatic values when covering large areas than when used on small areas. This is an optical illusion, and if areas are visible at the same time and it is desired that they appear similar, it is wise to equalize the effect by painting the large area a slightly lighter tone of the same color.

Colors affected by adjoining colors. A scientific fact of importance in relation to color surfaces is that they are greatly affected by adjoining or surrounding colors, and appear to change in color and value when certain other colors are close to them. A test can be made by taking two small squares of red. Place one on a purple background and one on an orange background. In each case the red square will appear to be tinted with the omitted primary color. The red placed on the purple background will appear tinged with yellow. The red on the orange background will appear tinged with blue.

The value of colors is also greatly influenced by adjoining color values, and a color may be made to appear either light or dark by contrast. Adjoining contrasts of light and dark colors accentuate the tonal values of each. A white object placed against a colored background will cause the background to appear dark, and, conversely, a dark-colored object placed against a white background will accentuate the tonal values of both surfaces; the white will appear lighter and the dark object will appear darker.

To illustrate this point, the illustration on page 780 shows the divisions

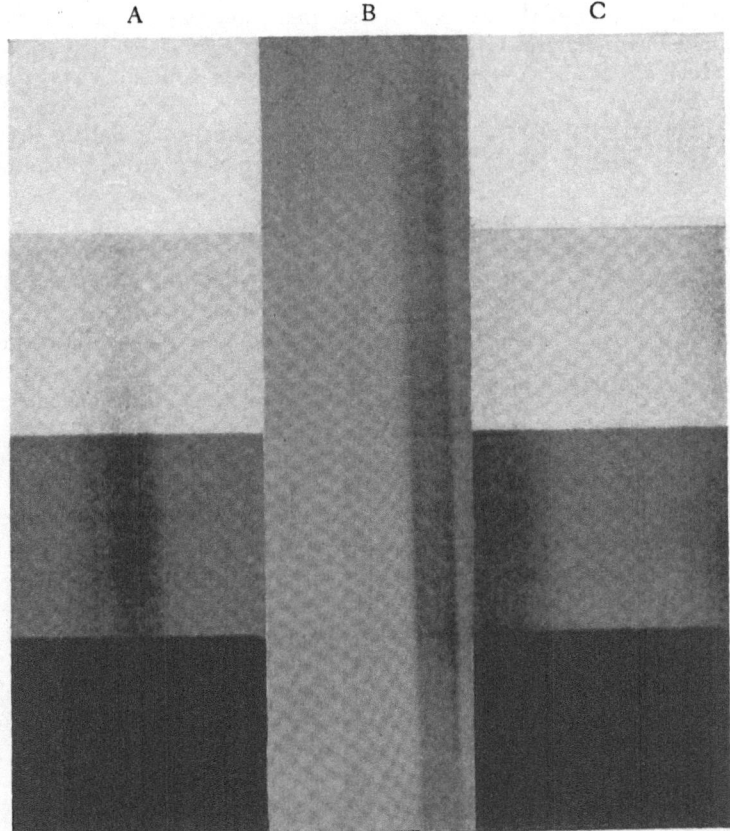

Diagram showing effect of adjoining tones or colors. Band B is actually the same color for its entire length, but it appears darker at the top in contrast to the light values of bands A and C. The dark values of A and C at the bottom of the bands cause B to appear light. The stepped gradations of A and C appear lighter where they adjoin the next darker step. Each step is actually a flat tone.

of gray tones. Bands A and C show a stepped series of flat tones in juxtaposition, light at the top and dark at the bottom. Band B appears to be graded in the reverse manner and looks dark at the top and light at the bottom. As a matter of fact, band B is a flat tone throughout its entire length, and if a sheet of paper is used to cover up the graded bands A and C, the even tone of band B will be seen. By this experiment it is obvious that colors may be made to appear either lighter or darker according to the tonal values of the colors adjoining them. These tests show the importance of working out complete color schemes for rooms in advance, so that samples of all the colors to be used in a room may be seen at the same time. They also illustrate the importance of analyzing the size of the intended areas to be covered and the influence of neighboring colors on one another.

The effect of natural light on colors. The quality of light is perhaps the first thing the trained decorator considers in planning the color scheme of any room—whether or not sunlight enters the room, and for what portion of the day it is there. In rooms that are particularly sunny, it is advisable to subdue the sunlight. Thus, in rooms with a southern exposure, it is the custom to use the cool colors. This will not only help soften the glare, but it will help give an agreeable effect in the heat of summer, when the sun actually becomes a problem. The decorator will then have an opportunity for variety in the use of the warmer colors in rooms or portions of the house that face north, thus bringing warmth and the effect of sunlight where it is most needed.

The next most important point in planning a color scheme is the consideration of the quantity of light which penetrates the room. The number, location, and size of the windows will have to be carefully studied, the kind of material that is to be used for draperies and sash curtains, and the area of the window that may be covered. Needless to say, darkening a room by partially or completely covering the source of light darkens the appearance of every color in that room, and often so neutralizes them, that a cheerful color scheme is turned into an uninteresting or gloomy effect. The quality of light in a room largely governs the choice of colors, but the tonal value of those colors will depend upon the amount of light penetration permitted by the curtain treatment, and upon the amount and character of the artificial light, if the room is for evening use.

These are very important features to consider, and they accentuate the importance of trying out color schemes in advance in the actual room where they are to be placed, and under conditions as similar as possible to those finally to be encountered. Many colors absorb so much light that it is impossible ever to have a bright room when they are used. An example of this may be found in a room panelled to the ceiling in dark oak. Both the material and the color reflect very little light; and while this may not be a disadvantage in some types of rooms, it may be a serious one in others. The decorator must consider in advance the amount of light he can afford to sacrifice in a drapery treatment in order to carry out the color effect he may be planning.

The effect of artificial light on colors. A treacherous element in interior decoration is artificial light, with its effect upon colors. The use of artificial light in theatrical productions is well known, and the remarkable changes upon a stage that can suddenly be made with a spotlight are common knowledge. Such changes may be pleasing or exceedingly disagreeable to the eye, and an understanding of the general theory of artificial light, particularly that of the common electric light, is necessary if the best results are to be obtained.

The ordinary electric light casts a warm light yellow or orange glow, but these colors may be altered by using slightly tinted or colored bulbs, and light of almost any color may be produced with modern electric illumination. It is impossible to describe the exact effect of different colored lights upon various colored surfaces, owing to the great number of hues that may be produced and the variability of the brilliance of the light. In general, however, the following results have been proved:

WALLS WITH RED AS A DOMINANT PIGMENT

Yellow light makes them appear red-orange.
Blue light makes them appear purple.
Red light makes them appear gray.

WALLS WITH BLUE AS A DOMINANT PIGMENT

Yellow light makes them appear green.
Blue light makes them appear gray.
Red light makes them appear purple.

WALLS WITH YELLOW AS A DOMINANT PIGMENT

Yellow light makes them appear gray.
Blue light makes them appear green.
Red light makes them appear orange.

WALLS WITH GREEN AS A DOMINANT PIGMENT

Yellow light makes them appear bluish green.
Blue light makes them appear yellowish green.
Red light makes them appear gray.

In general a light thrown on a wall of a similar color tends to neutralize the color, owing to the fact that all other colored objects in the room are given the same tint as the wall color, so that there is less contrast for the color of the wall, and it therefore appears to lose part of its tonal value.

The color of electric bulbs may be also influenced by the color of the shades or the shade linings.

If a room is intended for evening use to a greater extent than daytime use, a preliminary test should be made showing the effect of the intended artificial light upon the color scheme.

The effect of texture on colors. Rough textures, because of the great number of small shadows produced, make colors appear darker than do smooth surfaces. Very smooth textures that have a glaze or sheen reflect light and cause colors to appear lighter than would be the case with a dull finish. It is important to keep this point in mind in selecting colors for any large areas in a room. A pile carpet may give entirely different color values when seen from different directions, depending upon whether one looks into the pile or at the side of the pile. A wall may be painted a much darker tone, if a glazed finish is used. Dull-finished painted surfaces must always appear darker than glossy-finished ones.

Colors used in period rooms. Each of the historic periods of art has had its characteristic color scheme. In the periods of antiquity, this was in part due to the limited number of permanent pigments; but in the 16th century pigment chemistry began to be developed and in recent years there has been a great expansion of pigment production from a great variety of sources. During the Egyptian, Greek, Roman, and Gothic periods the most used colors were rather strong in primary and secondary hues; but with the Renaissance neutralization commenced. In Italy and in 17th-century France the colors used for walls and textiles were rather dark. In the tapestries of the late Renaissance a great many neutralized browns and greens were seen. Spanish Renaissance colors were usually brilliant primary and secondary hues, although those used by El Greco, the painter, were off-grays, and generally sombre tones. In 18th-century France, color schemes ran toward pale tints of neutralized colors for the large areas of woodwork and walls, while in textile patterns so-called pretty tints of the primary and secondary colors were extensively used. Patriotism dominated the Directoire period, and strong reds, whites, and blues were the rule. Under the influence of David in France, in the early years of the 19th century, considerable severity marked the use of color, and many of the color schemes show a dominance of off-grays and blacks. Some Empire textiles, however, show rather brilliantly colored backgrounds with pattern motifs in dull gold. Josephine had a more cultivated taste and undoubtedly influenced the colors for the interior of Malmaison which are in pale dull blues and grayed purples, medium dull browns, and flesh colors. The English colors of the 18th century are generally well neutralized and tend toward darker vaues than the French. The Wedgwood pottery colors are typical of these with neutralized blues, greens, browns, and black. The Adam colors are dull blue, pale yellowish green, light gray, lavender, and other tints that harmonized with the light satinwood and Angelica Kauffmann decorations. During the Victorian period—the so-called mauve decade—colors were often dark, such as eggplant, bottle-green, tobacco brown, and dull red and purple. American Colonial colors for woodwork show a great range of hues from light to dark and well neutralized. In provincial and peasant interiors colors were largely limited to textiles and painted decoration and were usually bright and gay. The general trend of all modern coloring for interiors is toward the use of very few colors, mainly in large areas of light, strongly neutralized tints.

But occasional dark backgrounds are used where there is ample illumination in the room. Brighter colors are used for small accents.

Color schemes from textiles and papers. The rather limited range of colors in which textiles and wallpapers are made limits somewhat the selection of color schemes. While this may appear to be a handicap, it is a great advantage to the beginner, inasmuch as it often limits the number of possible color schemes for a room, requiring the consideration of but a few, and so simplifying the selection.

After a color scheme for a particular room is abstractly formed in one's mind, and after the general character, scale, dimensions, and orientation have been taken into consideration, the textiles and wallpaper (if wallpaper is to be used) should first be decided upon. It is a hopeless task to approach the wholesaler of these materials without something definite in mind in the way of cost, quality, color, and pattern. Several samples should be selected and brought to the actual room in which they are to be used, and a final decision should then be made before any paint colors are chosen.

The reason for this is perfectly obvious. The colors in textiles and wallpapers are limited and fixed, while paint may be mixed by an experienced painter to any color desired. The error in reversing this process is obvious. If multicolored materials are used, it is customary to repeat some of the same colors in other portions of the room. If chintz curtains are to be employed, for instance, it is often advisable to select the most neutral tone in the chintz pattern as a paint color for the walls of the room, using possibly a slightly lighter or darker tone for the trim. Other colors may be used in either plain or striped materials for the upholstered pieces, while the floor covering may be an Oriental rug of similar tones or a plain rug of one of the drapery tones.

Developing a color scheme. The most practical method for working out a color scheme is to build it up from some existing textile, floor covering, wallpaper, picture, or other surface color, using the more neutral values for the large areas and properly proportioning the additional colors. This scheme is not possible in every case, and a decorator must arbitrarily develop in his own mind a composition that will be suitable, taking into consideration the size and purpose of the room, the amount of light, frequency of occupancy, and other conditions that have already been mentioned.

If Munsell charts are not available, small books of color samples are usually obtainable from paint stores, or one may purchase elaborate color sample books at artists' supply houses. A decorator may prepare a color scheme with water-color or tempera paints, mixing them with a white pigment to make them opaque. On page 785 is shown a sample chart for preparing a color scheme for a single room. The size of each color sample

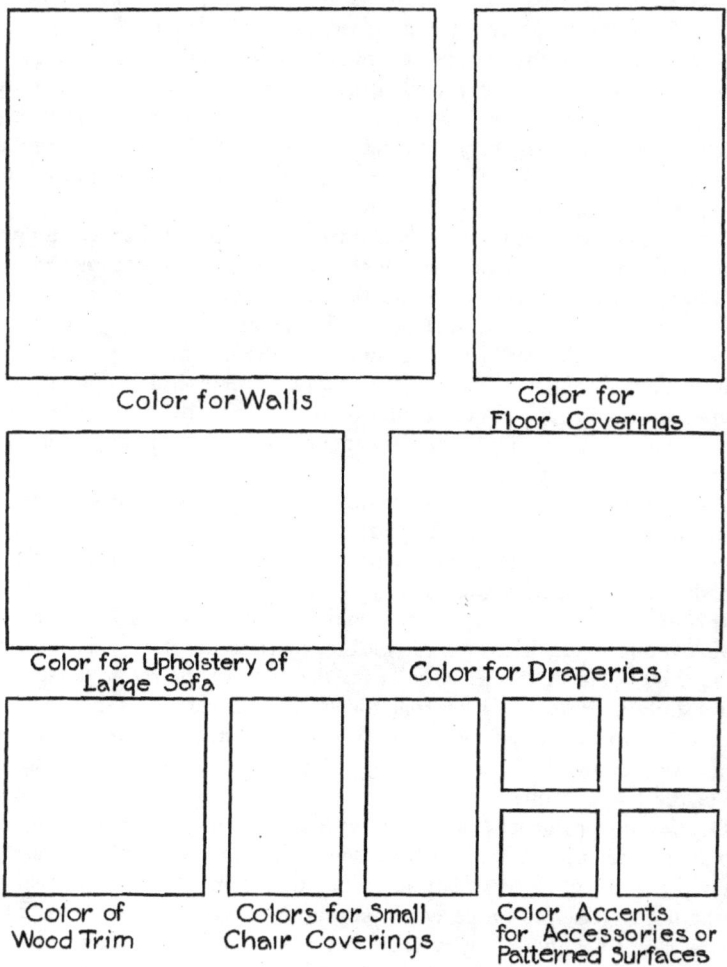

Sample chart for the presentation of a color scheme. The spaces should be filled in with paint or actual samples of textiles, wallpaper, etc., following general rules laid down for planning a color scheme for a particular room.

is proportioned to the relative area of color distribution in the average room. The walls and floor are indicated in the largest squares, with secondary areas and color accents in the smaller ones. This chart may be traced and used in its actual size, or it may preferably be doubled in size and drawn on a sheet of heavy paper. Sample color schemes may also be worked out with paint in combinations with actual textile and wallpaper swatches, if such are available.

Important points to remember. Any two hues may be used together if they are at the proper degree of neutralization. They should preferably contrast in tonal and chromatic value. The largest areas should be the most neutral, secondary areas of an intermediate chromatic value, and small areas and accents brightest.

It is preferable to have three steps in tonal value in one room. With light walls and dark floors, draperies and upholstery should be an intermediate value. With dark walls and an intermediate tonal value on floor, furnishings should be light, etc. With this principle, contrasts are orderly and maintain unity with variety and interest.

When bright and multicolored patterns form the basis for a color scheme, the bright colors may be repeated in the large areas (walls and floors) but in a neutralized value. Do not use over three hues for the large areas. The repetition of hues in various parts of the room aids the unity of the scheme.

In general, it is more simple to harmonize colors that approach each other, i.e., yellow-greens with yellow-reds, and blue-greens with blue-reds, etc.

Uninteresting color schemes are usually those of insufficient contrasts. Contrasts that are too strong are not restful. The colorist must decide the proper relationships.

Neutral colors are formal. Brighter values are more informal and gay. A neutralized color appears more neutral in a small area than it does in a large area.

If color contrast is lacking in a room, contrasts should be obtained by other methods, such as texture, line direction, line character, size and shape of furnishings, plain and patterned surfaces, and furniture and accessory interest, etc.

In working with house-painters' pigments, burnt sienna, burnt umber, raw sienna, and raw umber are good neutralizers for all colors. In the former two, the red-orange quality also acts as a warming agent for violets, grays, and whites.

Procedure and résumé. There is no procedure in planning the color scheme for a room that is applicable to all cases. A decorator must often start by considering some existing feature or piece of furnishing that cannot be changed and from which the balance of the scheme must be developed. He must also consider the general purpose of the room and the preferences of the owner. He must decide in advance whether the room is to be gay and young in character or dignified and mature. Other considerations must be the size of the room, the degree of formality, the frequency of use, the purpose of the room, and the amount and type of illumination. These points should influence him as to whether a warm or cool scheme is preferable, whether a light, medium, or dark tonal effect would be most suitable, and if and where patterns are to be used.

The general procedure would then be about as follows:

1. Consider the general color character to be expressed and decide tentatively which type of scheme is to be used.
2. Consider the amount of natural or artificial light to determine in general the tonal values of the main areas.
3. Distribute the tones or patterned surfaces in their respective locations. See that they are evenly balanced throughout the room, and that an orderly, but not excessive, contrast occurs between important color areas such as draperies and walls, upholstery and floor covering, and upholstery and walls.
4. Select the definite hue families and patterns for each area, starting with the largest and ending with the accents. Use the tertiary and quaternary hues for backgrounds if possible.
5. Make a final decision as to tonal and chromatic values for all surfaces. Walls and ceilings should seldom be stronger than a B chromatic value and may, at choice, range from 5th to the 8th tonal value in a light room and preferably a 9th tonal value in a room with little light.
6. Obtain samples of all colors and materials and examine them in their final lighting conditions. Visualize the areas in which they are to be used and keep in mind that colors covering large areas appear in stronger chromatic values than the same color in small samples.
7. Color accents should be distributed as far as possible in all parts of the room.
8. Dark colors reflect greater light if they are finished in a semigloss.
9. Keep all color schemes as simple as possible. Usually three different colors for the dominant and medium areas are sufficient.

Bibliography

BIREN, F., *Selling with Color*. 1945. An excellent analysis of the use of color in industry.

BOSSERT, H., *An Encyclopedia of Colour Decoration from the Earliest Times to the Middle of the XIXth Century*. V. Gollancz, Ltd., London, 1928. Colored illustrations with explanatory text.

BURRIS-MEYER, E., *Colour and Design in the Decorative Arts*. Prentice-Hall, Inc., New York, 1935. A thorough illustrated treatment of color and design in all fields of art and applied art.

BURRIS-MEYER, E., *Contemporary Color Guide*. Wilhelm Helburn, Inc., 1947. Sample color schemes.

CARPENTER, H. B., *Color: A Manual of Its Theory and Practice*. B. T. Batsford, Ltd., London, 1933. Excellent study of color with good color illustrations.

HOLMES, J. M., *Color in Interior Decoration*. The Architectural Press, London, 1931. A thorough treatment of color and its application in interiors.

Munsell Book of Color. Munsell Color Co., Baltimore, Maryland. Separate charts showing variations of each of forty hues of the Munsell color system.

COLOR IN MODERN FRENCH DECORATION

There is a tendency to associate jazzy colors and strong, harsh contrasts with the modernistic color schemes. This primitive trend of color combination is true of modern Austrian decoration but is not true of modern French. The French draw their greatest inspiration for modern color schemes from the Cubists, and together with forms initiated by Picasso and translated into concrete form by the architect-decorator we find the use of restrained color, closely related tones, and a contrast of value and intensity rather than hue. The French refer to these colors as "sad colors".

In these "sad" color schemes there is usually a quantity of brown of different values or different values of gray shading from silver gray to black. The use of these neutral colors is decidedly modern. A room in the neutral tones of beige, brown, and cream, oyster-white, gray and dull greens suggests a typical modern French color scheme. The subtle contrast of values forms the chief interest in such a color combination—gray against white, beige against brown and dark green against tones of light green. These combinations may lack the snap of stronger contrasts of complementary colors, but we do not tire of them so soon.

Kohlmann uses a combination of neutral tans and browns accented by burnt orange or relieved by pink and silver grays. However as he progresses his love for strong virile color seems to overcome his desire to follow the popular "sad colors" and one notes the added brilliance in his later interiors. Among these one sees such combinations as pinkish-tan walls, brown woodwork and carpet, with rug and upholstery of burnt-orange and dull red-violet. The furniture is a combination of gold laquer and walnut. There is a yellow vase in the room. Another room combines a bright blue wall with green drapes and upholstery, and tan and brown woodwork and rugs while still another scheme uses tans and browns with yellow-green, green-blue and silver. A warm color scheme by Kohlmann combines a dull and bright intensity of both cardinal red and red-violet with browns and tans, and, for accent, yellow and green books in a wall case.

A harmony of tan and salmon pink is characteristic of the interiors of Matet. One cannot refrain from calling to

...DIO. THE WALLS ARE PAINTED LEMON-YELLOW. THE STAIRWAY METAL CHROMIUM. THE TABLE IS PALISANDER AND NICKEL. BENCHES UPHOLSTERED IN BEIGE VELOUR WITH PALISANDER BASES. LINOLEUM YELLOW. CURTAINS YELLOW AND CITRON.

D. I. M., Decorators.

mind the color-prints of Utamaro and wondering how much direct inspiration for the modern trend of coloring may have come from them—salmon-pink and tans, silver, grays, and blacks in combination.

A chambre-studio by Louis Sognot has salmon-pink walls, a light brown carpet, furniture of palisander and a silver-gray door and gray upholstered divan. Two chairs are covered in light cream and a picture gives an accent of turquoise. A bedroom by Noémi Skolnik has salmon-pink walls, palisander woodwork and furniture, gray floor, and gray upholstery on bed and chairs. Yellow curtains, a yellow and salmon-pink rug and lavender tops to the book cases and window shelves complete the scheme.

Another room by Noémi Skolnik, a chamber for a young girl, combines tans, a light and dark value of pink, and a light gray-green. The end of the room has brilliant botanical paintings of flowers in red, yellow, and lavender.

R. Mallet-Stevens harmonizes yellow, tan, and gray, with accents of dull red and a bit of bright blue in books and vase.

The color of René Prou is always bright and refreshing. His Salon in a Palace in the 1928 Salon had a combination of blue-gray walls with green palm trees painted upon them and rose velour on light and dark brown furniture. In the 1929 Salon he showed a Salle Commune with light tan walls and brown furniture combined with dull brick red. In the windows are deep pink flowers in alternating blue and yellow pots and one chair is upholstered in a cretonne repeating these colors, another chair in blue, and still others in striped material repeating the same colors.

Leleu exhibited a dining-room in the 1929 Salon des Artistes Décorateurs which was Egyptian in its coloring of yellow-tan, red-brown and blue-green. The furniture was caucasian walnut and the chairs were covered in tapestry made from a design by Jean Beaumont.

.The interiors of Djo-bourgeois are decorated with fresh, cool greens and yellows usually relieved by neutral grays, but the pure bright color dominates the neutral and the result is gay rather than somber. One room by Djo-bourgeois has a chintz print of geometrical design in green and grays—one of the designs by Elise Djo-bourgeois which are used in all of the interiors by Djo-bourgeois—and the colors are repeated in the metal legs and green marble top of a large table. The furniture is built on simple straight lines and its constructive necessities are its only ornamentation.

COLOR IN MODERN FRENCH DECORATION

Pierre Chareau also uses very restrained color schemes in which one color is set off by the neutral tones of large wall spaces, rugs, and beautifully polished surfaces of simple woods.

Ruhlmann and Paul Follot are traditional in their use of color, and while they use a quantity of neutral gray and beige, it is always combined with soft and almost delicate blue, pink or green. They seldom use dark browns and even in furniture construction seem to favor the lighter woods with the darker wood used in lines of inlay.

Maurice Dufrène is the real colorist of the modern French school. He is not limited by one or two set schemes of coloring but can use the gamut of color combinations and play a new and unusual harmony with each scheme. One finds the frequent use of related schemes and one also notes the employment of black to set off and give added contrast to the other colors.

The walls of the private office of M. Dufrène are hung with water-colors of rooms designed by him and executed by Galeries Lafayette, and, waiting for my appointment with M. Dufrène, I had ample time to study them. I noticed a kitchen design in which the tile floor was deep blue, the walls red and the table yellow. A dining-room had a black and white tile floor, white walls and furniture, green chair seats and curtains and a gray marble fireplace. Another dining-room labelled "Neptune" was done in green, purple, blue, and a bit of dull pink.

Brilliant color and strong startling contrasts are used by the Martine School, but this school cannot be said to be part of the modern French trend of decoration. It is closer akin to the revival of brilliant peasant design and coloring, and its main beauty results from color rather than from the forms of its furniture or its dynamic architecture.

The materials of modern French decoration have to a great degree influenced the color schemes. Metal pipes, wrought iron and glass, all find dominant places in the construction of the modern interior and thus before the fabrics of decoration are introduced into a room there is already a quantity of neutral metallic tones. A polished aluminum staircase may give a dominant neutral tone to one room, while a wrought iron door grille would suggest the introduction of dull black in another room. The use of marble tops for tables and cabinets usually brings in neutral browns or grays although marble may be obtained in almost any color. Leath-

California Apartment of Templeton Crocker. Living-Room.

ers, cowhide and pigskin, and even exotic animal skins are used for upholstery, and while sometimes dyed, are favored most when retaining their natural colors. Chamois gives soft creams and yellow; and snake skins give tones of brown and tans. Porcelain also plays an important part in the modern interior and closely modulated tones of white often form the main note of a color scheme. White porcelain walls, white leather, white fur rugs, cream-white porcelain pottery upon glass shelves all offer subtle contrasts of tone and texture possible of conception and perhaps of appreciation by only the artist's eye. Another symphony in one color was seen in a room which had walls hung with walnut colored straw marquetry as a background for rolls of antique Chinese silk painted in browns. Dunand has decorated a dining-room in neutral brown tones. It is in the California apartment of Templeton Crocker. Rays of different toned gold laque arraché radiate on the walls. The ceiling in three levels is in a soft gold and the light from concealed sources is reflected from the various planes. The dining table and the service tables are of red-brown lacquer with crushed inlaid eggshell tops. The chairs are of the same lacquer, upholstered with brown grained leather.

The living room of this same apartment again shows the use of restrained coloring. Ivory and brown are the prevailing tints. The walls and ceiling are of parchment applied in squares, and the same material forms screens which cover the radiators and the outline of the piano. The low square built sofa and chairs are upholstered in deep ivory Morocco leather and the numerous small tables are covered with brown and white sharkskin, dark brown pressed straw, or parchment. The fireplace mantel is framed in gilt bronze and a large table is of the same bronze. Cabinets of dark brown straw appliqué hold the radio and phonograph. The curtains are of hand woven oyster-white silk. Many of the lamps in the room are of rock crystal with shades of mica. Ivory and metal are combined in other lamps. This room is by Jean Frank of Paris.

Another room which reminds one of the coloring of cubist painting is the breakfast room. The walls are of black lacquer with designs of tropical colored fish and silver rays of light. The ceiling is a canopy of glass, gray and white set in a silver frame above which are the lights. A pink and silver lacquered table has accompanying chairs of pink and silver metal tubes.

COLOR IN MODERN FRENCH DECORATION

The carpet is black and the curtains are of heavy salmon-pink silk.

Another tendency in Modern French color schemes is to prefer cool colors. There are two main cool colors—blue and green. These hues are closely related and the range of harmonies is rather simple. Most shades of green harmonize with each other and most shades of blue also harmonize. As cool colors suggest distance a room decorated in these colors has a feeling of spaciousness. Maurice Dufrène often uses a combination of blue and green. In the 1928 Salon a bedroom by Rapin had a blue and green scheme made dominant by wave effects frescoed on the walls. A quantity of fabrics, especially cretonnes, are designed which are a combination of blue and green tones, and one sees harmonies of various intensities of green with no other color but a bit of black. And again one recalls the influence of the Japanese—the colour prints of Hiroshige in this instance.

Color Harmony

Effects of Modified Colors

Because of their brightness and strength, the pure colors tend to be garish and strident. In large doses they would tire us out. This fact has led to the Law of Color Areas which states: *The purer the color, the smaller the area it should occupy. Conversely, the more a color is tinged, the larger the area it may occupy.* As a result, the pure colors find only restricted use as accents, while tints, shades and grayed colors find wide use in home decorating.

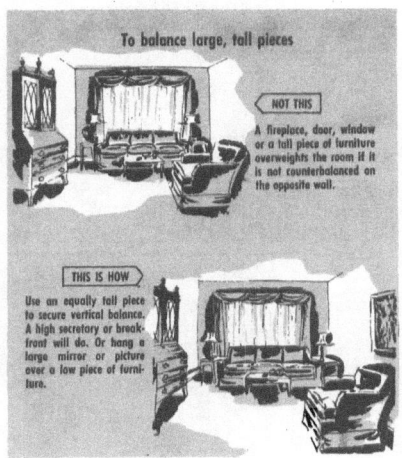

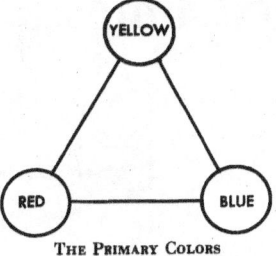

THE PRIMARY COLORS

Tints, we may note, have the psychological effect of femininity, airiness and grace. Along with white, they also tend to increase both apparent size and height, so that if you wished to create an effect of

not been tinged or modified in any way. Not every color, however, that goes by the name of any one of the twelve normal colors bears more than a vague family resemblance to its prototype. Thus, blues differ widely among themselves, as do reds, greens, violets and all the other colors. These differences are due to modifications of the normal colors resulting from tingeing.

One type of modification alters the degree of *lightness* or *darkness* of a color. Through the addition of varying amounts of white (or of water to our paints), we may lighten a normal color and produce different *tints*. Similarly, through the addition of varying amounts of black (or of pigment to our paints), we may darken a normal color and produce different *shades*.

Besides altering the value of a color, we may produce modifications in its *strength* or *brightness*. This we do by adding progressively larger amounts of gray to a hue until the hue loses its intensity and becomes neutralized altogether—that is, becomes indistinguishable from gray.

Intensity is thus the comparative strength or weakness, brightness or grayness of a color, depending upon the amount of gray it contains. The smaller the amount of gray in a color, the higher is its intensity, and vice versa. Colors which have been grayed are referred to as *muted* colors.

Color Harmony

Have you ever admired the beauty of the sky, with its myriad soft colors blending magically into one another? There are few wonders in this world which can equal the miracle of color.

Words cannot do justice to color. If you want to know color, it is absolutely necessary to experience it. Look at colorful paintings which delight you. Notice the colors the artist employed and how deftly they blend with one another. Do the same with pieces of fabric, with colored pottery, with Nature. Our world teems with color. To develop your color sense, you must revel in color and steep yourself in its lore.

The Color Circuit

We can build up the universe of color by starting with three *primary* hues—red, yellow and blue—as our fundamental blocks. (See *Diagram* on page 12.)

When we combine pigments of the three primary colors, we obtain gray—a neutral color. If, however, we mix two primary colors together at a time, we obtain the three *secondary* colors, green, violet and orange, as follows:

Yellow + blue = green
Blue + red = violet (or purple)
Red + yellow = orange

The six colors we now have form the *standard* colors. Arranged as in *Diagram* on page 13, each secondary color falls between the two primary colors from which it is formed.

By mixing any two neighboring colors of *Diagram 1* together, we derive the six *intermediate* colors:

Yellow + green = yellow-green
Blue + green = blue-green
Blue + violet = blue-violet
Red + violet = red-violet
Red + orange = red-orange
Yellow + orange = yellow-orange

From our three primary colors we have now built up the twelve *normal* colors. These colors provide the basis of color schemes for our homes. For reference, let us arrange these twelve hues in the form of a color wheel. (See *Diagram* on page 13.)

Modifying Colors

As the normal colors appear on a color wheel, they are at their brightest, purest and strongest. They have

Color Harmony

spaciousness or raise the apparent height of a ceiling, you would choose a tint.

Shades, on the other hand, exercise the opposite effect. They are masculine in feeling and, hence, well suited to use in a boy's bedroom or, perhaps, in a study. Like black, they give the impression of smaller size and lower height.

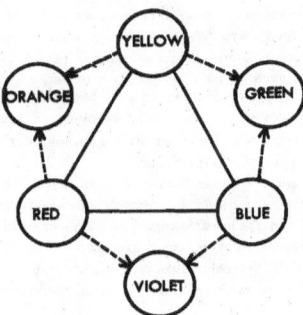

THE STANDARD COLORS

Graying a color, finally, has the effect of increasing its subtlety and interest and making it more pleasant to live with.

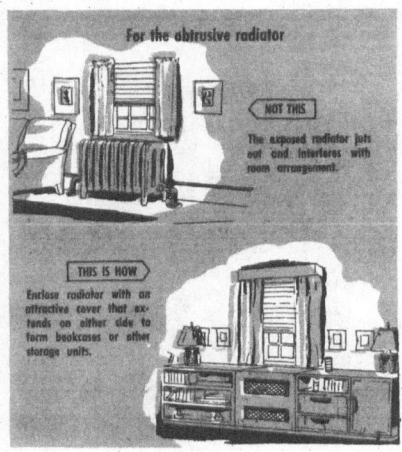

In practice, of course, you are not called upon to determine the precise degree of variation in value and in intensity of colors. As a home decorator, you simply designate or pick out colors which already are modified. But in appraising a color scheme, a sample of fabric, a wallpaper or in designating paint colors for a wall, you will assure more pleasing results if you can answer the question, "Will this color gain in effectiveness if it is tinted or shaded or if its grayness is increasd or reduced?"

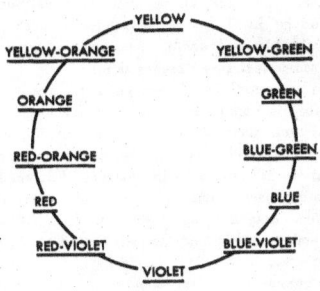

THE COLOR CIRCUIT

Color Harmony

Color Schemes

If we want our homes to share in the beauty of color, we must select an attractive color scheme that will achieve our decorative effect. The chart, *Colors for Your Purpose*, on page 17, offers you clues as to the types of colors you may select to procure different decorative effects.

Color schemes themselves we may select in either one of two ways. We may choose a color combination that we admire and that already exists, awaiting our use, such as we may find in a flower, a painting, a colorful piece of china or in a piece of fabric. Or we may devise our own color harmony on the basis of the color wheel and an understanding of the different types of color schemes.

The color schemes which we can devise through the color wheel are, in general, of two types, the *related* and the *contrasting*. The monochromatic and the adjacent color schemes are both of the related type, while the complementary, split complementary and the triad color schemes belong to the contrasting type.

A *monochromatic* scheme is based on the use of one underlying color. Variations in this color are obtained through the resourceful use of blending and contrasting values and intensities and, very often, through the use of one or more neutral colors. While the use of one main color assures unity, the possibility of lack of variety requires skillful handling.

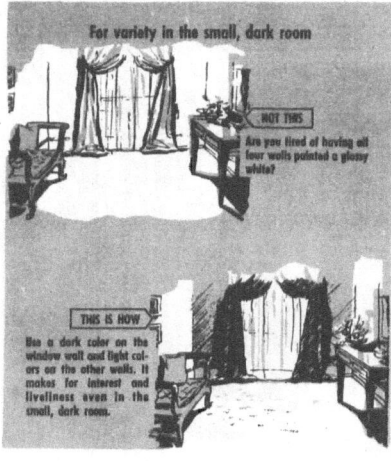

The Neutral Colors

Neutral colors such as white, gray and black are widely used in the home. White, which includes cream, ivory, oyster and off-white, embodies a feeling of delicacy and quiet and, like the tints, increases apparent size and height.

Black is often used in smart, sophisticated interiors. It has an air of modernity and richness and, like white, provides an excellent contrasting field for other colors. Like shades, black reduces apparent size and height. Today black lacquer is much used, often with bleached woods, in modern rooms as well as in rooms featuring Regency decor.

Gray is neutral in its expression, the reason perhaps for its popularity as a color for large background areas such as walls and floor covering. Gray goes well with other colors, neutralizing and toning them down as well as keying together different hues of a color scheme. The one precaution to observe in selecting a gray is to avoid the dull, drab battleship grays and choose instead the warm toned grays, such as rose gray.

The browns are shades of orange of low intensity. Along with tan, beige, taupe, silver, gold, mahogany and walnut, the browns, however, are usually thought of as neutral.

R_x for Smartness...

A decorating prescription
may well read...for smartness,
take walls, windows, floor and treat
in a contemporary manner...select
attractive period pieces of furniture...
arrange in handsome groupings...Thus,
do your background in tones of one
fashionable color or vary the color
progressively from floor to ceiling...
add interesting textures in your draperies,
carpeting, upholstery, a fine finish
in your furniture woods...your
period pieces then take on fresh,
new, smart beauty!

(Above) A simple, almost ascetic fireplace in a plastic white wall forms the focal point of this gorgeous living room done with fine French Provincial furniture. At the window, covered with an imposing louvered screen flanked by patterned draperies, stand a pair of easy chairs with round bolsters and made extra comfortable for lounging with aproned ottomans. The low, square cocktail table, in front of the fireplace, has a black marble top and a built-in planter.

(At right, Below) A corner done in a dark color forms the background for a deep-tufted Madame Recamier sofa. A two-faced lady's desk, with its sides carved in a lyre motif, stands at right angles to the window. The drapery is a branching floral with a large repeat. The same fabric is also used in the deep cornice, shaped with a French Provincial curve outlined with fringe on the bottom. The luxurious carpet is woven with a sculptured Greek key motif, a design that is repeated in the shade of the lamp in the corner.

(Above) A sheer drapery on a ceiling track here separates the living room from the dining room. Patterned fabric at the windows of both areas also extends ceiling to floor and omits cornices. One club chair picks up the pattern of the window fabric. Marble is found in the round cocktail table which is 18th century in style. The over-all effect is one of richness and formality, with a feeling of spaciousness.

(At right) Provincial furniture with Old World charm against today's suave background highlights this attractive dining room setting. The walls are fashionably dark in tone, with white trim and dining appointments. A pair of scales serve as fruit bowls on the oval cabriole-legged table. A sculptured floral carpet, with a ground of hard twist yarn, introduces a pleasant pattern into the room.

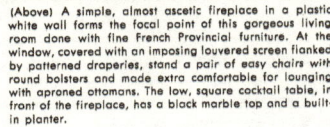

Color Harmony

With monochromatic schemes, often used very effectively in modern rooms, textures assume enhanced importance. The use of varied textures achieves variety through differences in the reflection of light and in the casting of soft shadows. Occasionally, too, a chair or an accessory is done in a contrasting hue to provide a desirable accent.

Adjacent color schemes—the other type of related harmony—simply select colors which lie side by side on the color wheel. The different hues are then keyed together, that is, their common element is strengthened to assure unity. Through the interplay of light and shadow, rough textures serve to key colors together, as do neutral colors which dull colors that otherwise contrast too sharply.

Adjacent color schemes usually are quiet and soothing, for strong, disquieting contrasts are absent. The colors best adapted to adjacent schemes are those which fall between the primary colors on the color wheel. Unless the related colors differ in value and in intensity, however, the scheme may lack zest and snap. We may overcome this through introducing a primary accent. With green and yellow-green, yellow may serve as an accent, while with green and blue-green, blue suggests itself.

Of the contrasting schemes, the *complementary* type—typified in the green-red combination—enjoys the widest popularity. Complementary colors are those colors which lie exactly opposite each other

on our color wheel, such as yellow and violet or blue and orange. When mixed together, complementary colors form gray. Thus we may mute a color not only by adding gray but by adding its complement. Altogether, there are six pairs of complementaries on our twelve-interval color wheel. Such pairs present the greatest degree of hue-contrast and, consequently, are more vibrant than are the related schemes.

Complementary colors, however, may produce too sharp a contrast for our purpose. We may soften the contrast somewhat by using, not the complement itself, but the colors which lie to either side of it. Thus, with yellow as our starting-point, rather than using violet in a complementary scheme, we may use blue-violet and red-violet to form a *split complementary* scheme.

Split complementary schemes rest on the fact that the two split complements, upon mixing, form the complement itself. Since the complement of a secondary color is a primary color, there are no true split complementary schemes based on a secondary color. Secondary colors, as well as primary colors, may however appear as members of split complementary schemes, as in red-orange, green and blue.

The remaining type of contrasting scheme, the *triad*, consists of three colors equally distant from one another on the color wheel. Our twelve-place color wheel offers four triad schemes:

Color Harmony

COLORS FOR YOUR PURPOSE

PURPOSE	MAIN COLOR CHARACTER	ACCENTS	COMBINE WITH
FORMALITY	Subdued cool colors or rich full bodied colors.	Black, Gold, Silver	Vertical lines. Smooth textures. Formal balance
INFORMALITY	Clear bright colors. Warm colors.	White, Pewter, Copper	Horizontal lines. Rough textures. Informal balance
HOSPITALITY	Warm colors. Deep reds. Rich browns.	White, Gold, Copper	Curved lines. Rich textures. Soft lighting
SOPHISTICATION AND MODERNITY	Subdued background colors. Marked contrasts in value and intensity.	Black, White, Strong color	Straight lines. Varied textures. Cove lighting
QUIET AND RESTFUL	Colors close in value. Soft muted colors. Cool colors.	Gray, Tinged gradations of color	Horizontal lines. Little pattern. Dull or rough textures. Indirect illumination
GAY AND VIVACIOUS	Warm colors. Clear bright colors. Marked contrasts in value.	White, Vivid colors	Diagonal lines. Spirited patterns. Rough or shiny textures. Direct lighting. Informal balance
FEMININE	Soft delicate pastels. Dusty tints. Tints of lilac and lavender.	White, Grays, Gilt	Curved and horizontal lines. Smooth textures. Floral patterns
MASCULINE	Strong deep shades. Browns. Tans.	Vivid colors	Straight vertical lines. Plaids and stripes. Rough textures, leather

PSYCHOLOGICAL EFFECTS OF ART ELEMENTS

LINE		COLOR	
TYPE	EFFECT	TYPE	EFFECT
HORIZONTAL STRAIGHT	Restful, quiet, informal; reduces apparent height	RED, ORANGE, YELLOW	Warm, hospitable, gay, informal; advancing, reduces apparent height, increases apparent size
VERTICAL STRAIGHT	Dignified, masculine, formal; increases apparent height	BLUE, BLUE-GREEN, BLUE-VIOLET	Cool, reserved, receding, increases apparent height, reduces apparent size
OBLIQUE STRAIGHT	Dynamic, restless; as corner-cornered placement of furniture, reduces size of room	GREEN, VIOLET	Neither warm nor cool; neither advancing nor receding
BROKEN STRAIGHT	Animated, gay	WHITE	Neutral, may be formal; receding, increases apparent size
CURVED	Graceful, feminine, soft, gay, cheerful, rich; softens effect of straight lines	BLACK	Neutral, sophisticated; advancing, reduces apparent size
FORM			
SQUARE	Obvious proportions, tends to be uninteresting	GRAY	Neutral, middle value between black and white
OBLONG	Pleasing in ratios 2:3, 3:5, 5:8; more interesting than squares	GOLD, SILVER	Neutral; formal
TRIANGLE	Lively; balanced	COPPER, BRASS	Neutral; informal
		TEXTURE	
CIRCLE	Obvious shape; tends to lack interest	COARSE, ROUGH, LOOSELY WOVEN	Informal, masculine; advancing, increases apparent size and height; softens light; keys colors together
OVAL	Subtle, more interesting than circle	SMOOTH, SATINY, TIGHTLY WOVEN	formal, feminine, glossy; receding, decreases apparent size and height

41

Red, blue, yellow—primary triad
Green, violet, orange—secondary triad
Yellow-green, blue-violet, red-orange — intermediate triad
Blue-green, red-violet, yellow-orange — intermediate triad

A modification of the primary triad, in which yellow is omitted or is restricted to a minor role, offers a pleasant harmony.

Color Distribution

Whether you have devised a color scheme or have adopted one, the question of where in the room to allocate your colors faces you.

Let us imagine that you have adopted a scheme from a swatch of fabric consisting of a gray background with a claret red geometric design and a small amount of yellow and pale blue—a triad scheme. The fabric looks cheerful and gay, warm and bright—precisely the qualities you desire for your room.

Since the room, let us suppose, is a large one, we may use the laughing yellow of the print as the background color of our room. Had our room been small, we would have chosen the pale blue for the wall. We then distribute our colors as follows:

Wall............pale yellow with white woodwork
Floor covering................claret red or wine
Draperies.................the print fabric itself
Sofa...........pale blue, trimmed with dark red
Easy chair......................the print fabric
Side chair...................golden yellow stripe
Accessories........gray, bright red and touches of deep blue

The steps that we follow in working out a color scheme are now apparent. We decide upon our decorative effect. The use to which the room will be put determines the furniture and accessories we shall need. We then devise or adopt a color scheme for the room which will carry out our decorative purpose and express our individualities. We assure that we achieve harmonious unity and pleasing variety. We determine which color will be dominant, which we shall use for the background. The rest is simply a matter of allocating colors throughout the room. If you follow the order in our example above, you will find that all this can be done easily — and effectively.

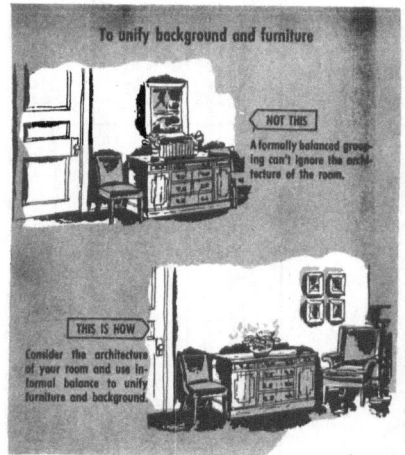

Color and Coordination

COLOR

THERE IS no factor in decorating a home that is more important, more exciting, more fun to achieve than a good color scheme. When buying home furnishings, it is extremely useful to know how to use color and how to coordinate a color scheme. The eye appeal of color can contribute enormously to the success of any room plan.

The scientist has taken light apart, has analyzed it, and put it together again. He has placed his findings at the disposal of the manufacturer, retailer, and homemaker. This has been tremendously helpful, because it has given us the means of using color intelligently to gain the effects we want.

When a ray of sunlight is passed through a prism, it is broken up into a series of colors called the spectrum. Of these spectrum colors, three are called "primary": red, blue, and yellow. All the other colors are called "secondary," because they are formed by mixing two or more of the primary colors.

1. Red and yellow make orange
2. Yellow and blue make green
3. Blue and red make violet

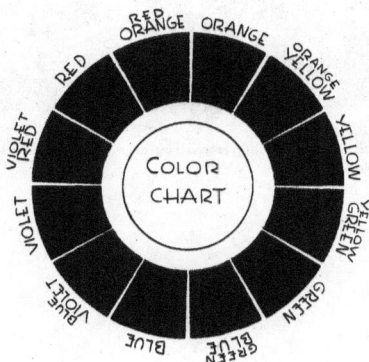

Opposite colors are contrasting or complementary. Adjoining colors are harmonious or analogous.

(*Courtesy of Popular Home, United States Gypsum Co.*)

Harmonious or analogous scheme built around two plain colors with terra-cotta bookshelves providing an accent color.

(Courtesy of Marshall Field and Co. and Popular Home, United States Gypsum Co.)

Color scheme of room, inspired by chintz on sofa, combines cool dark green, warm beige, and carnation pink.

(Courtesy of *Popular Home, United States Gypsum Co.*)

Color scheme for western exposure stems from drapery and sofa printed cotton, combining a floral with two plain colors in chair cover and rug.

(Courtesy of Popular Home, United States Gypsum Co.)
A warm scheme for a north room, combining a brick red wall with a plaid drapery which repeats the wall color.

(Courtesy of Popular Home, United States Gypsum Co.)
A contrasting or complementary scheme using bachelor-button blue with cherry red and chalk white.

COLOR AND COORDINATION

Obviously, a great many gradations of each mixture are possible, because different amounts of the primaries may be used. Each variation is called a "hue." Addition of black to a hue darkens it to a "shade." Addition of white to a hue lightens it to a tint.

In former years, color was not the vital factor in decoration it is today. Some of you may recall the drab era of living rooms done in grayed shades of taupe and mulberry, rust and green, or of living-room suites upholstered all alike in wine, green, or blue. Everyone still knows of many rooms that are a hodgepodge of unrelated colors. Fortunately, most people today are aware of the importance of color harmony, although they may not be able to achieve it.

Usually, people go to one of two extremes; either they try to use too many colors or too few. It is best to balance the colors in a room, remembering that they must be related to each other either through color harmony or through color contrast. In color harmony the colors used must be next to each other in the spectrum, or they must contain some of the same colors. In color contrast, the colors should be as far from each other in the spectrum as possible and be exactly opposite in their components.

Examples: A dining room in yellow and green would have a color scheme based on color harmony, because yellow and green are adjacent to each other in the spectrum, or color wheel. The rug might be green twist-weave broadloom; the walls, pale yellow; the draperies, a yellow chintz with green leaves; while the dining-chair seats might be yellow-and-green-striped textured cotton.

A living room in a contrasting color scheme might use dark green, rosy red, beige, and white. Contrasting schemes are stimulating, exciting, gay. The wallpaper might be patterned in red roses with green leaves on a white ground, and the curtains white ruffled tiebacks. The woodwork might be white; the carpet beige; the furniture, covered in plain rosy red and in stripes of the red, green, and beige.

There are as many kinds of color schemes as there are bridge hands in a deck of cards. Rules are made only as guideposts for the new homemaker. They will help you to know something of the fundamental laws of color harmony. When you have mastered the rules, your use of color may depend on your personal color needs and preferences.

One of the first questions to ask yourself about any room is, "What exposure does it have?" We know that rooms facing north and east get less sunlight than rooms facing south and west. Therefore, a room with a north or east exposure calls for warm colors, whereas a room facing south or west does not. Colors, like people, have personalities. The warmest colors of the spectrum are red and orange, the tones of fire and the sun. Less warm is yellow, which reflects sunlight; and the circle grows cooler as it approaches yellow-green. Green, the color of nature's landscape, is downright cool, while blue-green and blue are the coolest of all. Blue-purple is a touch warmer, purple is warmer still, and red-purple comes back into the warm range.

Most rooms fare best with a combination of warm and cool colors. This will depend not only on the exposure of the room but also on the temperament and tastes of the owner. The appropriate use of color also takes into consideration the size and purpose of the room. Light colors make a small room seem larger and dark colors make a large room seem smaller. This is why bedrooms, which are usually smaller than living rooms, are often finished in lighter colors. Also, light colors are considered more intimate than dark colors, and bedrooms are the most personal rooms in the house. In making an appropriate scheme for any room, large areas of color, like the walls and floors, should be considered first.

The lighting in a room is vitally important to the color scheme. A scheme that looks beautiful in a store under fluorescent lights can become dark and muddy in your home under an incandescent bulb. Always select colors under the same light that you have at home. If your room is dark and must be lighted when in use, plan your scheme for artificial light. If, on the other hand, the room gets a normal amount of sunlight, be governed by its exposure; that is, choose a cool color scheme for a room with a great deal of sun and a warm one for a room with little or none.

Some colors are more stimulating than others. Clear, bright colors, like reds and yellows, are found in dining rooms and game rooms, which are used for family gatherings, entertaining, conversation, and general sociability. Blues, greens, and wood tones are more restful and are often used in living rooms and bed-sitting rooms. In some rooms of this type, reds are used in small quantities as an accent color. A balance of stimulating and restful colors, of cool and warm colors, of light and dark colors, prevents monotony and insures interest. The proportions of each should be determined by the size, exposure, and use of the room.

Color can be repeated in small rooms adjoining one another. It unifies them, so that one seems to flow into the next. If you have a small house or apart-

Dark colors help to disguise architectural faults. *(Courtesy of Mademoiselle's Living.)*

ment, you can achieve a sense of greater space by using tints and shades of the same color in all the rooms. For example, if you put the same dark green covering on the floors of the living room, dining room, and the hall that connects them, you will increase the feeling of space throughout. You will also give yourself greater freedom in the choice of color accents, and by repeating the accents in connecting rooms, you will accomplish a most satisfying color scheme.

White has the same effect on a room as have all light colors. It makes the room seem larger. Also, white in off-shades helps to create a feeling of spaciousness. If you want a light color to enlarge your room, make the walls, ceiling, and woodwork all one tone and combine them with a floor covering that is a shade or two darker. Do not choose a bright color but rather a pale color. Then use dark accents. Conversely, if your color scheme is dark, have light accents. For example, try white woodwork in a room with dark green walls.

If a room has some unpleasant architectural feature which you would like to disguise—such as unevenly plastered walls, exposed pipes, or an overscaled mantel—do not have it done in a light color. In a case like this, dark walls with light rugs and draperies and bright color accents would change the mood of the room from gloom or ugliness to one of attractive cheerfulness.

One of the most sympathetic background colors for a room is gray. There are many shades: the warm beige-grays and mauve-grays and the cooler ice-grays, blue-grays, and slate-grays. The gray color family is a fine complement to most furniture tones, and gray carpeting is becoming to almost all floors. Gray is a color that can stand the tests both of sunshine and artificial light.

COLOR COORDINATION

What does color coordination mean? Quite simply, coordinated colors in rugs, fabrics, paints, and wallpapers go together harmoniously. They are the stores' answer to the need of ensembling home furnishings. The ready-to-wear clothing industry had been coordinating color for many years before the home furnishings retailers and manufacturers realized the benefits of the idea.

In a coordinated group of furnishings we find things that belong together and are harmonious in color, design, scale, and period with the minimum of effort. There are quite a few such coordinated groups on the market today. They are assembled in each of the three major style categories—formal Traditional, informal Provincial, and Modern. They are directed to the homemaker who feels that she does not want the services of a professional decorator but who, nevertheless, wants her home to be attractive and in good taste. These groups are really foolproof because for them designers and manufacturers have combined to produce furniture, rugs, fabrics, wallpaper, paints, and accessories, all of which are carefully correlated.

COLOR AND COORDINATION

HOW TO CORRELATE BY COLOR

You may be a person with strong color preference who is replacing only part of a color scheme or you may be one of those who wants a completely new scheme and does not know where to start.

If you are the former, begin with your strong color preference and apply this color to the important areas in the room, such as the rug, the walls, the sofa, or the windows. If you are the latter, the simplest thing to do is to look at fabrics that contain interesting combinations of color until you find one you like. Then pull out the three most important colors in the fabric and use them as the basis for your scheme.

Example: If it is a living room you are furnishing, you might start with a large, beautiful cotton print in coral, slate gray, and green. Then your scheme might include

1. A plain material in slate
2. A plain or self-patterned material in coral
3. A stripe combining coral and green

This scheme uses repetition and contrast in color, with a good proportion of plain and patterned fabrics in the proper scale to give the room variety and interest.

HOW TO CORRELATE BY PERIOD

We all know that there are three major trends in furniture. Are we also aware that there are three equally outstanding trends in fabrics, because fabrics must either go on furniture as upholstery or with it as draperies? The three big furniture trends are

1. Eighteenth-century English
2. Early American or Provincial
3. Modern

Since eighteenth-century styles are the most formal, it is important to know what kinds of upholstery were used at that time and what kinds of formal materials are available today.

FASHIONS IN FURNISHINGS

Upholstery and drapery fabrics used in the eighteenth century were

Damask	Taffeta
Brocatelle	Rep
Brocade	Petit point
Tapestry	Leather
Chintz (formal patterns)	Velvet and velveteen
Printed linen	

The colors used were rich and warm—crimson, royal dark blue, gold, and peacock green.

All of these fabrics can be purchased today. However, in today's colors we find more variety and subtlety. Furthermore, textured fabrics are often combined with printed cottons or glazed chintzes to make rooms gay and livable.

Early American styles are informal, and Early American fabrics and rugs were appropriately simple in design and homespun in texture. The fabrics used in New England were

Cotton (dyed in primary colors)	East India prints
Needlework	Homespun
Crewel embroidery	

All of these are appropriate today. Primary and secondary clear colors—red, blue, yellow, green, and orange—are good in small-patterned fabrics, such as conventionalized florals, calico patterns, checked ginghams, vine-patterned chintzes, informal scenic designs, and homespun plaids.

Rugs used were

Hooked and braided rugs	Woven cotton rugs
Rag rugs	

To these, we may add Modern shaggy rugs in lovely gay colors, flax or linen rugs in tweed mixtures, and copies of old, geometric-patterned hooked rugs.

In Modern rooms, texture and color are all-important. Almost any plain material, textured or smooth, can be used in Modern decoration. Texture is more important than design, although plaids, stripes, geometric patterns, overscaled and free-hand-drawn florals and leaves are all appropriate. Carpets in solid colors, both textured and plain, are good. Shaggy and deep-pile rugs or rugs with a sculptured effect in high and low pile are also popular.

COLOR AND COORDINATION

It is well to recognize two kinds of Modern—the formal and more elegant Modern, and the simple, informal Modern that leans toward the Provincial. For Provincial Modern, Indian mats are in keeping, as are cotton-textured and shaggy rugs. The deep-pile and sculptured rugs in solid pastels are appropriate only with formal Modern.

HOW TO CORRELATE BY PATTERN AND SCALE

By "pattern" we mean the way in which a design is laid out on a fabric —in a stripe, a large framed picture, a vine or small all-over motif, or a detached floral. By "scale" we mean the size of the design itself. No materials will combine well in a room unless they are properly related in pattern and scale. Here are a few simple rules:

1. Any stripe or plain fabric may be combined with any patterned fabric.
2. Patterns may be combined with each other only when they do not conflict; that is, there must be enough difference in their sizes and layouts so that they do not compete with each other.

- *Example:* DO NOT use two large striking patterns in the same room.
   DO NOT use two designs with the same type of layout, such as two stripes, two diagonals, or two large framed florals.
   DO NOT use a large floral fabric with a patterned wallpaper or patterned rug. If your carpet or wallpaper has a pronounced design, your fabrics should be plain or striped.

Bad. Too many patterns.

Good. Combination of pattern, stipe, and plain.

Bad. Too many patterns.

Good. Combination of pattern, stripe, and plain.

DO USE (1) a floral, (2) a stripe, (3) one or two plain materials in colors matching those contained in the floral. This Rule of Three is the safest formula. You may also use a floral with two plain fabrics which match it in color, and omit the stripe.

HOW TO BUILD A COLOR SCHEME

1. You can begin with the fabric for a living room

   a. Find a floral fabric with red roses and green leaves on a white ground to start your scheme.
   b. Then combine it with a green-and-white-striped wallpaper, white ceiling and woodwork.
   c. Use the floral fabric for draperies and slip covers of fireside lounge chairs.
   d. For the sofa and window valances, use a plain red textured fabric which repeats the red in the floral.
   e. Choose a plain green carpet, matching the green of the floral.

   This combination follows the Rule of Three: you now have a floral, or patterned fabric, a stripe, and two plain fabrics of colors contained in the floral.

COLOR AND COORDINATION

2. You can begin with the rug for a dining room
    a. The rug is a plain beige broadloom.
    b. Find a wallpaper with a blue background and a conventional design of fruit or flowers in beige, burgundy, and green.
    c. For the chair seats, choose a narrow multistriped fabric in beige, burgundy, and green.
    d. The draperies may be beige to match the rug.
        Again we have used the Rule of Three: here are stripes, a floral, and a solid color which is the base of the scheme.

3. You can begin with the wallpaper for a bedroom
    a. You may start with a gray wallpaper which has a framed floral pattern in blue and rose.
    b. For the bedspread choose a fabric in the same rose as the floral in the paper.
    c. Select a solid gray carpet.
    d. A gray-rose-and-blue-striped fabric may be used on the boudoir chair, for the dust ruffle of the bed, and for the tiebacks of the white ruffled organdy curtains.
        This scheme combines a floral, a stripe, and two plain fabrics in another version of the Rule of Three.

4. If you live in a dirty city
        DO NOT try to use ruffled organdy curtains or silk lamp shades.
        DO USE glazed chintz for draperies and tightly woven fabrics —such as denim, mohair, ticking, or other dustproof materials— for upholstery. Leather or one of the new coated materials would also be good.

    a. You may begin with a floral carpet in coral, gray, and olive green.
    b. Paint the walls a plain gray like the gray in the rug.
    c. Use a coral-and-gray-plaid chintz for the draperies.
    d. For the sofa, select a coral dustproof coated fabric.
    e. Repeat the drapery chintz on the fireside lounge chair and on a pair of sofa pillows.

(Courtesy of Feliciti Reynolds, decorator.)

Traditional old-fashioned nosegay paper matching the glazed-chintz dust ruffles on beds.

Provincial wallpaper with matching draperies. *(Courtesy of Better Homes and Gardens.)*

Traditional medallion paper for an entrance hall. (*Courtesy of R.K.O. art director, Albert D'Agostino.*)

A Disney print on washable paper. (*Courtesy of United Wallpaper Co.*)

A group of photographed textiles on wallpaper designed by Dorothy Liebes. *(Courtesy of United Wallpaper Co.)*

Silk-screen printed contemporary wallpapers designed by William Justema. *(Courtesy of Katzenbach and Warren, Inc.)*

FASHIONS IN FURNISHINGS

f. For a pair of occasional armchairs, find a solid-color fabric in olive green.

This scheme is colorful and practical. It combines a floral with a plaid and two plain materials. Again the Rule of Three has proved its value.

5. How to match curtains with wall color

Whether you should match your curtains with the walls will depend on the architectural details of your room. Before you start any color scheme, consider the following factors. If there is formal balance between the windows, the draperies or curtains can be in contrast to the wall color. Should the house have an informal plan, with windows placed at random, it is best to match curtains and walls. You may do both in solid plain colors or buy a companion paper and fabric. In either case, matched walls and draperies will give a feeling of unity to the room.

WALLPAPERS

The rules for using wallpapers are much the same as those for using fabrics. Colors and designs must be carefully related to the style, size, and purpose of the room. If the room is large, you may use a pattern in a large scale; if the room is small, the pattern should again be in proportion. When the architecture of a room is undesirable, a bold, dashing wallpaper will distract the eye from its structural faults.

In papering adjoining rooms, you should once more apply the Rule of Three. Do not use two floral papers or two stripes in connecting rooms. If one room is papered in stripes, the next should have a plain wall or one in a floral paper that harmonizes with the wall color of the first. If you are doubtful of your own ability to mix papers, look at the "companions" available in most stores today.

Living and Book Rooms

For Traditional living rooms and studies, use conventional flowered papers or stripes. In Provincial interiors, small all-over floral designs or papers simulating pine paneling are suitable. For Modern rooms, choose marbleized patterns, free-drawn or stylized designs, or some of the new "photographed" papers of hand-woven textiles.

COLOR AND COORDINATION

Dining Rooms

The wallpaper in a dining room should be gay and lively, because you want a friendly atmosphere there to stimulate conversation. For Traditional rooms, scenic patterns, brilliant florals or fruits in all-over, framed, or striped designs are equally good choices. Provincial dining rooms may have a small medallion paper or a small fruit or floral pattern in bright colors. In Modern rooms, plaids, stripes, free-drawn florals, or wood-weave papers are appropriate.

Bedrooms

In bedrooms with Traditional schemes, framed florals or stripes may be used. For Provincial bedrooms, calico and percale patterns, polka dots, or nosegay papers in delicate pastels are suitable. Stripes or plaids, geometric-patterned or free-drawn florals are the best papers for Modern bedrooms. For nurseries, circus, Mother Goose, and Walt Disney characters all appeal to the young. In some children's rooms, papering only one wall and painting the other three is a good formula, because too much design in a sleeping room is considered overstimulating. Many of the new nursery papers are washable and stainproof. This is a point worth investigating.

Powder Rooms, Foyers, and Alcoves

For small rooms that require dramatic treatment, such as powder rooms, foyers, and alcoves, try an amusing, whimsical paper in Victorian or peasant design or a free-drawn Modern pattern. Such papers give sparkle and an individual flare to closetlike interiors.

With experience and a little imagination, you can make endless numbers of beautiful color schemes with fabrics and wallpapers. The more you attempt, the more adept you will become. It is like learning to play the piano. At first you will make many slips and mistakes. It is always best to begin with a simple scheme for a small room. After you have succeeded with this, you will have more confidence and can undertake a larger room with a more elaborate plan. The ability to make a lovely color scheme will give you the thrill and pleasure of creative effort, for it will be something you have worked out yourself and not bought ready-made. It will reflect your own taste and personality.

What colors say

HAVE YOU ever admired the beauty of the sky, with its myriad soft colors blending magically into one another, accented here and there but all forming a miraculous pattern? There are few wonders in this world which can equal the miracle of color.

It is our purpose, in this chapter, to give you an appreciation of this vast symphony of color. It is our purpose to quicken your senses to the color which surrounds you and which unconsciously shapes your moods and spirit. Without irreverence, we shall try to take this complex subject out of the sky and present it in a fashion that will enable you to use the rich palette of color in decorating your home.

Color is one of the prime means through which you can bring beauty into your home. It is one of the chief means you will use in expressing your decorative purpose. With color you can create a mood, an atmosphere. **Color can give your home grace and** charm, an air of restfulness and contentment. Color is a powerful tool at your disposal. Through its wise use you can achieve much. Misused, color will mock all your efforts. Your home then will be uninteresting and drab,

To highlight a piece of furniture

NOT THIS ◀ Furniture placed against a dark background seems smaller and less colorful.

THIS IS HOW ▶ Place furniture against a light background to make it seem larger and more colorful.

or garish and unpleasant, restless and uncomfortable.

YOU MUST BE AWARE OF COLOR

Words cannot do justice to color. To one who unfortunately is blind from birth, no amount of description can convey the drama and experience of color. If you want to know color, it is absolutely necessary to experience it. Try, if you can, to describe the color *red*. You have to perceive color, live through the experience of a rainbow or of a beautiful autumn woodland scene, fully to appreciate the glory and splendor of color.

As a prerequisite to a full appreciation and understanding of color, you must become alive to its beauty. You must develop a genuine color awareness. Look at colorful paintings which delight you. Notice the colors that the artist employs and how deftly they blend with one another. Do the same with pieces of fabric, with colorfully designed pottery, with Nature. Only then can you begin to understand the power of color. Our world teems with color. To develop your tastes, to broaden and enrich them, you must revel in colors and steep yourself in their lore.

In this chapter we shall present the rudiments of color. We shall describe how the universe of color grows out of three primary, irreducible colors. We shall describe how colors are tinged and softened, making them pleasant and easy to live with. You will find out what colors say, so that you can have your colors express the mood and atmosphere you desire to create.

THE RUDIMENTS OF COLOR

We all are more or less familiar with colors. But simply knowing the names of a few colors is not enough. It may, as a matter of fact, lead to confusion. Suppose that you and your husband decide that the chairs in your dinette should be painted red. You call in a painter and order that they be painted this color.

In this instance three different persons are thinking of the one color red. Yet each may be thinking of a very different red. One may be thinking of a deep shade of red with a lot of black in it. The second may be visualizing

Pleasing unity in walls and woodwork

NOT THIS ▲ A busy pattern with woodwork in strong contrasting color produces confusion and disunity.

THIS IS HOW ▼ Woodwork in a soft background color of the walls blends perfectly, giving a feeling of unity.

a vivid scarlet while the third person may be recalling a pale rose tint.

Each of these three colors—or hues, as they may be called—has red in it. To that extent they are members of the one family. But how differently each of these reds lends itself to decoration! The deep red or the pale rose may be used with pleasing result for large areas. The vivid scarlet, however, should be restricted to small areas, limited to accessories as an accent, or used in a room such as a breakfast room which is not occupied for long periods of time at a stretch. The scarlet is not an easy color to live with. A little of it in decoration goes a long way.

The vivid scarlet is a *pure* color—strong, unmitigated and loud. It expresses a fiery warmth, the hot blood of temper. The pale rose tint has so much white added to it that its nature has been subdued. While it still yields some warmth, the addition of white has made it far more pleasant and amenable. Pale rose has a note of lightness and delicacy. The dark shade of red, produced by the addition of black, gives a feeling of strength. It has a masculine effect. This shade may be used for pleasing contrast or to add a note of dignity.

The pure colors are the colors which Newton obtained when he broke up the rays of sunlight by means of a prism. The band of colors which are thus obtained form the spectrum. The colorless rays of sunlight are separated into all the colors which compose it. Whenever we view a rainbow, with its band of colors, we see a natural reproduction of the spectrum. The prism merely duplicates this phenomenon.

Pure colors are those undiluted with white, black or gray. Because of their very purity, these colors do not lend themselves happily to lavish use in home decoration. They tend to tire us and grow monotonous, owing to their lack of variety and subtlety. They may, however, be used with good result as touches of contrast and accent. They may be used as the color in accessories or as part of a patterned material in upholstery, drapes, rugs and wallpaper.

THE PRIMARY COLORS

It is a remarkable quality of pig-

ments and paints that we can build up all our hues from as few as three of these pigments. These three pigments are the colors red, yellow and blue. Very aptly, they are called the three *primary* colors. They themselves cannot be formed by mixing other colors or pigments. They cannot be reduced into any component hues. They themselves, however, can produce all the other pure colors! When they are mixed together in various proportions, they give us the basis of our whole palette of color.

THE SECONDARY COLORS

When we mix equal amounts of any two of these primary colors, we obtain a *secondary* color. As we may mix any one of these three primary colors with either one of the other two, we can form three new secondary colors. Each primary color has a hand in thus forming two secondary colors. These secondary colors are new, pure hues. They differ from any of the three primary colors. They have an individuality of their own. Unlike the primary hues, however, the secondary colors are derivative and may be broken down into the primary hues which compose them.

If we mix equal amounts of yellow and blue, we obtain green. A mixture of equal parts of yellow and red will result in orange, while an equal mixture of red and blue will yield violet. The three secondary colors, then, are green, orange and violet. When produced by a mixture of equal amounts of the primary hues, they are at their sharpest, in the strength in which they appear in the spectrum.

A wallpaper that seems to undulate affords a striking background for this exceptional master bedroom. The bleached oak headboard of the studio bed is functional, providing cabinets and shelves. The bedspread is a green rayon taffeta, the curtains a beige rayon and cotton net and the wallpaper is a pale green with dark green patterns. The chest is soft green, the carved broadloom rug is in forest green.

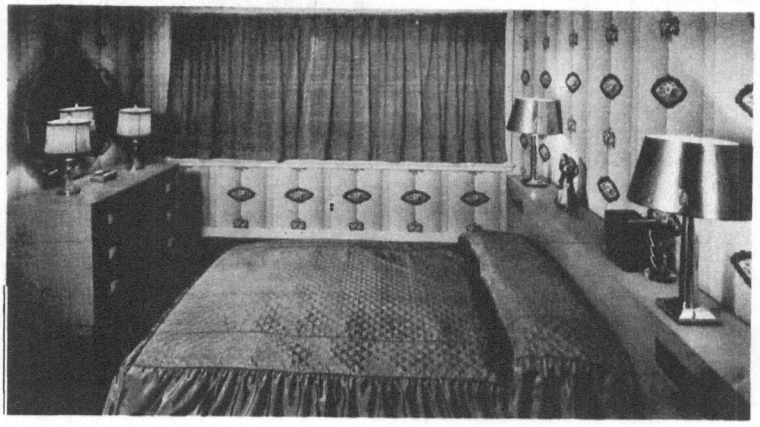

WHAT COLORS SAY

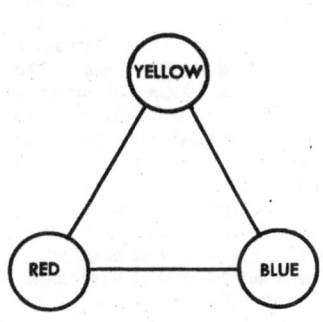

DIAGRAM 1
The Primary Colors

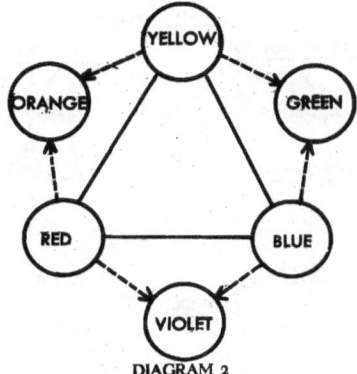

DIAGRAM 2
The Standard Colors

If we arrange the three primary colors and the three secondary colors as illustrated in *diagrams* 1 and 2, we so place the colors that we can see at a glance which primary hues go into forming each secondary color. In each instance the secondary color results from the mixture of the two primary colors which flank it. Thus orange, in *diagram* 2, falls between yellow and red and these two primary colors form orange. The primary and secondary colors together comprise the six *standard* colors.

THE INTERMEDIATE COLORS

We can, furthermore, mix any two colors in *diagram* 2 that are adjacent to each other. The six colors that result are the *intermediate* colors or hues. The process of forming these six intermediate hues is as follows:

Yellow plus green	yellow-green
Blue plus green	blue-green
Blue plus violet	blue-violet
Red plus violet	red-violet
Red plus orange	red-orange
Yellow plus orange	yellow-orange

In each instance of this process we combine a primary with one of the secondary colors which the primary helped originally to form and which lies next to the primary in our diagram. For convenience, we usually place the name of the primary color first in designating these six intermediate hues. With these six intermediate hues, we now have the twelve colors upon which we shall base our color wheel. Prepared in this way, these twelve hues are each at their purest. They have not been tinged. For this reason, these twelve hues are known as *normal* hues.

THE COLOR CIRCUIT

Arranged in the color circuit as in *diagram* 3, the family relationships of the twelve hues are readily apparent. Yellow and blue, both primary hues, upon combination, form the secondary hue green. Yellow and green produce the intermediate hue yellow-green. Similarly, yellow and the secondary hue orange form yellow-

67

CREATIVE HOME DECORATING

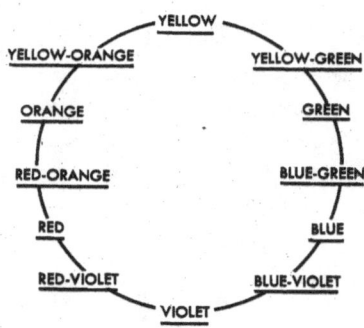

DIAGRAM 3
The Color Circuit

By continuing this process in the formation of our other secondary colors, we can have three hundred colors in our color circuit *without* a single intermediate hue. And when we think of the number of intermediate hues that we can produce through using this wide range of secondary hues, the number of colors multiplies fantastically. Though we can thus multiply at will the number of colors to suit our needs, the principles of the twelve-place color wheel that we shall use and the principles

orange upon mixture. With three primary colors, we have obtained a total of twelve colors. This color circuit is the basis of our color wheel.

We can readily imagine still other colors falling between any two hues that are adjacent to each other in the color circuit. In fact, the number of colors which in practice can be produced from the three primary colors is simply amazing. Thus we have seen that equal parts of red and yellow produce orange. But we can obtain *gradations* of orange through using one part of red and ninety-nine parts of yellow. True, the orange that we obtain from this proportion is much closer to yellow than to red.

We can continue this process of manufacturing colors. We can increase the amount of red progressively by one part while decreasing the amount of yellow by a corresponding part. In this way we can produce one hundred gradations of orange between red and yellow!

VALUE

We can produce other kinds of variations in the twelve colors of the color circuit. We all have noticed that sometimes, when writing with a pen, we get some lines that are darker or lighter than other lines. The color of these lines, however, remains the same, for we are using the same ink. This difference in color is a variation in *lightness* or *darkness* of the color. Such variations are differences in the *value* of a hue.

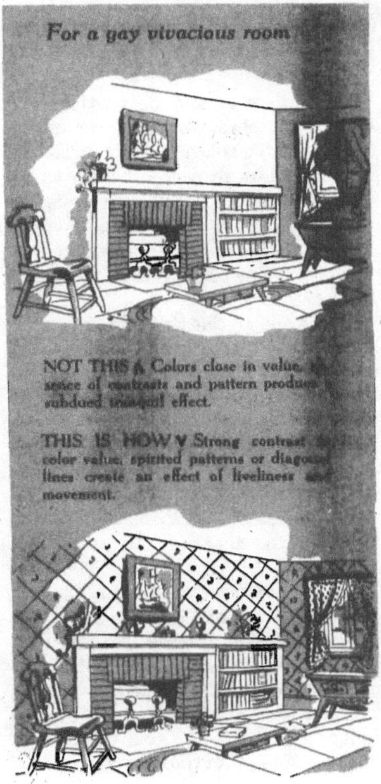

A *tint* of a color, therefore, is a color value that is lighter than the normal value of the pure color, while a *shade* of a color is a value that is darker than the normal value of the pure color. Tints and shades are produced in paints and pigments through the addition of white or black respectively to the color. Not only are we able to achieve gradations in hues but we are thus able to produce gradations in value within any one hue.

We may darken any hue in our color circuit until it approaches black in its shade. Or we may lighten any hue until it approaches white in its tint. Any hue, therefore, may be put into a scale going from its deepest shade through its normal value to its lightest tint. This scale corresponds to the progressive changes of black through gray to white. *Diagram* 4 shows this comparison in value between blue and the scale. While we here present a five-place scale for simplicity, the eye can register differences equal to ten distinctions in value.

For a gay vivacious room

NOT THIS ▲ Colors close in value, absence of contrasts and pattern produce subdued tranquil effect.

THIS IS HOW ▼ Strong contrast in color value, spirited patterns or diagonal lines create an effect of liveliness and movement.

WHITE	BLUISH WHITE
TINT	BLUE TINT
GRAY	BLUE
SHADE	BLUE SHADE
BLACK	BLUISH BLACK

DIAGRAM 4
Scale and
Corresponding Values of Blue

CREATIVE HOME DECORATING

To give a square room more pleasing proportions

NOT THIS — The use of the same color treatment on all 4 walls gives the room a boxlike appearance.

THIS IS HOW — Paint or paper one wall in a color different from the others.

In *diagram* 4 the scale goes from black, at the bottom, to a shade of gray, to full gray in the middle. It then passes through a tint of gray to white. The corresponding values of blue progress from a bluish-black to a medium blue shade. The normal value of blue is at the center. The blue then goes upwards to a medium blue tint and ends in a very faint bluish-white. If you look at the color wheel on page 65, you will see examples of tints and shades of each of the twelve colors. The tints and shades are arranged on the outer rim of the circle, beyond the pure colors to which they respectively refer.

EFFECTS OF VALUE

Tints and shades are widely used in home decoration. They make it possible to repeat a hue while at the same time altering it subtly yet perceptibly. Through the use of varying values which we obtain by tinting and shading, we can insure unity and secure contrast, emphasis and variety in our color scheme.

As with size and proportion, our eye judges colors through comparison. If we use two colors in tints or shades that are close to each other in value, then the effect of the difference between the hues themselves is minimized. The over-all impression that we gain is one of increased unity and harmony.

However, if the tints or shades of the colors we use vary widely in value, then the eye notes the contrast. Moreover, the degree of difference between the color values appears greater to us than actually it is on the basis of the scale. The difference between the two values is reciprocally widened. We may, as a result, thus obtain a contrast too marked for unity and harmony.

In fact, contrasts between sharply varying values of the same hue often strike us more forcefully than contrasts between two different hues of the same value. Color value is accordingly a powerful ally in securing unity and variety. You should remember and observe these facts when

WHAT COLORS SAY

deciding upon the color scheme for your home. Simply because you select two kinds of red for your color scheme does not automatically insure that these reds will go well with each other or with the other colors in your scheme. If one red is a light tint and the other a medium shade, the two reds may clash.

Through choosing colors alike in value, whether the colors are the same hue or not, you increase the harmony between them. When done skilfully, variations in value can produce very interesting and effective contrasts. In each instance, however, you have to get the proper values for your color scheme!

When a tint is used as a background, through contrast a shade would look still darker when placed against it. Colors likewise appear darker than they actually are against a white background, while against a dark background or black, colors appear lighter.

Objects also appear to differ in size as a result of the value of their coloring. Light values and white give the impression of greater size. Dark values and black, on the other hand, appear to decrease the size of an object. This applies to both room and furniture. To increase the apparent size of a room or of a piece of furniture, you would paint it a light tint or even white. And you would paint the room or furniture a dark shade if you wanted to reduce its apparent size.

In home decoration you secure an effect of unity, quietness, restfulness and reserve by keeping all your color values nearly uniform. The greater the contrast in value the greater is the effect of gayety, liveliness and movement. The light color values go best with a light background, the dark values best with a dark background. Such close values may produce beautiful effects, but may also tend to monotony. Light tints add to the femininity of curved lines, while dark shades emphasize the masculine effect of straight lines.

Selecting furniture for the large room

THIS IS HOW> A large room can stand massive pieces. Large sized pieces give the feeling of strength, durability and dignity.

NOT THIS < Do not smuggle an out-of-scale diminutive piece into a roomful of large furniture.

CREATIVE HOME DECORATING

INTENSITY OR GRAYING

Besides altering the value of a hue through the addition of white or black, we can produce still another variation by adding gray to a color. Gray is used in altering the *strength* or *weakness* of a color. If we mix pigments of the three primary colors together, we produce gray. The colors have neutralized one another.

Gray is a *neutral* color along with black and white from which it may also be produced. We obtain gray also when we mix yellow and violet. Violet consists of red and blue. By adding yellow to violet, we actually are mixing together the three primary colors. We produce gray whenever we mix a primary color with the one secondary color in which the primary is not originally a constituent.

The addition of gray reduces the *intensity* of a color. The pure colors of the spectrum or the normal colors of the color wheel are at their fullest strength of intensity. They are saturated. We can weaken these colors progressively by the addition of increasing amounts of gray until finally we neutralize the colors entirely. The colors are then indistinguishable from gray.

Intensity is thus the degree of grayness that a color possesses. It is the comparative strength or weakness of a color. The smaller the amount of gray in a color, the greater the intensity of that color; and vice versa. Colors which have been grayed are referred to as *muted* colors.

PURE RED	GRAYED RED	REDDISH GRAY
FULL INTENSITY	MEDIUM INTENSITY	LOW INTENSITY

DIAGRAM 5

Variations In Intensity

Diagram 5 shows three intensities of the color red. From the full intensity of the pure red, at the left, an increase in the amount of gray produces a red of medium intensity, as shown in the middle block. A still greater increase in the amount of gray gives a red of low intensity. The red of full intensity, being a pure

WHAT COLORS SAY

color, contains no gray in its composition. Both the other reds have, however, been grayed. If you refer to the color wheel on page 65, you can see examples of varying intensities of each of the twelve colors. The intensities are within the circle of the normal colors, running toward the center of the wheel.

EFFECTS OF INTENSITY

The strength or weakness of a color is equivalent to its brightness or dullness. A dull finish is one that has been grayed. It is a soft color, of low intensity. A pure color is at its full intensity. It is exerting its fullest individual psychological effect. The pure normal colors of the color wheel, accordingly, are strident, garish, unrestrained.

For this reason colors at full intensity can only be used in moderate amounts if we want to avoid the effect of loudness and vulgarity. In moderation, colors at full intensity introduce accent and interest. Bright, intense colors should be used only in small areas and as elements of a pattern. For in large doses they tire us out. The grayed colors are less bold and startling. In exchange for their loss of intensity they have gained in subtlety, quietness and good taste. The grayed colors, therefore, invite use for large areas.

When we use two or more colors in a room, we should avoid too great a difference in the intensity of these colors except for accent and contrast. We should likewise avoid too great a correspondence in their intensity. The intensity of colors is heightened by contrast. A patch of bright blue stands out more sharply when it is surrounded by an area of blue lower in intensity. A grayed green placed against

a green background of stronger intensity appears grayer. It looks less intense than it does when alone. In each of these instances the contrast in intensity has heightened the particular effect.

Against a gray background, the intensity of a hue is increased. Still greater emphasis will be secured, however, when a hue is set in contrast to a background of either white or black. White and black strengthen contrasts in both value and intensity. Against a dark red background, pure red appears both lighter in value and grayed in intensity. The differences of both value and intensity have been deepened by the contrast.

In dealing with color, it is accordingly possible to alter both the intensity and the value of hues at the same time. When we vary colors in both these respects, we achieve the richest and most subtle effects. In practice, of course, you are not called upon to determine the precise degree of variation in one or both of these qualities. As a home decorator, you merely designate or select colors which already possess these variations. But in appraising a color scheme for your own use you will assure more pleasing results if you can answer the question, "Will this color gain in effectiveness if it is tinted or shaded or if its grayness is increased or reduced?" A knowledge of the facts governing these variations will prove of value to you in attaining the very best results.

WHAT COLORS EXPRESS

Now that you are familiar with the rudiments of color, you should become acquainted with what colors express. What the intermediate colors say depends on the primary and secondary colors that enter into their composition. If you know, therefore, what the six basic colors say, you will know what colors express. These six colors say what they have to say most emphatically when they are pure. They are then bold, outspoken and unsubdued.

Of course, colors themselves don't actually talk. They do, however, arouse a reaction in human beings who are alive to them. In this sense, accordingly, colors do say something. What they say is the feelings which they produce in us. And these feelings are not to be brushed aside in your effort to secure a pleasing and tasteful color scheme in your home.

WARM AND COOL COLORS

Certain colors have already been referred to as *warm*, while others have been said to be *cool*. To complete this classification, we may call still other colors neither warm nor cool. The

WHAT COLORS SAY

warm colors are red, orange and yellow. All the hues in our color wheel which contain these colors share in this warmth. The colors grouped around blue in the color wheel are the cool colors.

Green, which contains equal amounts of yellow and blue, is neither warm nor cool. And violet which contains equal amounts of red and blue resembles green in this respect. As the greens and violets go toward the warm colors, they gain in warmth, while they partake of coolness as they approach blue. Thus, yellow-green grows warm in expression as its gradations contain increasing amounts of yellow. As blue-green increases in blueness, it grows cool.

Warm colors are important to the decorator who is concerned with the exposure of a room. A northern exposure, with little sun, can be cheered up with warm colors. A sunny southern or western exposure, however, may produce a feeling of coolness through use of the cool blues. In a very sunny room, yellows in large areas will result in glare.

The amount of light that a room receives is usually, in this day of towering buildings, of more importance than the fact of geographic exposure. If your room lacks light, then the use of light tints rather than dark shades is indicated. A light room, however, may use the shaded colors without serious diminution of natural light.

The warm colors *advance*, while the cool colors *recede*. Red and orange, the warmest of the colors, seem to go toward the observer. Blue, blue-green and blue-violet give the effect of withdrawing. Warm colors, in consequence, increase the apparent size of objects while they decrease the apparent size of a room. They can create the effect of greater intimacy in a room. Cool colors act in the opposite fashion and produce the effect of diminishing apparent size of objects while they create an effect of spaciousness in a room. This power of advancing or receding applies equally to a wall, a ceiling, a chair or a picture.

Together with the use of horizontal lines, warm colors may therefore serve to lower the apparent height of a ceiling or increase the size of a piece of furniture. Cool colors and vertical lines increase the apparent height of a ceiling or decrease the apparent size of a piece of furniture. These effects of color are of importance in restoring or creating proper proportions.

Warm colors are not only exciting and cheerful, but they give an effect of buoyancy, liveliness and activity. By their power of bringing an object nearer to the observer, warm colors lend added emphasis and significance. They tend to give a room a note of intimacy. Warm colors blend well with one another and thus assist in producing unity. Used in touches in a room that is predominantly cool, warm colors introduce a note of contrast. They accent a grouping or an object.

The cool colors have the opposite effect. They are restful, soothing, quiet colors. They produce an effect of aloofness and reserve. Through their power of withdrawal, cool colors give an effect of spaciousness. Cool colors may, if used exclusively, result in disunity. They tend to emphasize the distinctiveness of individual pieces of furniture and of accessories. As a result, the room will not seem to hold together. Too much cool color in a room, also, makes for somberness. The effect is a depressing one.

These general effects hold, not only for the related intermediate hues, but for the tints, shades and grayed intensities of the colors in the color wheel. Changes in value and intensity from the pure color modify these effects. Such changes introduce subtlety sophistication and charm. And changes in value and intensity do make it easier to gain both harmony and contrast with colors. Besides these general effects of warmth and coolness, advancement and recession, we associate more specific feelings with each of the colors themselves. We shall consider the feelings we associate with each of the six standard colors.

WHAT THE STANDARD COLORS SAY

Yellow, a warm color, is the sunniest and brightest of colors. The most cheerful of the colors, it suggests light and gayety. In home decoration, we may use yellow glass curtains to in-

WHAT COLORS SAY

troduce a feeling of sunniness in a dark room. For large areas we may also use tan, sand, bisque, beige and champagne, as well as pale yellows.

Red, the badge of courage, is full of vigor and fire. It is the most highly stimulating and exciting of the colors. But red is also associated with restlessness and violence. For these latter reasons red should be used with restraint. The shades of red—crimson, for instance—tend to darken a room and impart a somber effect. Red does carry a feeling of richness, hospitality and warmth, however. It makes an excellent contrasting color. In the red family, the pastels are very pleasing. Rose, coral, shrimp, raspberry, currant, cherry red and burgundy are all widely used.

Blue, the coolest of the colors, suggests a feeling of serenity and restfulness. It induces a feeling of unruffled dignity and tranquility. Blue-green and blue-violet are widely used in home decoration. Avoid cold blues. Tinted blues, such as Wedgwood and robin's-egg, are good background colors. Turquoise, delft, delphinium, slate-blue, navy and iris find popular favor.

Green has a calm and restful effect. It is one of the least strident of the six standard colors. More than any other color, green is the color of Nature. With increased blue, green is cool. With more yellow in it, green becomes lighter, gayer and warmer. Green, in home decoration, profits by addition of an accent. Soft apple, lime, chartreuse, mint, leaf and moss greens are widely used for walls and floor covering. Emerald, hunter, olive, and malachite are popular for accent and contrast.

Orange combines the sunny cheerfulness of yellow with the vigor and warmth of red. Very intense orange, however, crackles with heat and may become irritating. Among the oranges, rust, copper, apricot, rosewood, peach and henna especially recommend themselves for use in home decoration.

Violet is a rich, aloof and dignified color. It is not an intimate color. As the blue in it is increased, violet tends to express coolness. With more red, violet becomes warm. Mauve, mulberry, pansy-purple, fuschia and eggplant find ready use in home decora-

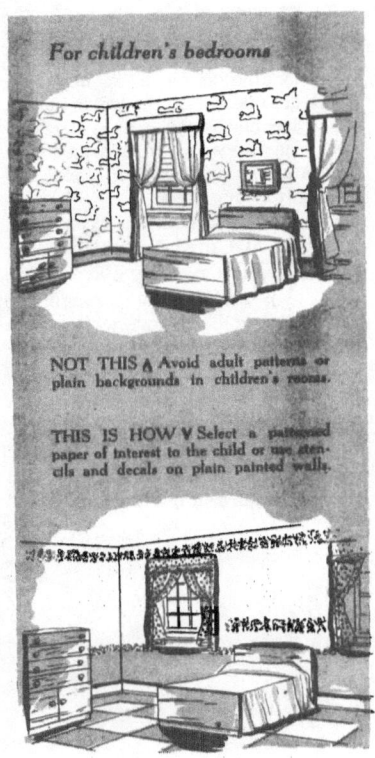

For children's bedrooms

NOT THIS ▲ Avoid adult patterns or plain backgrounds in children's rooms.

THIS IS HOW ▼ Select a patterned paper of interest to the child or use stencils and decals on plain painted walls.

tion while lavender or lilac are feminine colors reserved for bedroom and boudoir.

THE NEUTRAL COLORS

In addition to the colors of the color wheel, white, gray and black are frequently employed in home decoration. White embodies a feeling of delicacy and quiet. White goes best with cool colors. Black, the lowest of the colors in value, is frequently used in smart, sophisticated backgrounds. It has an air of modernity which seems to mock at the cares and travails of life. Black serves as an excellent contrasting field for colors, besides lending a touch of opulence. Black goes best with the warm colors. Black lacquer is much used together with bleached woods in modern rooms and is also widely used in rooms featuring Regency style.

Gray is neutral in its expression. The blue and green grays are cool, the yellow and red grays are warm. Battleship gray—made through the admixture of black and white—is a depressing color. A blue-gray or green-gray is soothing and goes well in a room with a dominantly warm color scheme. A rose toned gray is very pleasing in a room in which cool colors dominate. Gray goes well with the pure colors. It gives the effect of neutralizing them and toning them down.

Gray is growing more and more popular in home decoration, being widely used for walls, rugs, upholstery and drapery. Gray combines very effectively with both tints and shades of many colors, especially the warm ones. Gray and beige are used very effectively together. The one caution that need be observed is to avoid the dull, drab, listless grays.

Grays vary from pale silvery tones to deep gray-browns. The browns are formed by mixing any hue from red-violet to yellow-orange with dark gray until the hue itself is hardly distinguishable. The light browns, tan and beige are very interesting background colors, offering the home decorator wide opportunity. Like the grays, these colors are enjoying widespread popularity.

You are now acquainted with what colors say. In the following chapter we shall tell you how you may originate color schemes of your own. We also give you twenty complete color plans for various rooms and period styles of furniture. These plans are illustrated in full color. They are for formal and informal rooms in both traditional and modern styles. If you want to adopt any of these schemes for your home, a chart lists the full details of the first sixteen of these rooms.

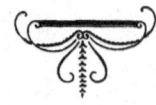

Color schemes for your home

THE BEAUTY that we find and cherish in Nature is very largely the beauty of color. We all enjoy color. We are attracted and stimulated by it. We want our home to share in the beauty of color. The choice of a pleasing color scheme will bring beauty and distinction into our home.

In going about the selection of a color scheme for our home, we may resort to either one of two methods. We may choose color combinations that we admire and that already exist, awaiting our use. Such a combination we may find in a flower, in a painting, a colorful piece of china or in a piece of fabric. Or we may devise our color scheme through the use of a color wheel.

Either method can give very pleasing results. What is essential to success with either method is an inner feeling for color. This feeling can be acquired only through developing a consciousness of color. If you wish to attain good results with color, no quality is so basic to you as this quality of color consciousness.

You can develop a feeling for color through noticing colors more analytically and carefully. When you observe a sunset, try to distinguish the various

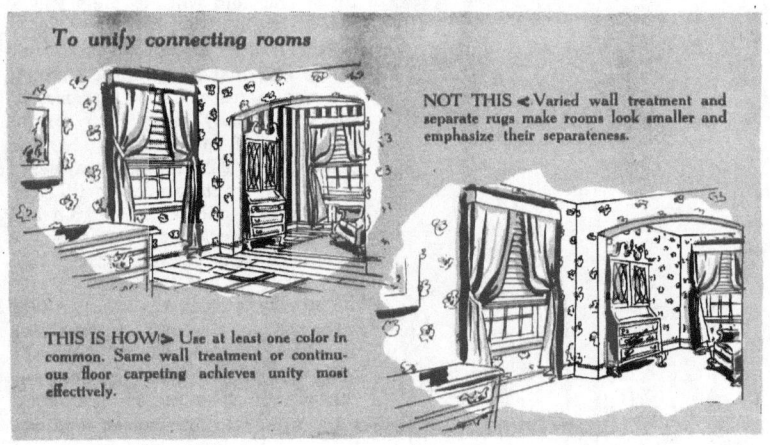

To unify connecting rooms

THIS IS HOW▸ Use at least one color in common. Same wall treatment or continuous floor carpeting achieves unity most effectively.

NOT THIS ◂ Varied wall treatment and separate rugs make rooms look smaller and emphasize their separateness.

colors. See which colors blend together. Notice how the contrasts are achieved. Try especially to determine how the colors have been tinted, shaded and muted. With a little practice, you will be able to distinguish these variations. You will find a new pleasure in colors, and an increased confidence in your ability to express your moods, convey your feelings and attain your decorative purpose through them.

Your first question in arriving at a color scheme for yourself is the decision as to which colors you will use. This decision will rest upon your individual color preferences. It will depend on the use to which the room will be put. It will be tempered by the decorative purpose which you desire to achieve. And it will depend upon the style of furniture which you use in decorating your home.

COLORS FOR YOUR PURPOSE

The decorative purpose you select as your own may be any one of several general kinds. You may want your home to express formality, or you may prefer it to express informality. If you want *formality*, you will use either subdued colors or rich fullbodied colors with rich textured materials. With subdued colors, you will also express reserve and quiet, while the fullbodied colors will be rich and gracious. Either of these two effects are compatible with formality. Black and gold will also help you to carry out the feeling for formality.

Pewter and copper are restricted to the informal room, while silver is a formal accessory. For *informality*, you will usually select clear, bright colors. But if your furniture style is Colonial New England, you may select turkey and cranberry reds, with light browns and yellows like saffron and mustard. The colors for this style are vigorous, forceful and strong, the colors that we find in Nature.

You may want to have a room that is feminine or masculine in tone. For the *feminine* room you will use soft, delicate pastels, with smooth textures. You will stress curved and horizontal lines. Tints of lavender or lilac are distinctly feminine. The keynote of the feminine room and of the masculine room as well, is set by its colors, accessories and textures. In the

To restore proper scale

NOT THIS ▲ A small picture over a broad piece of furniture produces an incongruous effect.

THIS IS HOW ▼ Two small pictures hung side by side will restore proper proportion.

COLOR SCHEMES FOR YOUR HOME

COLORS FOR YOUR PURPOSE

PURPOSE	MAIN COLOR CHARACTER	ACCENTS	COMBINE WITH
FORMALITY	Subdued cool colors or rich full bodied colors.	Black Gold Silver	Vertical lines Smooth textures Formal balance
INFORMALITY	Clear bright colors. Warm colors.	White Pewter Copper	Horizontal lines Rough textures Informal balance
HOSPITALITY	Warm colors. Deep reds. Rich browns.	White Gold Copper	Curved lines Rich textures Soft lighting
SOPHISTICATION AND MODERNITY	Subdued background colors. Marked contrasts in value and intensity.	Black White Strong color	Straight lines Varied textures Cove lighting
QUIET AND RESTFUL	Colors close in value. Soft muted colors. Cool colors.	Gray Tinged gradations of color	Horizontal lines Little pattern Dull or rough textures Indirect illumination
GAY AND VIVACIOUS	Warm colors. Clear bright colors. Marked contrasts in value.	White Vivid colors	Diagonal lines Spirited patterns Rough or shiny textures Direct lighting Informal balance
FEMININE	Soft delicate pastels. Dusty tints. Tints of lilac and lavender.	White Grays Gilt	Curved and horizontal lines Smooth textures Floral patterns
MASCULINE	Strong deep shades. Browns. Tans.	Vivid colors	Straight vertical lines. Plaids and stripes Rough textures, leather

CREATIVE HOME DECORATING

A Monochromatic Color Scheme uses only one hue of the color wheel. This hue is usually varied in value and in intensity to achieve an interesting, smart effect.

An Adjacent Color Scheme uses any two or more colors that lie side by side on the color wheel, varying them in value and in intensity to attain pleasing harmony.

A Complementary Color Scheme adopts any pair of hues that lie directly opposite each other on the color wheel. One hue dominates, the second provides contrast.

A Split Complementary Scheme consists of a combination of three colors—a primary or intermediate color plus the two hues that lie on each side of its complement.

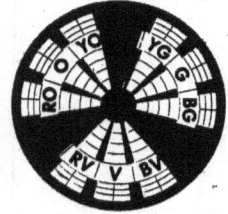

A Triad Color Scheme is a combination of three hues that divide the color wheel into three equal parts; a 12-place wheel contains four different triad harmonies.

COLOR SCHEMES FOR YOUR HOME

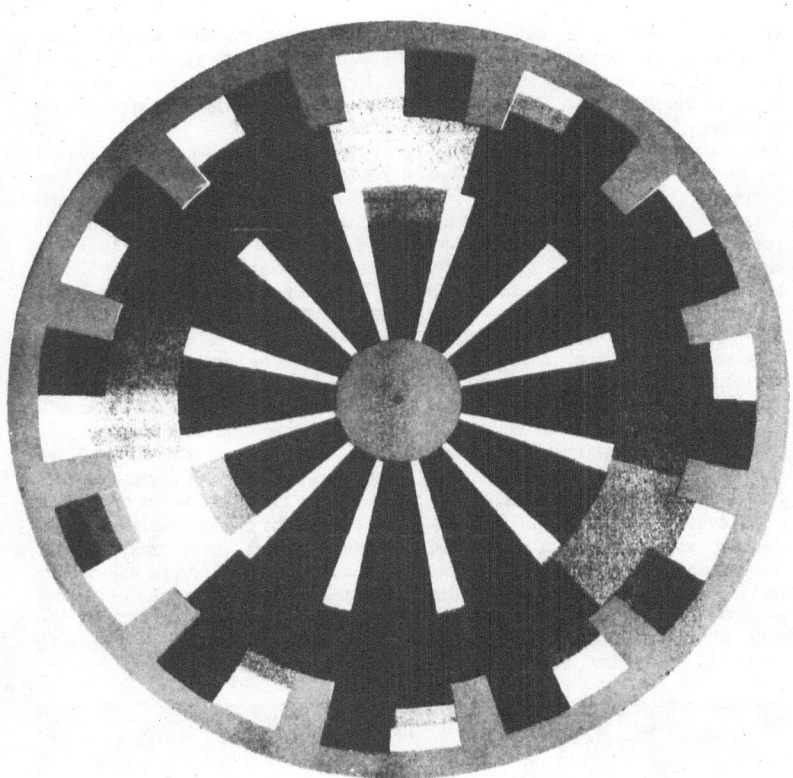

COLOR WHEEL

This color wheel consists of the twelve normal, pure hues and their gradations in value and in intensity. The tints and shades which constitute values of each color are arranged in scale on the rim outside the pure colors of which they are gradations. The muted, grayed, intensities of the pure colors fall within the circle of normal colors, running toward the neutral gray center of the color wheel. With this color wheel you can devise any of the five types of schemes shown on page 64 for your home. Chapters 3 and 4 describe how you can do this.

masculine room, you will feature muted colors or strong, deep shades, with coarse, rough textures and straight vertical lines. Vivid colors are used for relief. Tans, browns, deep reds, moss and olive greens may be used to further your decorative purpose.

If you want a *quiet, restful* room, you will keep the colors that you select close in value. Cool colors, especially soft blues and greens, enhance the feeling of repose. The colors will be soft and muted. Pattern will appear only sparingly in such a room. And horizontal lines will be stressed. For the *gay, vivacious* room, however, you may use clearer, brighter colors. Its colors will be the warm clear yellows and the bright reds. And there will be marked contrasts in value.

To achieve *sophistication* and *modernity*, you may select a subdued background with strong color accents in the foreground. Blacks and whites may be used for contrast. And you will secure added variety through contrasts in value and intensity.

Sophisticated rooms may be built around one single color, with novel effect through tinging this color or through introduction of a strong color accent.

The room designed to bespeak *hospitality* will use warm colors. In formal rooms with this effect you may use the deep rich colors, but in informal rooms the colors selected may be clear and bright.

Your decorative purpose will accordingly tell you which colors will best fulfill your aim. By selecting suitable colors your room will speak with one voice. You will then translate your plans into reality. And you will achieve your plan and purpose.

Your preferences will be broadened and enriched through a growing consciousness of the beauty of colors and an awareness of the precise expressiveness which you may attain through the use of tinged colors. For the tinged colors carry the significance of the pure colors along with all the subtle overtones which variations in value and in intensity give.

THIS IS HOW ▸ General illumination suffuses the entire room with light and thus produces unity.

NOT THIS ◂ Direct, local lighting creates strong contrasts between areas of a room.

COLOR SCHEMES FOR YOUR HOME

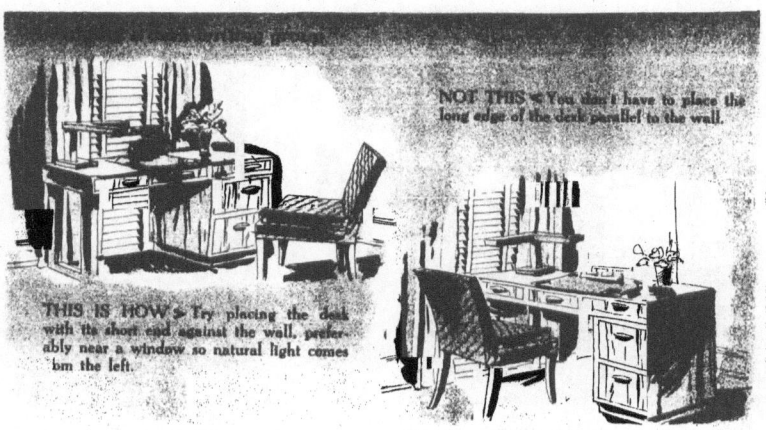

THIS IS HOW ▸ Try placing the desk with its short end against the wall, preferably near a window so natural light comes in from the left.

NOT THIS ◂ You don't have to place the long edge of the desk parallel to the wall.

COLOR AND FURNITURE STYLES

How your choice of furniture styles will influence the color scheme you finally adopt will be fully treated in subsequent chapters. Chapter 9 deals with the problem of harmonizing your furniture with its background. A chart clearly indicates what goes with what. The kind of furniture you select will be based on the use to which the room will be put. The style of the furniture will rest in part on your preferences. In part it will rest on the mood you wish to achieve and the decorative purpose you wish to express. Before you have a knowledge of the characteristics of different styles, it would hardly be enlightening to discuss this question in detail.

MONOCHROMATIC COLOR SCHEME

The color schemes which we can produce through the aid of the color wheel are in general of two types, the *related* and the *contrasting*. The monochromatic and the adjacent color schemes are both of the related type.

The complementary, split complementary and triad color schemes belong to the contrasting type.

A *monochromatic* scheme is based on the use of one underlying color. Variations are obtained in this scheme through the resourceful use of blending and contrasting values and intensities of this color. This method is a difficult one to handle. The danger that it faces is, of course, the ever-present one of lack of variety. The use of one main color does insure unity. But the achievement of variation is tricky. And without variation, we sacrifice interest and liveliness. We get monotony and boredom.

Monochromatic schemes have, however, been very deftly used in modern interiors. The values and the intensities have been successfully adapted to express the purpose of the decorator. Textures attain an extremely important place in monochromatic schemes. The use of varied textures achieves variety through differences in the reflection of light and in the

CREATIVE HOME DECORATING

Color Scheme 1 — A formal Georgian room in an adjacent color scheme of blue, blue-green, a plum blue-violet and neutral dull gold gives an effect of dignity and richness.

Color Scheme 2 — Red with its two split complements, blue-green and yellow-green, sets the color harmony for this luxuriously formal English Regency room which deviates from tradition in its treatment of walls and trim.

Color Scheme 3 — A French Provincial city style room with an adjacent scheme of soft faded pastel blue, grayed pale Wedgwood and accessories in gilt, soft green and pastel prints creates an atmosphere of feminine grace and formality.

Color Scheme 4 — Faithful to the Victorian era is this formal living room done in an adjacent scheme of mauve and violet-tinged rose with a deep blue-green as complement.

For details of these four color schemes see chart on page 88.

COLOR SCHEMES FOR YOUR HOME

Color Scheme 5 — The charm and simplicity of Colonial New England furniture here receive a triad treatment that adopts the cranberry red and mustard yellow so typical of this quaint, informal style.

Color Scheme 6 — Brilliantly colored stencils highlight the complementary and adjacent scheme of this informal, carefree room decorated in the Pennsylvania Dutch style.

Color Scheme 7 — Gayety and cheerfulness mark this French Provincial country styled room which uses blue-violet, medium blue and faded gray-blue with bright red as accent in an adjacent scheme.

Color Scheme 8 — The natural finish of knotted wood furniture in the Modern country cottage style lends a spirit of informality and comfort to this room decorated in triadic red, yellow and blue.

For details of these four color schemes see chart on page 89.

casting of shadows. Occasionally, one piece of furniture or accessories in a different hue are used to provide a desirable accent.

Color Scheme 10 gives one such room done in monochromatic colors. This modern room uses various values and intensities of yellow. For accent it has a deep green chair. This contrast secures a pleasing variety. The over-all effect is a smart and sophisticated one, while the yellow radiates hospitality and good cheer and the subdued tones of the background provide a restful, easy feeling.

ADJACENT COLOR SCHEME

The second type of related color scheme is the *adjacent*. Very often, in fact, adjacent schemes are referred to as related schemes. Adjacent color schemes simply select colors which lie side by side on the color wheel as illustrated on page 64. They thus secure unity. Unity is also gained through *keying*.

Colors are keyed together when they are related to one another by a common bond. The colors of an adjacent scheme have a common element through their position on the color wheel. This common element is strengthened in keying.

Colors may be keyed in several ways. One way is by graying them. Their relatedness is then strengthened through their neutrality. Glazing a color is another method. In glazing, one color is painted over another and the mixture serves to mediate both colors. Or we may glaze colors through coating them with a varnish. Rough textures serve to key colors together through the interplay of light and shadow. Colors are also united through the use of neutral colors— white, black, gray, silver and gold. These neutral colors act as a tie between colors which might otherwise contrast rather sharply. Finally, we may add one color to each of the other colors in our scheme. By adding green to yellow and blue, we can key both these colors.

Color Scheme 1 pictures a formal Georgian room with an adjacent color scheme. The colors here employed are mainly blue, blue-green, a plum blue-violet and neutral dull gold. The effect is gracious, tranquil and dignified, rich and pleasant.

Color Schemes 3 and 7 are also examples of adjacent color schemes.

COLOR SCHEMES FOR YOUR HOME

Here, through a difference in color and texture, one room is definitely formal, the other definitely informal—this despite the fact that both rooms have a French Provincial style of furniture. The color contributes to the difference and expresses the varying moods. The former of these rooms uses a background of pale green Wedgwood blue and soft faded blue pastel. The accessories are in gilt, soft greens and printed pastels. All this gives the room an air of formality, richness and delicate lightness.

The latter of these rooms uses blue-violet, medium blue and a faded gray blue, with bright red as accent. Other accents are in grayed blue-violet. Pieces of copper are also used decoratively in this room. The effect is very informal, as befits its country style, with a feeling of simple gayety and cheerfulness.

Adjacent color schemes usually are quiet and soothing, for strong, disquieting contrasts are lacking. Their beauty often relies upon skilful keying. The subdued colors give an effect of spaciousness and repose. Unless the colors selected differ in value and intensity, zest and snap may be wanting.

The colors best adapted for adjacent schemes are those which fall between the primary colors on the color wheel. With green and yellow-green, yellow may be used as accent, while with green and blue-green, blue suggests itself.

COMPLEMENTARY COLOR SCHEME

One method of enlivening adjacent color schemes is through the use of *complementary* colors. Complementary colors are those which lie exactly opposite each other on our color wheel. The colors opposite each other fall at either end of a line as shown on page 64. The colors of any such pair are complementary to each other.

The greatest degree of contrast between hues exists between the complementaries. Thus yellow and violet, green and red, blue and orange are all pairs of complementary colors. They are thus contrasting colors. While colors that lie side by side on the color wheel are related through a common element in their makeup, complementary colors are not related. When blended together, complementary col-

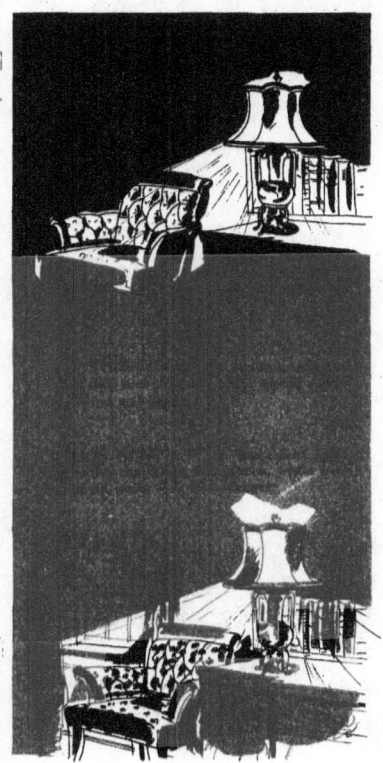

CREATIVE HOME DECORATING

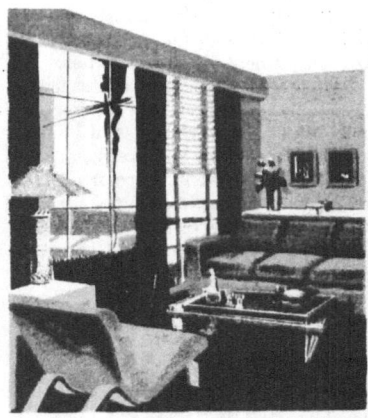

Color Scheme 9 — A monochromatic beige combined with complementary tones of red and green assures a pleasant setting for this Modern living room which conveys a hint of formality and a spirit of ease.

Color Scheme 10 — This Modern living-study room achieves livable sophistication through a yellow monochromatic scheme relieved by contrasts of green in accessories and chair.

Color Scheme 11 — A raspberry wall that contrasts with the soft blue-gray of the other three walls distinguishes this fine semi-formal room in the Classic Modern style and illustrates the variability of the primary triad color scheme.

Color Scheme 12 — Light wood contemporary furniture of traditional lineage joins with complementary tones of red and green to produce a gracious, pleasant formality.

For details of these four color schemes see chart on page 90.

COLOR SCHEMES FOR YOUR HOME

Color Scheme 13 — Coral, seafoam and chartreuse, a split complementary scheme, contribute to this attractive informal room furnished with Modern light and dark pieces.

Color Scheme 14 — This Modern blonde wood dining room, keyed to delightful informal entertainment, chooses a monochromatic scheme in coral and neutral colors with green leaves as a piquant accent.

Color Scheme 15 — A Classic Modern combination room, which stresses comfort and informality, selects a complementary harmony of dominant green and a deep red-violet.

Color Scheme 16 — The gay flowered print of the draperies forms the basis of this triad color scheme that gives this Classic Modern room a cozy, livable appeal with a charming semi-formal quality.

For details of these four color schemes see chart on page 91.

CREATIVE HOME DECORATING

ors neutralize each other and produce gray. Thus we may gray a color, not only through adding gray itself, but by mixing it with its complementary.

Color Scheme 17 presents a pleasing complementary color scheme for a bedroom. The dominant color is red, with green as its complement. The soft green bench and drapes add a quiet contrast to the reds. The soft rose tone used in this scheme is a color which is flattering to most persons. The general effect is quiet and feminine, with a note of formality and reserve.

With a change in colors, type of furniture and accessories, it is simple to convert this scheme for use in a masculine bedroom. The soft green would be changed for a dark, dull green. Rich shades of red would replace the rose tints, while tans and browns would replace the beige. The textures selected for the masculine room should be rough. With the appropriate change in furniture and accessories, the room would then be entirely masculine.

Oftentimes, adjacent and complementary color schemes are used together in decorating a room. As *Color Scheme* 4 indicates, such a combination of two schemes may be used with successful effect. In this room, the mauve and violet-tinged rose are related colors, while the deep blue-green is the complementary. Used with ornate Victorian furniture, the general expression is one of luxury and richness. Altogether this room appears florid and showy, a modern room in the traditional manner.

SPLIT COMPLEMENTARY COLOR SCHEME

When two hues are used side by side, the contrast between them is strengthened. The degree of difference is made more pronounced. This is especially true of complementary colors. For this reason, contrasting color schemes are more brilliant and colorful than are the related schemes. They are more vibrant.

True complementary colors often produce a too sharp and disagreeable contrast. The contrast can be softened

somewhat through using, not the complementary color itself, but the related colors which lie to either side of it. Thus, if we were to select yellow, rather than use its direct opposite on the color wheel, we could use the two colors on either side of violet—blue-violet and red-violet. Red, similarly, goes better with blue-green and yellow-green than it does with its complementary green. Such a contrasting color scheme is called a *split complementary*.

If in forming our split complementary we select a primary or an intermediate color, we can use the two colors which lie on either side of its complementary. Thus, on our color wheel, if we select the primary blue, the complementary color is orange. By using the blue with the colors on either side of its complementary, we get a split complementary scheme consisting of blue, red-orange and yellow-orange.

If we select the intermediate hue, yellow-orange, the split complementaries are violet and blue, while for yellow-green the split complementaries are red and violet. The basis for use of split complementaries lies in the fact that the two split complementaries upon mixing form the complementary itself.

This fact, however, limits us in selecting the starting color from which we can build up our split complementary scheme. We are limited to primary and intermediate colors as our starting point. We cannot begin our split complementary scheme from a secondary color.

The reason for this is that secondary hues have primary colors as their complementaries. Thus, green has red, violet has yellow and orange has blue. The complementary primary color, however, cannot be formed by any other colors. In other words, the split complementary of a secondary color cannot give the complement, as this latter is a primary color. Therefore, we are restricted to primary and intermediate hues as our starting point in forming a split complementary color scheme. This does not, however,

CREATIVE HOME DECORATING

Color Scheme 17 — Quiet femininity is the note of this formal bedroom which unites traditional and Modern furniture in a complementary plan of rose, pink and green.

Color Scheme 18 — Very pale shrimp pink and turquoise with soft white and gray are the complementary colors of this rich feminine bedroom in semi-formal French Provincial.

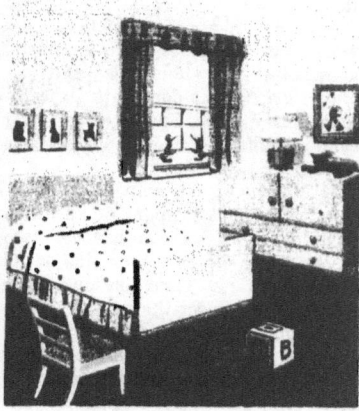

Color Scheme 19 — Tones of green in an adjacent scheme with complementary tints of pink introduce a restful charm into this delightfully sunny informal Modern bedroom.

Color Scheme 20 — The primary triad appears again in blue pastel walls, dull red linoleum, yellow curtains, pink beige wood with red knobs, a yellow bedspread with a navy blue and vivid red design, red leather chair and accessories in white, red and deep blue.

COLOR SCHEMES FOR YOUR HOME

Color contributes to the beauty of this pleasant Modern living room. The table-desk and triangular end table are decorative space-saving pieces of furniture.

Wallpaper	dusty rose pink pineapple pattern with green sprigs against a cocoa brown field
Draperies	bottle green
Rug	raisin
Sofa fabric	pink and brown tweed weave
Lounge chairs	one olive green; the other copper
Leather	on sofa, end tables and pull-up chair is light shell pink
Furniture wood	amber mahogany
Coffee table	gold and silver lacquer flecked on black lacquer

forbid using either secondary or primary colors within the scheme itself. This stricture holds only for the planning of such a scheme from an initial color.

One example of a split complementary scheme is given in *Color Scheme 13*. The blue-green and yellow-green of this modern room are the split complements of the coral. The over-all effect is one of informality or semi-formality, a quiet, cheerful room with a note of gayety and warmth.

TRIAD COLOR SCHEME

The remaining method of selecting a color scheme from the color wheel is through selecting the colors at the points of an equilateral triangle. These colors, on our color wheel, are exactly three colors apart from one another and divide the color wheel into three equal divisions. Thus, starting at yellow, we would get the other two primary colors. The three primary colors thus form one of the possible *triad* color schemes. This may be seen by referring to page 64.

Altogether, we can get four such triads on our twelve-interval color wheel. One triad consists of the three primary colors, the second triad consists of the three secondary colors. The remaining two triads consist of the six intermediate hues. Yellow-orange, blue-green and red-violet comprise one of these triads; and yellow-green, blue-violet and red-orange make up the other.

Color Scheme 5 pictures an Early Colonial room in the New England style. This room is decorated in a triad scheme. The effect in this instance is informal, with the charm and simplicity which characterize this style.

PRINCIPLES OF COLOR

In translating your color scheme into reality, the problems which you face are the same regardless of the manner in which you arrived at your scheme. The color wheel is an important ally of yours in working out your color schemes. The use of the color wheel can help you to select the specific colors in your color scheme. It can also help you to determine which colors go well together. You can similarly determine this through use

COLOR SCHEMES FOR YOUR HOME

of the alternate general method that was already recommended—that of adopting your color scheme from a flower, a natural scene, a painting or a piece of printed material. In each case you can see for yourself whether your colors will blend or clash.

With a knowledge of what the colors themselves may say, you can select a color that will harmonize with your decorative purpose. And select one which will express your own tastes and preferences. Color, while important, is not the only element you have with which to secure your aim. Your choice of furniture is also of importance. And your furniture will possess certain lines and textures. These two qualities, consequently, must also be ingredients in your recipe.

The problems that you face, therefore, do not arise from the selection of any specific color. Specific colors may easily be determined. You simply select the colors that you prefer, that will go well with one another and that contribute to the decorative plan you intend. But you still have a problem.

COLOR DISTRIBUTION

The problem is one that applies to both related and contrasting color schemes. It is the problem of determining the *distribution* of colors so as to secure both unity and variety. If you can decide upon a color for your large areas, such as the walls, ceiling and floor, then you have taken the step that will contribute toward unity. Contrast can be attained through using contrasting colors or tinged colors in the accessories.

The principles that apply to the distribution of color are, consequently, mainly matters of scale or proportion. The general principle has been noted in several variant contexts. It is this: *The stronger the intensity and the higher the value of a color, the smaller the area this color should occupy.* And the converse applies as well. *The weaker the intensity and the lower the value of a color, the greater area the color may occupy.*

The apparent size of a room, we have already noted, may be increased or diminished through the use of receding or advancing colors respectively. The effect of spaciousness may be enhanced through treating walls

CREATIVE HOME DECORATING

and woodwork, walls and floor covering, or walls and furniture in the same color. In small rooms, the use of light tints will also give the effect of greater space.

If the colors that you select for your scheme are close in value and intensity, then you need observe only the Greek rule of the Golden Section. This rule, you may recall, tells us to avoid precise, obvious divisions. We should preferably use divisions in the ratios of two to three, three to five, or five to eight. This insures added interest and also serves to make one color in your scheme the leader—the *dominant* hue.

If you select a triad color scheme for your room, you will violate this rule if you use each one of your colors in equal amounts. Instead, you should make one color dominant, use the second in moderate amount, while reserving the third for accent and contrast.

With all types of color schemes, it is necessary that one color be dominant. It is through dominance that the mood of a room is fixed. But dominating is not domineering. The brightest, most intense colors are usually reserved for emphasis and accent. In all color schemes, the neutral colors—white, gray, black, silver and gold—may be used. These colors are not considered in classifying the schemes as related or contrasting.

You need not, furthermore, follow any of the five types slavishly in using the color wheel. Each of the methods is flexible. Types of color schemes may be combined. And mention has been made of the enormously complicated color wheels that are possible. These wheels allow greater freedom and variety. Freedom may also be secured through adopting your scheme from Nature or a work of art.

BALANCE AND EMPHASIS

In apportioning the areas, it is especially important to take account of the tinged colors, of the values and intensities of colors. We have already seen how contrasts in value or in in-

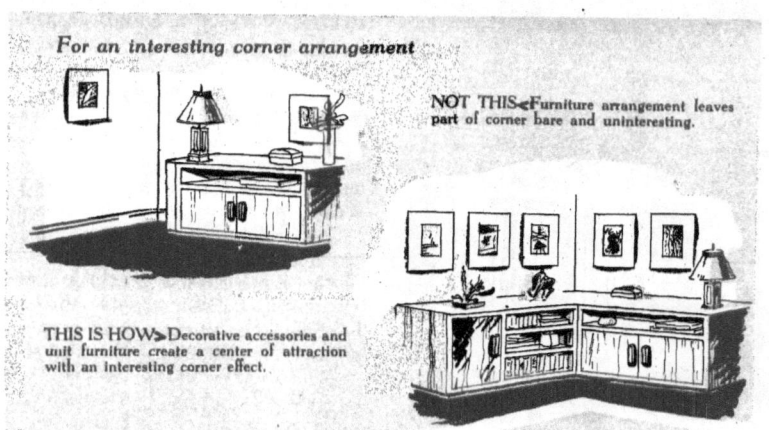

For an interesting corner arrangement

THIS IS HOW▸ Decorative accessories and unit furniture create a center of attraction with an interesting corner effect.

NOT THIS◂ Furniture arrangement leaves part of corner bare and uninteresting.

COLOR SCHEMES FOR YOUR HOME

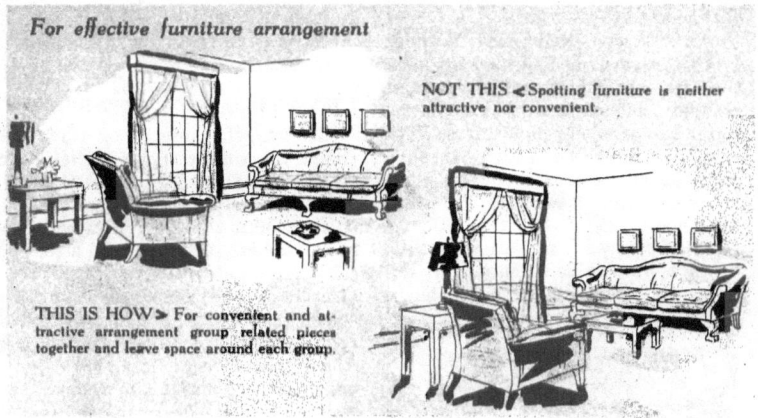

tensity are heightened. A small amount of warm color will serve as contrast to large areas of cool colors. A small amount of shaded color will stand out in contrast with large areas of tinted colors, while a touch of pure or brilliant color will accent large areas of muted colors.

The pure colors of the color wheel are not themselves well suited for wide use in a room. They must be varied in value and intensity. What they have to say is very strident. And it is said in an uninteresting manner. Pure colors, however, are often used effectively as accents. If we wish to secure accent, we must be sure not to relegate the accenting color to an isolated corner of the room. The accent should set off your more important groupings.

If we apportion our colors so as to make one color dominant, we still may have concern over securing balance among the subordinate colors. We achieve balance with colors through repeating the colors in different areas of our room. In a room in which only the drapes are blue-green, the room may seem somewhat out of balance. It is necessary, if this is so, only to repeat this blue-green in another accessory somewhere else in the room. And *for balance, colors should be distributed throughout the entire room, not concentrated in a single area.*

Emphasis is introduced through the use of contrasting hues, values or intensities. It is for this reason that the contrasting color schemes are important. Before we can achieve contrast, we first must have unity. For unity, we must select one color as the principal color of our scheme. The principal color need not be the background, however, even though the background covers the largest area. The background is the field against which objects that we want to emphasize will stand out.

We must remember that backgrounds are exactly what they are called. They must not obtrude. They should serve to set off the foreground. They should not distract attention.

Nor should the background be one that is hard to live with.

What is to be emphasized belongs in the foreground. The background, therefore, while dominant in area, is actually subordinate to the foreground in decorative importance. The emphasis that we secure through contrast will in consequence be given to colors that are used in lesser amounts.

This contrast may be secured through hue, value or intensity. But it is this contrast, this emphasis, which will enliven your room and give your room just that bit of difference so important to individuality and distinction.

TREATMENT OF CONNECTING ROOMS

If two adjoining rooms in your home are connected by a wide doorway or other architectural opening so that an observer can see from one directly into the other, you will have to give these rooms especial attention. For best decorative effect, these rooms ought to be considered as a unit. The color schemes that you adopt for these rooms should blend with each other. There should be at least one color in common between these rooms. This unity is most effectively achieved if the same wall treatment is used throughout both rooms. Continuous floor covering—carpeting, linoleum or similar rugs—will also serve the same purpose.

It will make for even greater unity if you use two colors in common. The two colors, in this instance, need not, however, be used extensively in each of the rooms. As is so often true, the factor that will finally determine the treatment is that of unity. And the way in which you attain this quality will depend upon the architectural features of your home. It will depend upon how much of each room is visible from the other, as well as upon the size of the rooms. If the rooms are small, it is advisable to use the same wall coloring throughout. If the rooms are large, greater variation is possible.

The simplest method of treatment is to begin with the more important room first. If your two connecting rooms are living room and entrance hall, then you will begin your plan

COLOR SCHEMES FOR YOUR HOME

with the color scheme for your living room. While here your problem is to combine both unity and variety in interesting proportions, the selection of a common color or colors will serve to secure unity. The use of a common color will result in producing the effect of greater spaciousness, as well as greater restfulness. If you emphasize the contrast in the colors of the two rooms, you will produce the opposite effect.

If your two connecting rooms are kitchen and dinette, both rooms may be treated in the same manner. Your kitchen will then take on some of the quality of cheerfulness, lightness and gayety that you want for your dinette. The present trend in home decoration is in line with your decorative purpose. Kitchens today no longer are the solid whites of ten years ago. Frequently the only white areas in kitchens are those of the mechanical units—the stove and the refrigerator. You can therefore repeat the scheme of your dinette in the kitchen.

In planning your color scheme, it is necessary to take account of the fixed decorations of the room. You must give thought to the walls, woodwork and floor. If the room is already partially furnished, you must consider these furnishings as well. To apply your color scheme requires consideration of only a few principles. These principles are those of proportion, balance and emphasis. You must also plan your color scheme to express the effects that you wish to achieve. With careful planning and forethought, you will achieve beauty and good taste in your home.

WORKING OUT A COLOR SCHEME

Now that we know the principles underlying the use of color, let us see how we would go about working out a color scheme for a room. If you want a modern, distinctive room, you might adopt a monochromatic scheme. The color you select will be one you like and believe is well adapted to express your decorative purpose. Let us say that this color is green.

For a monochromatic scheme, you will vary this one color in your room in accordance with your purpose. If you want a quiet, subdued room, masculine in tone, then you know that you will employ shades of green,

grayed greens and deep grays. You will, furthermore, use tans and browns. The tints of green which suggest lightness and femininity, if used at all in this room, will be restricted to accent only. All this is directed by the mood and atmosphere that you want to express and that colors and their tinges convey.

You may, accordingly, decide upon a dark green rug with chairs upholstered in moss green. For the background, you may use tan—tan walls with drapes that are tan in background and have a brown and green geometric plaid or striped pattern. We may feel assured that these colors will go well together. If you fear that the over-all effect may be somewhat somber, you may add a rich red leather chair and picture for vivacious contrast.

Suppose, however, you want to secure delicacy and femininity through a green monochromatic room. You will then use soft, pale tints, while limiting the use of dark greens and deep tans and browns. Your greens will be used with whites, pinkish grays or rosy beiges. You may do your background in white or in a pleasant pale green muted tint. The drapes, then, may be somewhat darker than the walls or white with a dainty leaf green pattern. For the rug you may select any one of a wide variety of hues. It may be moss green, a rosy beige, or a pinkish gray. It may even be a rich brown color. You may repeat the drapery material in the upholstery. Or, instead, you may select other soft green shades or light tints of green. And you might use white accessories with a small amount of green trimming. Your room will then reflect your purpose.

These are only suggestions for your guidance in working out just one type of color scheme for your home. We have by no means exhausted all the possibilities of a green monochromatic scheme. Regardless of the details of your final plan, this is the method by which you can work out such a scheme.

Let us see how we might build up a contrasting color scheme. The mono-

Choosing patterned wallpaper

NOT THIS ◅ Large sized patterns are out of scale in small rooms.

THIS IS HOW ▶ Choose small sized patterns for small rooms and reserve large sized patterns for large rooms.

COLOR SCHEMES FOR YOUR HOME

To Group Pictures and Furniture

NOT THIS ◀ The broken line arrangement fails to unify pictures or relate pictures to furniture.

THIS IS HOW ▶ Aligning bottom edges relates pictures of uneven size, unifying pictures and furniture.

chromatic schemes are difficult ones, resting as they do for effectiveness upon the subtle interplay of variations in value and in intensity. Complementary schemes do avoid the danger of succumbing to monotony.

The color wheel shows that red and green form a complementary pair. We shall use this pair, with green as the dominant color. In contrasting schemes you will recall, it is important that we clearly decide upon our dominant color. And our purpose will be to decorate a bedroom which will be quiet and restful, feminine and reserved in tone.

The reds that we may select will be soft dusty rose tones of pale pinks, for these are feminine colors. Our greens similarly will be light, pale and soft. The walls may be done in a very pale pink, a rosy beige or a light dusty rose. Any one of these will give a pleasant, soothing background with a touch of warmth and intimacy. For the floor we may select a pinkish-gray carpet or we may use a pale-tinted gray-green. The bedspread and drapes may be a soft green with a pink and dark green floral pattern. The chair may be a solid green, slightly darker than the drapes and the bedspread. The accessories might be in white and very pale pink.

You may want to work out your color scheme from a piece of printed fabric that you like. Adopting your scheme from such a source is one of the two general methods of deriving a color scheme, you will recall. Let us imagine that the fabric consists of a white background with a pretty floral design largely in claret red and that it uses yellow and pale blue in small amounts. This is actually a triad color scheme. The fabric looks cheerful and gay, warm and bright. And these are the qualities that we want our room to possess.

As we have the colors that we shall use, we must now consider how we shall distribute them in our room. How shall we allocate our dominant red and our subordinate blue and yellow? What colors shall we use for the walls, what for the floor covering and draperies? We must also decide upon the colors we shall use in our upholstery and accessories.

Since the room is large, we may use the laughing yellow of the print for the background color of our room. Had our room been small, we would have chosen the pale blue as the color of the wall. Using the print as our basis, we distribute the colors as follows:

Wall .... pale yellow with white woodwork
Floor Covering......claret red
Draperies ....the floral print
Upholstery
  sofa..............................pale blue
  large easy chair..the floral print
  side chair................golden yellow
  chair..........................grayed Wedgwood blue
Accessories...............white plus bright red and touches of deep blue

With Classic Modern furniture, the over-all effect that we have secured is informal or semi-formal, depending upon the textures of the materials selected and the arrangement of furniture throughout the room. Our room now welcomes us with a cozy and livable quality. It is illustrated in *Color Scheme* 16.

The steps that we follow in working out a color scheme are now apparent. We decide upon our decorative purpose, the effect that we intend to secure. The use to which the room will be put determines the furniture and accessories that we shall use. We then select the colors for the room. We choose as our colors those that will carry out our decorative purpose and express our personal preferences. We assure that we achieve harmonious unity and pleasing contrast. We determine that one color will be dominant. The rest is simply a matter of allotting areas for distribution of color. If you follow the order in the example immediately above, you will find that this can be done very easily.

The colored illustrations of twenty color schemes that accompany this chapter may serve you as a guide or offer suggestions to you for other

COLOR SCHEMES FOR YOUR HOME

color schemes. The charts give you all the color details of sixteen of these illustrated rooms. Practice with these color schemes. See how you may vary them. Ask yourself what colors you would prefer to use in place of those already selected. Try to decide what effect your variations will produce.

Working out color schemes is real fun.

Once you grow conscious of colors and their effects, you will find your life enriched and broadened. You will know beauty. You will gain deeper, finer experiences and a keener expressiveness. The study of color is deeply rewarding in its own right.

Vivacious colored and patterned draperies, repeated in the bedspread, highlight the sunshine corner windows of this bedroom. The pattern is in chartreuse and black on a white background. The pebble twist rug is a Sequoia tan, while the corner chair is covered in gray textured fabric. The light wood of the twin dressers contrasts with the tier table and a spacious mirror picks up the gay pattern of the bed.

CREATIVE HOME DECORATING

DEFINITELY FORMAL

Color Scheme 1	Color Scheme 2	Color Scheme 3	Color Scheme 4
GEORGIAN English, 18th Cent.	**ENGLISH REGENCY**	**FRENCH PROVINCIAL** (City Style)	**VICTORIAN**
FURNITURE WOODS Mahogany and walnut	**FURNITURE WOODS** Dark woods with black and gold	**FURNITURE WOODS** Walnut Natural fruitwoods	**FURNITURE WOODS** Dark with gilt trim
WALLS Creamy gold	**WALLS** Wallpaper—pale gray in striped satin effect	**WALLS** Pale grayed Wedgwood blue	**WALLS** Mauve
FLOOR COVERING Oriental — gold background with design in deep and light blue, bluegreen and plum	**FLOOR COVERING** Very deep bluegreen	**FLOOR COVERING** Aubusson (beige and pastel florals) or Broadloom in soft faded blue tint	**FLOOR COVERING** Yellow brown floral rug
DRAPERIES Floral print—gray gold background and blue, green, plum	**DRAPERIES** Grayed soft yellow green	**DRAPERIES** Striped satin damask, blue, bluegreen, and green and gold	**DRAPERIES** Deep bluegreen with gold tassels
UPHOLSTERY SOFA — soft medium blue frieze WING CHAIR — gray gold damask CLUB CHAIR — plum mohair SIDE CHAIR — needle point	**UPHOLSTERY** SOFA — rich red mohair CHAIR — champagne damask CHAIR — deep blue green but lighter than rug striped with gray	**UPHOLSTERY** SOFA — light turquoise CHAIR — petit point — gold and pastels CHAIR — soft deeper blue than walls or rug.	**UPHOLSTERY** SOFA — brilliant rose, violet tinge CHAIR — deep bluegreen floral damask with gilt trim CHAIR — plum
ACCESSORIES Lamp shades — cream, cream and green Bases — White alabaster, bluegreen alabaster Green leaves	**ACCESSORIES** Black Gold White	**ACCESSORIES** Gilt Pastel green French prints in pastels	**ACCESSORIES** Bright rose Gilt Dark brown
TYPE OF COLOR SCHEME Adjacent	**TYPE OF COLOR SCHEME** Split complementary	**TYPE OF COLOR SCHEME** Adjacent	**TYPE OF COLOR SCHEME** Adjacent and Complementary

COLOR SCHEMES FOR YOUR HOME

DEFINITELY INFORMAL

Color Scheme 5	Color Scheme 6	Color Scheme 7	Color Scheme 8
COLONIAL New England	**PENNSYLVANIA DUTCH**	**FRENCH PROVINCIAL** (Country Style)	**MODERN** Country Cottage
FURNITURE WOODS Maple Pine Fruitwoods	**FURNITURE WOODS** Walnut, pine and painted with stencils in brilliant colors	**FURNITURE WOODS** Natural fruitwoods	**FURNITURE WOODS** Natural finish Knotted woods
WALLS Light green blue with white wood trim	**WALLS** Pinkish white with terra cotta wood trim	**WALLS** White paint	**WALLS** Pale yellow
FLOOR COVERING Oval hooked rugs in beige and soft colors	**FLOOR COVERING** Braided or flat weave terra cotta and yellowish mixture	**FLOOR COVERING** Rag rug or any flat weave faded gray blue	**FLOOR COVERING** Braided or Mexican serapes Dark blue borders with tan, red, blue, white
DRAPERIES Mustard yellow—small calico print with deep blue and bright red	**DRAPERIES** Gay Dutch blue	**DRAPERIES** Toile de Jouy type light and dark blue print on white	**DRAPERIES** Red and white gingham with navy blue edging
UPHOLSTERY SOFA — brown CHAIR—cranberry red CHAIR — print, deep green blue on white	**UPHOLSTERY** SETTEE—small print of copper tans on Dutch blue Medium blue painted chairs with stenciled hearts and tulips in bright yellows, blues and lavenders CHAIR — burnt orange	**UPHOLSTERY** SETTEE — blue violet cushions CHAIR—red CHAIR—medium blue Chair cushions — same as drapes	**UPHOLSTERY** SOFA OR DAYBED Strong medium blue with yellow corded edges Chair—same blue Chair—grayed red
ACCESSORIES Cranberry red White Pewter	**ACCESSORIES** Deep blue glass Earth brown pottery	**ACCESSORIES** Copper Bright red Blue violet (grayed)	**ACCESSORIES** Yellow lamp shades Deep blue bases Deep blue and gray pottery
TYPE OF COLOR SCHEME Triad	**TYPE OF COLOR SCHEME** Complementary and Adjacent	**TYPE OF COLOR SCHEME** Adjacent	**TYPE OF COLOR SCHEME** Triad

CREATIVE HOME DECORATING

	FORMAL OR SEMI-FORMAL		
Color Scheme 9	**Color Scheme 10**	**Color Scheme 11**	**Color Scheme 12**
MODERN	**MODERN**	**CONTEMPORARY** (Classic Modern)	**CONTEMPORARY** (Classic Modern)
FURNITURE WOODS Bleached woods and lacquer	**FURNITURE WOODS** Light and dark (cream and brown)	**FURNITURE WOODS** Dark woods	**FURNITURE WOODS** Light woods
WALLS Gray beige	**WALLS** Old ivory	**WALLS** 1 wall raspberry 3 walls soft blue gray	**WALLS** Pale soft yellow green
FLOOR COVERING Very dark green	**FLOOR COVERING** Brown	**FLOOR COVERING** Soft blue gray of walls	**FLOOR COVERING** Gray beige
DRAPERIES Deep tan coarse net	**DRAPERIES** Deep yellow (mandarin)	**DRAPERIES** Patterned-gray background with yellow formalized leaf design	**DRAPERIES** Soft Green
UPHOLSTERY SOFA — gray beige darker than walls CHAIRS 1 red — clear, medium shade 1 green — same intensity 1 beige	**UPHOLSTERY** SOFA — deeper sand color than walls DESK CHAIR — deep green CHAIR — taupe CHAIR — yellow	**UPHOLSTERY** SOFA — gray (against raspberry wall) 2 CHAIRS — solid wine DESK CHAIR — yellow leather CHAIR — medium gray blue	**UPHOLSTERY** SOFA — grayed rose CHAIR — soft yellow green, deeper than walls CHAIR — topaz
ACCESSORIES Dark green leaves as accents Lamp shades soft rose beige Coffee table or vases and small accessories — vivid Chinese red lacquer	**ACCESSORIES** Dark green color of chair Daffodil yellow White	**ACCESSORIES** Lamp shades — white and raspberry binding Pottery — Wedgwood blue and bluegreen argenta	**ACCESSORIES** Rose red and dull gold
TYPE OF COLOR SCHEME Monochromatic background with Complementary	**TYPE OF COLOR SCHEME** Monochromatic with green accent	**TYPE OF COLOR SCHEME** Triad	**TYPE OF COLOR SCHEME** Complementary

COLOR SCHEMES FOR YOUR HOME

INFORMAL OR SEMI-FORMAL			
Color Scheme 13	Color Scheme 14	Color Scheme 15	Color Scheme 16
MODERN	**MODERN**	**CONTEMPORARY** (Classic Modern)	**CONTEMPORARY** (Classic Modern)
FURNITURE WOODS Light and dark	**FURNITURE WOODS** Light	**FURNITURE WOODS** Medium tones	**FURNITURE WOODS** Light and dark
WALLS Soft warm gray	**WALLS** Coral	**WALLS** Green	**WALLS** Pale yellow with white woodwork
FLOOR COVERING Sea-foam, a soft tint of bluegreen	**FLOOR COVERING** Gray brown	**FLOOR COVERING** Warm gray	**FLOOR COVERING** Claret red
DRAPERIES Chartreuse (grayed) with coral binding on edges toward center	**DRAPERIES** Soft slate gray	**DRAPERIES** Gray with deep violet red pattern	**DRAPERIES** Floral print—white with red, yellow and soft blue
UPHOLSTERY SOFA — coral CHAIR — chartreuse slightly darker than drapes CHAIR — print, white with green and eggplant	**UPHOLSTERY** Beige Brown	**UPHOLSTERY** SOFA—brown and tan mixture CHAIR — gray with green corded edge CHAIR—same as drapes	**UPHOLSTERY** SOFA — soft pale blue CHAIR — deeper gray blue CHAIR — same as drapes CHAIR — yellow
ACCESSORIES Chartreuse and rose	**ACCESSORIES** White and dark green leaves	**ACCESSORIES** Green and dull gold	**ACCESSORIES** Poppy red White Deep blue
TYPE OF COLOR SCHEME Split Complementary	**TYPE OF COLOR SCHEME** Monochromatic with color accent	**TYPE OF COLOR SCHEME** Complementary	**TYPE OF COLOR SCHEME** Triad

CREATIVE HOME DECORATING

MIXING FURNITURE STYLES

STYLE	SPIRIT	MIXES WELL WITH —
QUEEN ANNE (Simple) (More elaborate)	Comfort, Simplicity, Usually Informal Formal	Colonial New England. Early Chippendale. Cottage type furniture. Formal Georgian.
CHIPPENDALE (Early) Chinese and Smaller Pieces	Sturdy, Masculine, Informal Formal or Informal	Queen Anne. Hepplewhite. Sheraton. Duncan Phyfe. Modern.
HEPPLEWHITE	Classic, Elegant, Delicate, Feminine, Formal	Adam. Sheraton. Chinese Chippendale. Smaller Chippendale pieces. Louis XVI. Duncan Phyfe. Classic Modern.
SHERATON	Classic, Simple, Delicate, Formal	Adam. Hepplewhite. Chinese Chippendale. Smaller Chippendale pieces. Louis XVI. Duncan Phyfe. French Empire. Directoire. English Regency. Classic Modern.
FRENCH PROVINCIAL (City Style)	Feminine, Delicate, Gay, Graceful, Usually Formal	Louis XV. Louis XVI. Queen Anne. Simpler Georgian pieces. Duncan Phyfe. Classic Modern.
FRENCH PROVINCIAL (Country Style)	Simple, Sturdy, Quaint, Countrified, Informal	Colonial New England. Pennsylvania Dutch. Informal Queen Anne. Cottage & Farm House types.
DIRECTOIRE	Classic, Graceful, Formal	Sheraton. Duncan Phyfe. Federal American. English Regency.
FRENCH EMPIRE	Classic, Dignified, Imposing, Formal	Duncan Phyfe. Federal American. English Regency. Victorian.
COLONIAL NEW ENGLAND	Quaint, Picturesque, Simple, Sincere, Informal	Simpler Queen Anne. Early Chippendale. Pennsylvania Dutch. French Provincial—country style.
PENNSYLVANIA DUTCH	Quaint, Gay, Friendly, Sturdy, Informal	Colonial New England. French Provincial—country style. Informal Modern.
DUNCAN PHYFE FEDERAL AMERICAN	Classic, Elegant, Formal	Adam. Hepplewhite. Sheraton. Louis XVI. Directoire. French Empire. English Regency. Classic Modern.
ENGLISH REGENCY	Sophisticated, Rich, Elegant, Formal	Chinese Chippendale. Sheraton. Hepplewhite. French Empire. Duncan Phyfe. Federal American. Classic Modern.
VICTORIAN	Homey, Elaborate, Usually Formal	French Empire. English Regency. Federal American.
CLASSIC MODERN	Sophisticated Formal or Informal	Chinese Chippendale. Sheraton. Duncan Phyfe. English Regency. French Provincial. Organic Modern.
ORGANIC MODERN	Comfort, Restful, Simple, Flexible Informal	Some Classic Modern.

What Color Should It Be

SO you don't like all of the rooms you see that are supposed to be well decorated! On that we agree. The model rooms in many stores, many rooms shown in magazines, and some rooms I have done myself would drive me crazy.

This, of course, just goes to prove that there is no infallible set of rules that will always lead to the results you want. It is more important to have your room the way you want it, and the way you like it, than to have every detail perfect from a decorator's point of view, since decorators also differ in tastes and temperament.

However, if you build up resistance to the *idea* of a decorated room, to one that is "designed," an organized and a complete whole, you are blinding yourself to what your home really looks like. Maybe you will see your living room in this description of the typical American living room. "The front parlor has brownish walls, contains overstuffed furniture in brown velour and an upright piano."—*Life*, January 1, 1939, page 51. If this description does apply to your home—and I hope it doesn't—you have been careless. Drab overstuffed suites of furniture are sold because it is the easy way to sell furniture. People buy furniture suites because that's what they find in the stores. This creates, as you can see, a vicious circle.

Seriously study your own living room. As you sit and analyze it, does the room appear to be an organized whole? Does it have design? Has it a theme? Or does the room seem to be just a collection of miscellaneous objects?

Probably the color effect—or lack of it!—is the worst offender. Dollars to doughnuts, the colors are ordinary and conventional. In fact, there may be no apparent color scheme. And yet a color scheme will do more than anything else to hold together a miscellaneous assortment of furniture.

So if you are decorating on a budget, if your problem is to make-the-most-of-what-you-have, if you frankly can't afford your ideal, your best bet and most effective helper is color. When you can recognize the right color in the ten-cent store as easily as in super-shops, you will have uncovered a gold mine.

Soft French-blue paint really costs no more than drab tan paint and may actually be seen in the same paint folder. Sparkling yellow wallpaper costs no more than characterless cream paper. Delightful chartreuse and turquoise colored dress percales and denims in fast colors, for draperies and slip covers, may be found at the surprising outlay of twenty-five cents a yard. Even ordinary red, blue, or green twelve-cent fabrics, shown in mail order catalogues, offer fresh and vivid color.

Color has no price, so there is no excuse for not having a color-fresh room. In fact, an inexpensive fabric, right in color and used lavishly, will do more for a room than a skimpily used expensive fabric that is the wrong color.

So when a slim pocketbook is coupled with a decorating urge, color-mastery comes first.

To start with a clean slate, develope a clear, undimmed eye and sign away:

> All interest in so-called safe colors. They lead you into drab, uninteresting effects.

> Interest in fashionable colors. The right color for you and for your room is more important than any rumor about "what is being done this year."

> All idea that color is dangerous. Colors are probably more amiable than your best friend.

> All jitters over color selection—cultivate a strong, sure feeling.

There are scientific systems for using color, based on laws of physics, psychology, and physiology. I've spent months wrestling with these methods. I've read dozens of books, I've listened to lectures, and I've worked in color laboratories. But to be absolutely honest, when it comes to doing a decorating job, I forget all the systems and let my emotions rather than my head lead me.

These statements might suggest that color schemes could be pulled out of the air like magic. Actually ninety-nine and ninety-nine one-hundredths per cent of the decorators I know use absolutely no hocus-pocus. Let me whisper the secret: they

WHAT COLOR SHOULD IT BE

use ready-made color schemes. In other words, they find a piece of chintz, some wallpaper, a picture, a porcelain vase, a bit of old needlework, even a choice piece of old furniture, and the colors are taken from it or are prompted by it.

If it is a multicolored chintz, for instance, the colors for walls, rugs, and upholstering may be matched with those in the fabric. Thus the colors in the chintz serve as an exact color guide. Usually the chintz, picture, or vase which is the source of the color scheme is used in the room, but it is not necessary. For instance, you may see a porcelain vase in a museum with a fresh and inspiring color scheme. The colors may be used even if the vase is not attainable.

When presenting this theory another question which always comes up is this, "If I want to use a picture as a color guide, shall I always have to use the same color scheme?"

In most pictures there is an infinite variety of color, which can be used in different ways. For instance, I have a three-fold screen made from some old Victorian window shades, given me, when I admired them, by a nice old lady in Princeton, New Jersey. I'm very fond of the screen and it has travelled with me through many houses and apartments.

The ground color is grey. The border is tarnished silver with beige and brown acanthus leaves painted on a faded green ground. The central motif is a green and silver basket filled with pale periwinkle-blue fruit, treated with mica so that it glistens.

This screen has been used with sage-green walls, an earth-brown rug, and green and beige upholstering. It has been used with walls covered with silver teaboxpaper, and upholstering in periwinkle-blue and cloud-grey. Now the screen stands against a soapstone-grey wall. The same brown rug covers the floor but on one chair there is chintz with a brown ground and design in grey-green, creamy yellow, and a touch of blue. Antique green satin, grey velvet, and yellow striped satin are also represented in upholstery. The screen has still to be used with periwinkle walls.

These variations of color scheme merely indicate how a variety of color effects may be inspired by a single object. Your current mood will determine which colors you wish to accent.

POPULAR HOME DECORATION

Perhaps you can't consider doing your entire room over. Your problem may involve changing only one item in the room. In fact, here is a frequent question.

"The walls in my living room are a kind of cream color, the rug is blue. I have one rust colored chair, the sofa is brown, now what color shall I use for draperies and another chair?"

Such a haphazard approach to a color scheme will never lead anyone to a pleasant, interesting room. The only way I know of to make an interior sing with color is to start with a definite color plan and work it into every nook and cranny of the room, even if it takes three or four years to get it all finished. If you have such a color theme when you start, you never have to worry about what color new additions are to be. It is all settled for you, at least it is narrowed down to a choice of one or two colors. If you haven't already a color theme, don't just think about a color for the new chair. Determine an entire-room color scheme, which may be evolved over a period of time. The new chair, of course, should then be selected with the new color theme in mind.

In any case, my answer to questions such as the one above is, "Go out and search the entire town, if necessary, until you find a chintz, printed linen, or other fabric with a pattern in cream, blue, rust, and brown, the colors now used in the room. Use it for draperies and a slip cover on the new chair and pretend that the new fabric was your starting point instead of the finish."

I would like to add, "When you do over your room later, lady, remember that there are heavenly colors in the world. Instead of uninspired cream and blue and rust and brown, give your eyes a treat. Try pomegranate-red, seafoam-green, and white; or citron-yellow, lime-green, and earth-brown. Don't be a Mrs. Drab. Try some free-wheeling in color. Remember that a color scheme is one thing in this big temperate world that doesn't have to be moral—in fact, the other extreme may be desirable."

Here is a true story of a friend of mine. She was a New England girl, descendent of a line of clergymen. She was brilliant; she was pretty, but plain; she was a timid soul. She definitely had no glamour, and she was definitely on the shelf. Although her name was Jane, her friends called her Miss Mousey. You see, she was brought up in the stark Puritan colors of black and white, mouse-grey, taupe, and brown. In fact, she told me that the only colors that she was ever aware of were the colors in the American flag—

>White—for purity
>Red—for valour
>Blue—for truth

But after she graduated from Mount Holyoke (with honors) she came to the big, bad city and got a grand job in a department store. And there began her downfall. Or her uprising, depending on how you look at it. For she discovered a secret passion—she saw and coveted a big, red pocketbook, and it was as red and as scarlet as only red and scarlet can be. Her Puritan side said, "No, no" but she was haunted by that red purse. She dreamed about it at night; it pursued her wherever she went until finally she went completely haywire and in one mad, exotic moment she bought the red pocketbook, at the hitherto unheard-of price of sixteen dollars. Never before had she dreamed of paying more than three dollars for a purse.

Well, it's a tale with a happy ending, for she also bought a new red hat. Her dull little apartment became unbearable and she got hold of a color scheme—a good brassy color scheme of daffodil-yellow, white, and seafoam-green, with a dash of vermilion for good measure. Now she is a new woman. She has more friends, she is more interesting, she gives and receives more from life. In fact, she is on the verge of becoming a glamour girl. And the other day I heard her father fondly speak of her as "*his* colorful, imaginative Jane"!

And that is precisely what color can do for our houses and our spirits. It makes rooms warm and livable. It makes them sparkle. It makes them live. And there is no trick to it, if you just lift color effects you like from pictures or what-have-you.

Actually, there is nothing wrong with cream and blue used together in a room. It is a satisfying combination of colors. When the rust and brown are kept as minor elements they too add to the cream and blue theme. Or turn it the other way around and let the cream, brown, and rust lead with just one bold dash of blue and you have a scheme that is inevitably pleasant. But when no *one* color predominates, when there is no one central key which ties all of the colors together, the rust sofa, the blue rug, the brown chair, and the cream walls are just hard unrelated masses of color. So the theme idea—the picture, the wallpaper, the chintz that is a blend of all of the colors used in the room—is a desirable co-ordinator as well as an inspiration and guide in laying out the colors for the rest of the room.

TRAIN YOUR EYE

Even if there isn't a trick to the use of color, if you haven't had much traffic with color in the past, your young and tender urge may need a bit of coddling.

If your eye isn't used to spotting glamour colors, you may overlook them or, worse still, deliberately turn your back on them. So before you even select a picture, chintz, or bibelot you wish to use as a color guide, you will find it worthwhile to train your eye to *see* color.

Learning to use color is about the same as learning a language. Many people never acquire more than a nursery school color vocabulary. They see just the ordinary colors—pink, blue, green, and red.

If you are going to see and appreciate the subtle, interesting colors and combinations that are all about you, if your eyes are to respond to the possibilities of azure-blue, geranium-red, olive-green, or saffron-yellow, you will have to extend your color vocabulary.

Use the method a two-year-old uses in learning to talk. The child first learns single words. Next the words are linked in simple sentences. Finally whole compositions are undertaken. So it is with understanding color. First familiarize yourself with the thousands of available colors. Learn to *feel* them, instead of just to *see* them. Develop an emotional response to them. Only then will you be ready to put them together sensitively.

Take green for instance. Green isn't just green. It can be a thousand colors ranging from yellows just tinged with green through pure middle-value green, on to greens with varied amounts of blue in them.

Next consider greens as they range from the palest tint to greens that are almost black. If you took a paintbrush and mixed all of the greens that your eye can distinguish, you would use days, hundreds of pieces of paper, and pints of paint.

The room photographed at the left had a dark brown taste before it was remodeled. The furniture was all fairly new, but it had been moved into the room and forgotten, as a result there was not one feature in the room that attracted the eye.

Above see the same room and the same furniture handled with imagination and taste. The cretonne with its rosy-red ground and white flowers is the key to the color scheme. The wallpaper is white with a peppermint-pink stripe. Study the window design and the remodeled fireplace.

Now close your eyes and visualize greens in nature: grass, maple leaves, oak leaves, cedar, spruce green, the green of the Douglas fir, willow shoots in the spring, pale stocks of romaine, ice-green, the green of the sky at the horizon just after the sunset fades, sea-green, brownish kelp-green, dusty sage-green, olive-green, emerald-green, phosphorescent green of cats' eyes. All these are green. To think of them will help to make green a personal friend of yours.

Study the other colors in turn; red, yellow, blue, and violet until they bring similar pictures to mind. The reds will range through yellow-reds to red-violets. The yellows will start with the yellow-reds and range through pure yellows to yellow-greens. The yellow-greens merge into greens and blue-greens, and the blues start with blue-greens and end up blue-violets. The blue-violet hues slide into violet and meet up with reds in red-violets. This merging of one color into the next is best shown by a color wheel or rainbow.

The only value analyzing color has in decorating is to acquaint you with the infinite variety of each color. You must develop an impatience with just blue or just green. The thrill comes only when you find just the right blue or just the right green. As your color vocabulary grows, your color sense becomes more sophisticated. You will see and appreciate color harmonies that formerly escaped you entirely.

WORKING METHODS

If you can't think abstractly about color, think over things you like, and their color, and in that way you may find the key to your favorite color. The woods, the hills, sky, rocks, flowers, fabrics, Japanese color prints, Chinese porcelains, show windows, vegetable and fruit stalls, color pictures in magazines, costume ensembles, jewels, paintings, rugs, wallpaper, etc., all offer tremendous color inspiration.

It is our own fault if we starve our color sense, if we are mentally color blind. We have no one to blame but ourselves if we miss one of the most exquisite joys of life.

But that joy is not complete if you are always in the position of observer. Place yourself in the position of creator. Acquire the art of putting colors together. The satisfaction that comes from such an experience is worth working for and it comes automatically with decorating.

If you are taking your search for cultural development seriously, start right now making color collections. You will need one folder and two shoe boxes. Now as you leaf through magazines and see a color page that appeals, tear it out and put it in your folder for reference.

The pages you save may show fashions, foods, or automobiles. The subject matter of the illustration is of no importance if it shows an effective color combination.

In one box keep small clippings of fabrics, samples you get from stores, and other odds and ends. The swatches will handle more easily if they are all fairly uniform in size, say three by five inches. In the other box collect paper clippings. These may be squares from Christmas wrappings, wallpaper, etc.

To train your color eye, turn the clippings out on a table in front of you. Sort out all of the colors with blue in them, all of the reds, all of the yellows. Compose color schemes that appeal to you.

In one of my college art classes we mixed our own paints and made our own collection of color samples. The samples were cut in four-inch disks. Then a violinist came to the classroom and played for us, and as he played we developed color schemes suggested by the music. On another day poetry was read aloud and again we interpreted each poem in color. In this way we developed color dexterity.

WARM AND COLD COLORS

Probably the basic difference between colors is whether they are warm or cold.

The so-called warm colors are red and yellow, with all their related tints, shades, and variations—orange, coral, rust, pink, rose, burgundy, wine, mahogany, tan, beige, brown.

These are the colors which are associated with the sun, with fire, with warm Latin countries, with gypsies, with vitality and joy.

Gay, exciting carnival music naturally prompts color schemes in which light clear values of red, yellow, and orange dominate.

Translated into decorating, the warm colors have the same effect. In delicate tints the warm colors are young and spring-like and suggest young girls' rooms. In stronger values they become virile and masculine and seem right for game rooms and boys' rooms. See illustrations facing pages 23 and 295.

Warm, pleasant, hospitable living rooms are suggested when black is mixed with red and yellow to give brown, burgundy, and mahogany.

The cool colors, grey-green, blue, violet, are associated with the sky, grass, trees, distant hills, the ocean. Cool colors are not so intimate and exciting as the warm colors. They are restful and soothing; they are soft and pleasant to the eyes. They are more often associated with old age than youth; they are dignified.

These cool colors are indispensable in decorating and in light tints make ideal background colors. They make small rooms seem larger.

Incidentally, it is worth mentioning that white and grey are essentially cold colors. However, greys can be warm; there are pink-greys and yellow-greys, as well as cold green-greys and blue-greys.

Still thinking in terms of cold and warm colors, it is interesting to note that in almost all color schemes both warm and cool colors are used.

Who hasn't seen a blue room with cherry-red accent notes, a green room with bits of red and orange, a yellow room with grey, or a brown room with cool, sharp whites.

It is interesting and perhaps rather surprising to discover that when selecting favorite colors both warm and cold color will quite unconsciously be mentioned no matter how different the combinations.

When asked what colors she liked best, one of my friends selected chartreuse, blue-green, and blue-violet as her favorite assortment. These colors not only make a charming color scheme, but they also are attractive with her brown hair and blue-green eyes. Also notice that both warm and cold colors are represented.

Another friend quickly decided that she preferred peach, yellow, and blue. These too not only make an effective combination of colors, but they bring out Laura's golden-glinted brown hair and blue eyes. Moreover, both warm and cold hues are represented.

WHAT COLOR SHOULD IT BE

My personal preference is elephant-grey, seal-brown, and daffodil-yellow. With my brown hair and eyes this is easily understandable, and again there are warm and cold colors listed.

It does seem natural to like colors that are becoming and automatically to select warm and cold colors to use together. So again it is quite possible that your own favorite colors may be just the colors for you to use in a room.

While analyzing your own color reaction, decide whether you like an alive, vibrant room where vivid color plays a part, or whether you prefer soft, greyed colors that are less dramatic and exciting. Don't let timidity influence your answer. This problem is a matter of temperament as well as of personal coloring. Naturally, you should plan a background that brings out your own best points. You want your house to bring you out—not to eclipse you.

A friend of mine, a grey-haired woman, always surprises me when I see her in her own living room. Seen on the street or in a restaurant she is just a sweet middle-aged woman with a pleasant feminine quality. At home she is beautiful, a cosmopolitan. Invariably the walls of her living room, as well as the ceiling and woodwork, are an elusive, soft blue. The draperies are slightly deeper blue, with delicately pink Venetian blinds under fluted, ruffled, floor-length froths of curtain. There are rich pools of mirror glass and candle-filled crystal wall sconces that were picked up in Rome. The furniture is soft brown French walnut, and the upholstery is beige with perhaps one faded rose velvet bergere as well as a cocoa-brown one. The rug is a faded Aubusson in beige and blue, pink and brown.

This would be no room for a sportswoman, a wide-awake, impulsive gamin type of woman, or even a simple home body. The sportswoman would certainly feel happier with strong colors, blues, browns, and greens. She would want more pattern in the room and a less fragile air in general so that dogs, possibly, could roam at will and would not seem out of place.

A dark-skinned, dark-haired type of woman would again want higher keyed color. Spanish, Mexican, and even peasant color sources are rich with inspiration. Even the risky magenta and orange color combination is possible and becoming for dark coloring.

It is also obvious that your color scheme will inevitably be influenced by the climate of the section of the country where you live, and whether you live in town in a house or apartment, or whether you live in the country.

In a largely feminine household, the color scheme might well be different than in a home where the masculine contingent dominates. The age of the children, and the cat and dog questions, are other factors in developing color schemes. In fact, every element of your life enters in.

So, in addition to thinking about colors you like, think about colors that are becoming to you, to your taste and your habits. Only in this way can you work out a well balanced color scheme.

MORE TALK ABOUT COLOR SCHEMES

Perhaps you have wondered how many colors should be used in one room. There are no hard and fast rules. However, color schemes are simpler now than they have ever been because fewer colors are used.

Perhaps the wallpaper or chintz you have selected for your color key has ten or twenty colors in it. The trick is to select the color or two which please you most.

The easiest of all color schemes to develop are built around tints and shades of one color with plentiful dashes of white, black, or grey.

For example, perhaps you have several pieces of old blue willowware and you want to build a dining room around them. Paint the wall behind the buffet white. Hang your willowware on the wall over the buffet. Cover the other three walls with the well known blue and white Canton wallpaper. (It repeats the willowware design.) Paint the ceiling and all woodwork white. Use a blue rug and frothy, deeply ruffled floor-length organdy curtains at the window. Paint the chairs white and upholster them in blue. Leave the table and other pieces in red mahogany finish. It is all blue and white and it's a lovely room.

Even red can be handled in this way. The Russel Wrights (he is the well known designer) have a red and white bedroom. The walls are painted American-flag red. The ceiling, woodwork, Venetian blinds, rugs, bedspreads, and draperies are white. The furniture is blond maple and modern, of course.

WHAT COLOR SHOULD IT BE

Another red room that delights me is in a doctor's home in Ames, Iowa. It might be called a back parlor. The walls are pie-cherry red, the ceiling, woodwork, and draperies are white. But the rug is an old one dyed black. The sofa is upholstered in white leather, and there is a matching chair. The wood of the furniture is miscellaneous and is painted white, including an upright piano. It is a convivial room and inspires good conversation.

Even though in the examples given only one value of a color was used plus white this is not always the case. To create an effect of many colors, several tints and shades of a hue are often used. Thus, working with green in a living room, a pale grey-green might be used for walls and woodwork. A dark grey-green rug for the floor, a green and white striped sofa, a green and white chintz for draperies and slip covers on two club chairs, plus one white leather chair and a grey-green velvet chair with bushy white fringe in the seams would complete the room. Black lamp bases (Wedgwood or black marbleized wooden ones) would be striking and interesting.

Incidentally this green living room is made for flowers. Imagine how lovely rust-red chrysanthemums would be in it; visualize huge crystal bowls of yellow daffodils. See yourself greeting friends in this setting in a flaming red velvet gown!

TWO-COLOR EFFECTS

Probably the most common of all room color schemes are two-color ones, based on one cold color and one warm one. The combinations are endless; brandied-peach and magnolia-green, delphinium-blue and daffodil-yellow, shocking-pink and forget-me-not blue, coral and chartreuse, flag-red and navy blue, grey and wine-red, cream-in-coffee brown and French-blue, dove-grey and pale yellow.

In developing these two-color schemes, just as in the one-color plans, mix in liberal amounts of white, black, or grey, as well as tints and shades of the two colors. But even more important—one of the colors must dominate. Tints and shades of one color should be used for the largest masses and the other color should appear only in small amounts.

For instance, by introducing some red into the green room described above a two-color effect would result. The wing chair could be red, there could be a narrow red stripe in the green and white striped sofa. A framed print of Van Gogh's green and rose-red *Laurier Roses* over the mantel would tie the whole color scheme together. (Illustration on page 60.)

Instead of using one warm color and one cold color, harmonies may be approached by the effective use of closely related colors. Thus coral (yellow-orange) and chartreuse (yellow-green) are effective together. They are linked by yellow which is in each color. Again, blue, turquoise (blue-green), and chartreuse (yellow-green) are pleasing as there is a trace of blue in each.

A FEW PRACTICAL POINTS

If you follow these general outlines, if you experiment, if you delve within yourself and discover the colors that mean something to you, you will soon be exhilarated by your growing feeling for fresh color combinations. True, there are a few rules to tuck away in the back of your mind. You will find it easier to plan successful color schemes if you confine them to variations of only two or three colors plus the neutrals, white, grey, and black, used as blenders. You will discover that only one color, or at most two, should be used in large masses and that the third color should be intense in value but used very sparingly and only for accent.

For practical reasons you will have to check over your room and consider which things that you already have must stay as they are in your remodeling plan. If a rug must be used, take it into your color plans. You won't have to worry about furniture woods, which behave very well. For that matter, wood colors can be easily changed by painting or refinishing. Slip covers can bring upholstery around to a new color theme fairly inexpensively. The chances are that the draperies aren't, and never were, right.

Before you make a move to do any shopping, get your plan worked out to the last detail. Take with you actual fabric or paper color samples from your source boxes. With this in hand you are ready to go shopping. You will be charmed to find what a protection against confusion it is to have your color scheme worked out in advance and color samples in your hand when you go shopping. It will simplify matters unbelievably.

This is a silvery green and yellow room. It is delicate in color but beautifully practical. The grey wall paper has a delicate silver tracery. The woodwork is grey and the leaf patterned damask draperies and sofa cover are also silvery grey. At night yellow casement curtains are drawn to cover the white curtains. Pale turquoise blue printed linen on two chairs, tangerine velvet on the desk bench and turquoise blue on a love seat by the fireplace offer color relief. Decorators Grace Hyman and Rebecca Dunphy.

But notwithstanding your careful plans and notwithstanding the fact that you may find a fabric, a piece of wallpaper, or a rug that apparently matches your sample perfectly, don't get excited and make your purchase immediately. Get a sample, as big a one as possible. Take it home and try it in the exact location it is to be used. Leave it there. Look at it as the light changes through the day, and at night under artificial light. Your eye will tell you whether or not you are right.

Don't consult even your best friend about it. They are your room, your family, and your draperies. You yourself should know, better than anyone else, whether your choice is good. You are the one who will have to live with it. You know what you want. Make up your own mind. It is the only way to unlock your own mental and emotional doors to color understanding.

Such understanding of color will have twice the value of any known rules. In fact Brooks Atkinson, drama critic of *The New York Times*, has this to say about rules:

"Rules do no harm if they are kept in their proper place, which is a humble one . . . in order to keep things in proportion it is necessary to remember that rules are only a by-product of creation . . . that, unless they are so general as to be meaningless, they have to be revised when a genuine artist comes along."

Mr. Atkinson continued, "Someone was remarking the other day that Van Gogh would have been less great as an artist if he had ever learned to paint . . . For the basic thing in art is not a code of good behavior but an artist with mind and spirit and direct contact with life. He needs rules less than he needs freedom of expression."

Remember this when working out your own color schemes. Let them express you.

HOW TO USE COLOR

THERE are many learned and scientific ways to approach this all-important subject, but I'm going to take the simplest and most direct way and tell you how we plan color schemes in the Good Housekeeping Studio work. Consider in this order: the purpose of the room, the type, the exposure and the size. Naturally the choice of wall covering will differ for a hall, or a bedroom, and remember that the color in walls is the controlling factor in a color scheme because it occupies the largest area. Halls, living-rooms, dining-rooms generally demand some formality. Bedrooms usually are informal.

By type is meant, not size or shape, or height, of room, but the general period or atmosphere which the room will have, such as Contemporary in plate 76, or Colonial as in plate 77.

A sunny room with a south-east, or south-west exposure may have darker colors, such as wood paneling, and cooler colors such as gray. Rooms with little or no sun, especially north rooms, should have warm colors such as yellow, rose, and even red, while gray should be avoided. With dead white walls the draperies and furnishing may give coolness or warmth as needed. In a very small room, generally speaking, smaller patterns in wall paper, and neutral tones in plain color on the walls are best. Large rooms, especially when well proportioned, lend themselves to a great variety of schemes, no matter what the exposure.

Let us use as an example for assembling a color scheme the room illustrated in plate 76. This was a living room in our Exhibition House at Valley Stream, Long Island. The house was Colonial in character so we determined on a living room in the Contemporary feeling. The exposure was south-east with sun pouring in, so a cool green was chosen for the walls. The size being approximately thirteen by twenty-three feet the proportions were pleasant, and therefore presented no problem.

But as there are greens and greens, arriving at the right green for these walls was controlled by everything else to be chosen for the room. Years ago I invented for myself what I call the color card (plate 75), which I use as an artist would a palette. This is where the colors are mixed, and when found right lined up under each other to see if they blend. In this room 18th Century wood furniture was to be used with chintz, as the room was in a country house and was to be gay and colorful and yet have a hint of formality. It also had to be inexpensive as it was a budget house. The first step was to find the chintz. As suggested in the opening chapter of this book, a single piece of chintz may give you the complete color scheme for a room. It did so here. The gay floral pattern chosen had tones of rose, blue, yellow, and green on a white ground. The softest tone of green gave the shade for the walls; the stronger tone for the green and white striped curtains, and plain sofa pillows. A tannish-beige rug with a self-colored pattern blended with the general color effect of the chintz and with the natural pine and brown mahogany of the furniture. To try this idea of color, before buying any fabric we lined up the color scheme as in plate 75. We spread out an ordinary card folder, and pasted a sample of green for walls at top. For this we used an actual sample of paint, but a wallpaper sample could have been used. Next comes the contrasting wood trim. In this case it was a white cornice and venetian blinds so we put a piece of white paper on the card. This means that white was used in lamp shades and other places in the room. We put the sample for striped curtains with trimming under it. Then came a good sized sample of chintz which is used for the sofa and one chair, and next the striped material came again

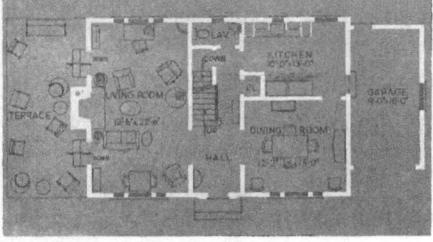

This is the first floor plan of the house in which the living room shown on plate 76 appeared. As the hall, dining room, and living room opened into each other, the same carpeting was used in all three, thus increasing their apparent size. This is a good idea to consider in planning related color schemes in a relatively small house

COLOR SCHEME FOR LIVING ROOM
GREEN ACRES HOUSE
VALLEY STREAM, LONG ISLAND

Walls: painted olive green like sample attached

Surbase, mantel, window, and door trim painted same olive green as walls

Venetian blinds and cornice at ceiling painted white

Draperies: Green and white cotton stripe, 36" wide, at 75c a yard. Draperies made with box pleats to hang to floor. Straight valance mounted on buckram

Trimming on Valances: white cotton fringe at 8c a yard

Sofa and one comfortable chair covered in chintz, 36" wide, at 49c a yard

Overstuffed chair and side chairs in green and white cotton stripe same as draperies

Wing Chair: olive green damask, 50" wide, at $4.75 a yard

Floor Covering: Beige fern-patterned rug, 12' by 21', approximate retail price $162.50

PLATE 75

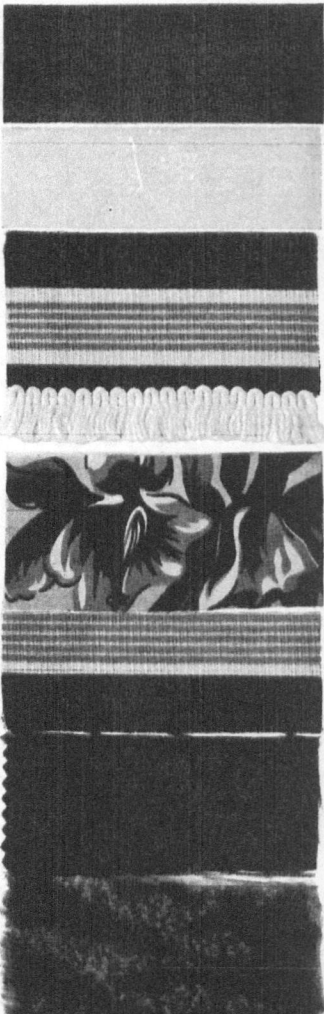

PLATE 76: Studying this picture will show how the entire color scheme grew naturally from the colors in the chintz

as this was used for chairs as well as window draperies. A deeper, serviceable fabric follows in olive green damask which covered a wing chair. Last of all came a sample of the rug. There is our color scheme lined up. If we find a jarring note, or feel uncertain about some color we take it out and try something else in its place using the colors in the chintz as a guide since it was chosen for the base of the scheme, and selected because it was attractive. Therefore it was well to follow the colors in it. The accents in it, such as pink and yellow, were used in the ornaments in the room and repeated in a picture. You yourself can easily paste up such a color card when you are determining the color scheme for your own room. You will find it a great help in making sure ahead of time that your room will present a harmonious whole. Another excellent way for the layman to decide if the colors to be used are right, is to pin a large piece of the wall covering on a screen or on the wall; tack up the curtain material near it, and throw the furniture fabric over a chair under it. Place a sample of rug under the chair and study the group of colors. Leave them over night and see if they are pleasing to you when you look at them with a fresh eye. If so, go ahead feeling confident that you have a color scheme you will like to live with.

Besides the actual colors there must be a proper distribution of color, and pattern. For instance as striped curtain material was used in four places in the room just described, it was well to cover one chair with it, to relate the curtains to the furniture. By the same token the green in the curtains was in the chintz used for fireside grouping, and the plain green sofa pillows. It is the right combination of plain and patterned surface that gives a harmonious feeling. Just a touch like the bowl of yellow tulips (any yellow flowers would have done) brought out the yellow in the chintz. The white cording on the green pillows, and the green and white rope edge on the white lamp shades blended all the colors pleasantly.

MAKING UP THE COLOR CARD FROM A DIFFERENT STARTING POINT

In the method of arriving at the color scheme of the room decorated in the Contemporary manner, a piece of chintz was used as a guide. Another way to arrive at a color scheme is when a definite color is wanted for the walls, or when the type of room demands a given treatment. Examples of both are shown here. In plate 77 in the Colonial room we determined we wanted a certain shade of blue which had been used in the restoration of Williamsburg, Virginia. It was the basis of the scheme. In plate 83 showing the French Provincial living room-dining room, paneled walls were wanted and the room was to have a definite French Provincial character. The color cards for these schemes were made up from the color of the backgrounds instead of from the chintz. And in both cases *type* had a controlling influence. Among the lovely Williamsburg colors which have taken the country by storm is the blue used for the walls of the living-dining room illustrated at right.

This was taken as a basic color and was put at the top of the card. The pine paneled chimney place, and wood cornice (true to type or period) came next on the card. Then the colors which belonged to the period were considered. Reason it out this way. In informal 17th Century and early 18th Century American rooms, pine or maple furniture would be used. Floors would be bare with scatter rugs. Getting our inspiration from the authentic furnishing of Williamsburg, we found red was used as well as certain types of India prints brought over in sailing ships. We decided upon maple furniture and India prints for curtains. The red and blue in the print had to be right with the blue of the wall. We found a print which was. Then we found a solid red for covering one chair, and because there was yellow in the print, we found a small figured chintz with the blue, red, and yellow in it for covering the barrel chair by the fireplace. Last of all we found the braided rugs (right for the period) of blue, red, yellow, and black. These we used in two sizes: a small rug for the fireplace group, and a larger one for the main part of the room. Each of these colors was pasted on the color card in the order shown in plate 75, and considered to see if they were right together. When they were found to be right, we went ahead with a definite picture of the room and the color scheme in our minds.

In passing, note the plan of this room. It makes a comfortable living-dining room and

In many houses the need for a little study for the man of the house outweighs the need for a separate dining room. The plan at the left shows how space was saved and a satisfactory living-dining room arrangement was worked out. In PLATE 77, opposite, you will see the fireplace end of this living-dining room with its lovely Williamsburg color scheme

PLATE 77

In the living-dining room above the soft gray-blue of the walls, determined the colors and the type of fabrics selected for the room

Quaint, old-fashioned Early American wallpaper set the color scheme in the little study at the right. The furniture is maple in antique finish; a hooked rug was used

PLATE 78

would be charming in small suburban or country houses. It contains all the furniture needed for comfort: soft, easy chairs, a good secretary desk, and a number of small tables, as well as a good dining table, serving table, and dining chairs. The plan shows a group of windows, opposite the fireplace, which could have the two side windows, or the center only, filled with glass shelves, on which could be put the interesting old red and blue glass of this period. This glass would definitely be a part of the color scheme.

In the French Provincial room (Plate 83) the same steps were followed. The color of the wood paneling was determined by type and put on the card. Then the period was studied to find the colors and types of fabrics used in old French cottages and small manor houses. There was no wish to be absolutely authentic but rather to recapture the atmosphere of such rooms, using modern and available materials. Reds and blues again were found, but of an entirely different sort. The rugs taking up large areas are of the rag variety of today but they were selected because of their informal character and color. As this was to be a practical room, again a solid color—blue—was used for the two couches (really beds) on each wall near the fireplace. This is a major color when put on the card. A fabric was found for the curtains with red in it, so the red was accented by the binding of the curtains, and the red couch pillows. This room serves a double purpose. The dining room portion is in the center of the room, and the living room group is in front of a deep recessed bay window. The furniture is French Provincial, and the attractive ornaments, lamps, and old French prints repeat the colors in the chintz and make a very gay informal room, just as attractive for winter ones, as for summer. As a matter of fact it is a summer cottage and faces south-east, so that the flood of sunshine keeps the room warm in color notwithstanding the wood walls and the blue rugs.

Color schemes for the two bedrooms, on the opposite page, were determined by type. In the room with the four-poster beds the theme was—"the Regency feeling." We therefore selected a gray wallpaper with a Classical feeling, practically colorless, and looked for an interesting chintz. When we found the chintz we liked we used it as the base for the color scheme and made up our color card accordingly.

In the Modern bedroom the theme was—"Modern." In this case we found a wallpaper of Modern design and used *it* as a base for the color scheme and then made up the color card. The same method was followed for the Modern living room, Plate 85.

Accessories play an important part in color schemes, and contribute greatly to livableness. Many a woman follows a correct color scheme, has nice furniture in the various rooms of her house, good pictures or prints hanging on the walls, and yet the room or house is cold. It lacks livableness. It has no charm. And if you look further the chances are that it will be found to be rather uncomfortable. One of the things that add greatly to comfort is the use of proper accessories—lamps to read by on small tables near comfortable chairs, ashtrays for those who smoke, vases of flowers or pottery containers for ivy and other potted plants. And all these accessories may be cleverly used to point up a color scheme. Let us suppose that your living room has gray walls, a deep blue rug, and curtains and a slipcovered chair or two of chintz with a blue background and a design in gray and sepia, with just a touch or two of soft rose and creamy yellow. A color scheme of this sort would be used in a sunny room, as it is predominantly cool in effect. To point it up, and prevent it from seeming too severe, accessories in yellow and soft rose are used. For example: a gray pottery lamp with a warm yellow shade, and yellow shades on other floor and table lamps; vases and ashtrays repeating the rose of the chintz, and perhaps a vari-colored pottery bowl in yellow, brown, and deep rose to hold potted bulbs.

Glance through the illustrations in this chapter and see how much the accessories contribute to the color scheme. In Plate 76, for example, observe how the black lamp repeats the black of the hearth stone and gives character to the color scheme as a whole. The little mantel figurines in green and crystal glass repeat in a deeper tone the green of the walls and the curtains. In Plate 77 pewter acessories were freely used, both because of their period suitability, and because their soft, dull sheen added a needed note to the color scheme as a whole. See how the desk blotter is edged in the red of the wing chair with the quill pen repeating this color. Little things, to be sure, but they make all the difference to the general effect of a room.

In the Modern bedroom, Plate 80, white and crystal accessories accent the white pattern of the wallpaper and the clear white curtains.

Again, in the French Provincial Living Room, Plate 83, the accessories were chosen to repeat the dominant colors—blue, red, and white. On the table at the left a white vase of flowers balances the white lamp at the right. Little ornaments on the shelves above the two couches again repeat these three colors. So look to your accessories—they can do much to make or mar a color scheme.

Definite period requirements set the color note in this Regency bedroom. The wallpaper in gray, with an architectural dado and cornice pattern, and the soft green rug form a pleasing background for the formal chintz of the period in green with sepia and gray flowers. Particularly interesting is the use of black and gold Chinese Chippendale beds combined with mahogany furniture inspired by Sheraton. Two chairs, also in black and gold, are typical of the Regency period. Accessories are of crystal suitable to the period with a few notes of pale yellow china

PLATE 79

PLATE 80

Here is a bedroom in the Modern manner with a color scheme in dusty shades which are so restful and attractive. A Modern wallpaper in dull dusty pink with a large floral motif in white and coppery brown covers three walls; the fourth is painted the color of the background of the wallpaper — interesting and simple to do. Against this wall stand the beds of palest bleached maple with bedspreads of pale beige chenille. The carpet is a slightly deeper shade than the wood of the furniture and the floor length glass curtains are of white voile. Dressing table, easy chair, bench, are covered in coppery quilted chintz

PAINT, WALLPAPER, AND FABRICS IN RELATION TO PERIOD

Rococo patterns are to be found in wallpapers, rugs, and fabrics, and are finding their place both in 19th Century and some Modern rooms. Due to its ornate character it is well to use this type of thing sparingly; when used with restraint it may be charming.

In a living room for instance the walls could be hung with a paper such as that shown in Plate 81. This has a definite period feeling of the 19th Century, whereas the other materials suggested, with the exception of the dull satin stripe, which belongs with the wallpaper, are rather Modern in character. This is an example of what is being done today in combining fabrics of Modern texture and coloring with the well-defined designs of the 18th and 19th centuries. Rococo is a broad term for the rather florid designs of the second quarter of the 19th century. Oddly enough, it can be used charmingly as an accent in Modern rooms to relieve the straight lines. In the group illustrated a deep brown was chosen for the color of the rug. For the sofa, which is usually found in a living room, the dull satin stripe of brown, beige, and green was used. The curtains on the other hand were soft beige corresponding to the stripe in the upholstery. Brown fringe harmonizing with the stripe in the upholstery finished the edges. To give accent to the tans, browns, and creams of the color scheme, the rather vivid green in the striped material was repeated in a diagonal weave fabric for use on one or two upholstered easy chairs.

Although generalization in color may be helpful, perhaps an example illustrated by the color group in Plate 82 will make it clearer to the layman. Take, for instance, the Regency period which was an outgrowth of French Empire and English 18th Century. Furniture of this type might well be combined with modern fabrics to give that freshness to decorating which is desired today. In the lower group on the opposite page is a suggestion for a dining room. A modern carpet in soft gray was chosen to be used with a wallpaper of gray and white stripe. Against this neutral background a modern chintz with striking color is suggested. The predominating gray (deeper than the walls) is splashed with fruit, ears of corn, and leaves in vivid greens, soft coppers, and browns. To bring the note of gray which is in the curtains into the room it was used in solid color for the chair seats.

This group illustrates the choice of a design to suit the purpose of the room. In a dining room a wallpaper with the horn of plenty spilling grapes and fruits is a suitable theme, just as this chintz with the ears of corn and grapes is delightful. Look for chintz with this in mind. In fact ask for such designs as there are many on the market.

Another attractive color scheme for a dining room of almost any period feeling, is the use of gray walls, painted or papered (if the room is sunny) with plain red curtains. Pattern should be brought into the room by pictures or paintings of fruit and flowers.

An attractive color scheme for a Colonial bedroom (which unfortunately we cannot show) is the following. A wallpaper with a soft gray-blue ground has tiny figures of the Colonial period in old-pink and periwinkle blue. The rug chosen to go with this is in a deeper shade of the blue, while the curtains are a soft dusty pink with a light brown stripe. This gives the three essential colors: blue, rose, and brown. In a bedroom the other area of importance is whatever is used for the bedspread and for glass curtains. In this case white organdie with a blue leaf and dot design is used to drape the four-poster bed and to make the full petticoat on a draped dressing table. This sheer white and periwinkle blue repeating the color in the wallpaper is most attractive. Beige is used for the chair coverings. Either antique maple or mahogany furniture of the Early Colonial period would blend admirably with this color scheme. The accessories are in crystal, with touches of periwinkle blue and the rose of the draperies. This is a case again where a wallpaper of a definite period, Colonial, can be combined with fabrics of modern texture in the clear modern colors for draperies, upholstery, and floor covering. It requires some skill, but if you will assemble the samples of fabrics and see for yourself by the use of the color card if they combine well, you will find yourself getting some interesting and individual effects without losing the character of the period which you wish to reproduce.

PLATE 81

PLATE 82

SUGGESTED COLOR SCHEMES

LIVING-ROOMS

Type	Walls	Rug	Furniture	Upholstery	Curtains	Accessories
Contemporary	Slate blue	Honey beige	Mahogany; black lacquer	Burgundy; beige and white; off-white chintz with gray-blue and burgundy in design; striped rose and white chintz	White spun rayon with burgundy cord valances	Black, gold, white, burgundy, silver
18th Century	Terra cotta pink	Two-tone brown	Mahogany; black and gold	Plum, cream, brown, and pink	Plum and cream stripe	White, beige, pink, and dark green
Modern	Mauve pink	Beige and mauve	Honey color mahogany in Swedish modern design	Gray-blue; mauve and brown; beige and white	White net	Crystal, white, and plum

HALLS

Type	Walls	Rug	Furniture	Upholstery	Curtains	Accessories
Contemporary	Gray paper with white and brown design—white woodwork	Mahogany brown linoleum with white and gray design	Mahogany, black lacquer	Brown leather, gray damask	White tweedweave rayon	Brown glass, black, silver
18th Century	Terra cotta pink and white—terra cotta pink trim	Brown two-tone	Mahogany	Plum and pink	White	White

DINING-ROOMS

Type	Walls	Rug	Furniture	Upholstery	Curtains	Accessories
18th Century	Cocoa brown with white design; woodwork—cocoa brown and white	Beige	Pine; black lacquer	Green and white	White with brown trim	Dull gold
18th Century	Gray, white, and plum—pink trim	Brown	Mahogany; gray lacquer	Pink	Plum and beige stripe	Silver, crystal; gold and white china
Modern	Mauve pink—woodwork off-white	Beige and mauve	Honey color mahogany in Swedish Modern design	Beige	White; yellow gold	Crystal

136

PLATE 83: French Provincial is a charming style, suited to country cottages, which should not be overlooked

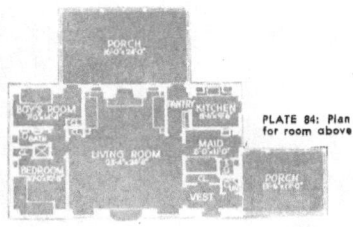

PLATE 84: Plan for room above

PLATE 85: A Modern cottage living room

Type	Walls	Rug	Furniture	Upholstery	Curtains	Accessories
BEDROOMS						
18th Century	Pale beige paper; white trim	Cinnamon	Mahogany; white lacquer and gold	Beige; nasturtium pink; white and pale green	Beige; pink and white	White, pink, and brown
18th Century	Gray and yellow figured paper	Soft green	Mahogany	Gray, white, and yellow	Bright yellow	Light and dark green, yellow, and white
Modern	Dusty pink paper with white and coppery brown design	Beige	Honey colored mahogany	Dusty pink; beige	White	Crystal, white, coppery brown
BOY'S ROOM						
Nautical	White paper with nautical design in red and blue	Blue, red, and white mixture	Rock maple	Blue, red	Blue and white	Nautical
MAN'S ROOM						
Modern	Warm beige—woodwork beige—window frames white	Beige tufted	Honey colored mahogany	Green; green and beige woven fabric	Dull green	Ivory, copper, brown, beige
STUDY						
Cottage—Mexican Feeling	Soft green, beige and copper	Beige and dark green plaid	Walnut	Green and beige	Beige	Brown, green, rust
POWDER ROOM						
Contemporary	Gray and yellow paper	Gray marbleized with white and yellow design	White plaster dressing table, festooned in ivory fringe	White fringe top on bench	White	Crystal

HOW TO USE COLOR

Most of the homes I visit—and my work calls me into hundreds of homes each year—are in themselves mute but eloquent testimonials of the ignorance of even the more cultivated people, of the real possibilities of color as applied to home decoration.

Not that we err by using garish or overly brilliant colors in our homes. We go to the opposite extreme and limit our palette to the low-keyed, sad-eyed grays, dull browns and taupes. Those who have graduated from the monotones of browns (what Oscar Wilde called "brown ambiguities") that were so popular a few years ago have adopted the even more uninteresting, colorless taupe as the dominant hue of their living rooms: taupe upholstery, taupe rugs, taupe draperies.

In a great many homes, however, there is no apparent dominating hue, but an assemblage of furniture, rugs, draperies, upholstery and pictures which in color are for the most part unrelated to each other and in many instances utterly hostile to each other.

Even in the homes where the hand of the professional decorator is manifest, the timidity of the mistress—or master—of the house in many cases has so emasculated the color scheme that all that the color expresses is a quiet, well-bred, characterless nonentity. Very rarely does one have the joy of finding a room in which rich, deep, glowing color has been used intelligently and freely. We are afraid of color. The pictures on our walls prove it. Look at them! How dull they are! How gray and drab and sad toned. Black and white lead in popularity, with sepia and gray close seconds.

This is the protest I hear most frequently when urging Mrs. Home-maker to make her home the abode of joyous, harmonious color. "But, Mr. Crane, I want my living room to be quiet and reposeful." And I feel like answering, "The most quiet and reposeful place known to man is the tomb." Living rooms *should* be reposeful—the keynote of the living room should be comfortable restfulness. But I know of nothing more conducive to an atmosphere of comfort and restfulness than a fine harmony of deep-toned, rich color in the appointments of the room.

I feel quite sure you will agree with me that the Six-Hundred-Dollar living room described in Chapter II is wholly comfortable and restful in looks and appointments. Yet the color of everything in it, from the walls to the upholstery, is rich and definite. But the colors first of all are beautiful in themselves; secondly, they are suited to the exposure of the room; thirdly, they harmonize with each other, and finally, they express the strength and sweetness of character of the people for whose use the room was furnished and decorated.

COLOR OUR NATURAL ENVIRONMENT

The fact is we live in a world of color. No pigments or dyes ever have been invented which are brilliant enough to reproduce the colors of nature under the morning sunlight. Color is our natural and lifelong environment. Why then, shoo it out of our homes? Why? Because, as I said before, we are afraid of it; not of color itself, but of the tragic mess we make of it when in our ignorance of the laws of color association we essay to use it.

THE REVERSE OF THE SHIELD

Having displayed one side of the shield, it is only fair that I show the other; and I am pleased beyond measure to be able to say there is another and totally different face to this subject of color in home decoration; this is that within the past three or four years, particularly in larger cities, a tremendous vogue for color has utterly transformed the homes of the great majority of people of cultivated taste.

HOW TO USE COLOR

And this vogue, since it is sponsored not only by people of taste and discrimination, but also by the leaders of that vague and more or less exclusive domain which is featured in the Sunday newspapers under the head of "Society," is bound in time to become universal. Fortunately, in this new and growing enthusiasm for rich, strong, harmonious color in our home environment, the example set by "Society" can exert only a wholesome and beneficial influence over the home life.

MUST USE SOME COLOR

Now here is a significant and vital fact: Whether you know anything about color or not—whether you love it or fear it—the very moment you undertake to furnish a home that *moment you begin to use it!* For every article of furniture, every rug, lamp or picture you place in your home has color; it is its color, in fact, that makes it visible. And since you *must* introduce color into your home, the part of wisdom is to make that color contribute to the comfort and pleasure of all that dwell in that house. More than that, color is not only the master key to beauty in home decoration, but it is the chief ally and first aid to the home-maker of limited means, for color offers *the most economical way to achieve beauty.* Manifestly, therefore, the first lesson for the amateur home decorator to learn is how to use color in order that she may avail herself of this tremendous decorative asset.

All I shall attempt to do in this study is to outline some of the simplest, most practical and useable facts about color—such as the characteristics of the more common colors, the way they act on each other, on rooms and on people; what colors may be used together; how to distribute the colors in a room; what particular color combinations are most appropriate for the various rooms of a house and, in short, how to go about it to build a color scheme for any given room.

I shall begin by showing the relationship of the commoner colors to each other—simplifying the process by the use of the accompanying color chart.

As every one knows there are three colors that cannot be produced by combining any of the other colors—RED, YELLOW, BLUE; from these three, in conjunction with black and white, all the other colors are produced. For this reason they are called the *Primary Colors*. These you will find in the small circles at the apexes of the triangle.

Midway between these three colors, in the middle spaces, outside the triangle are three other colors—Orange, Violet and Green, which are called *Secondary Colors* or *Binaries*. They are formed by combining two primaries, yellow and red, producing orange; red and blue, producing violet; and blue and yellow, producing green.

Then on either side of these secondary colors are other areas containing what are known as the *Tertiary Colors*—colors formed by mixing a primary and a secondary together; for instance, the product of yellow (a primary) and orange (a secondary) is yellow-orange; while the union of red with orange yields red-orange.

A mixture of red and violet makes red-violet, violet and blue mixed together produce blue-violet. Then again, uniting green with yellow gives us yellow-green, while a union of blue and green yields green-blue.

These twelve hues are by no means the limit to which these color divisions can or do go—the spectrum showing an almost infinite number of colors, one great authority on color dividing the chromatic circle into seventy-two parts. These twelve, however, together with black and white and the grays, are sufficient for our use in home decoration.

The diagram can be used to show at a glance what colors are blood relations—or colors that have a common element: For instance, red-orange, orange, orange-yellow, yellow, yellow-green and green, all contain the common color, yellow; therefore they can all be safely used in combination. So, too, all the colors that have blue in them—green, blue-green, blue-violet, violet and violet-red, being unified by their common constituent, are, therefore, useable together in color harmonies.

The diagram also indicates the various complementary relationships of color. For example, green, being composed of blue and yellow, has for its complementary the remaining primary, red. Violet, a product of red and blue, has the third primary, yellow, as its complementary; while orange, composed of red and yellow, takes the remaining primary, blue, as its complementary. The diagram shows these complementary relationships by means of the arrows in the triangle. Following the arrow from the circle entitled yellow, we come

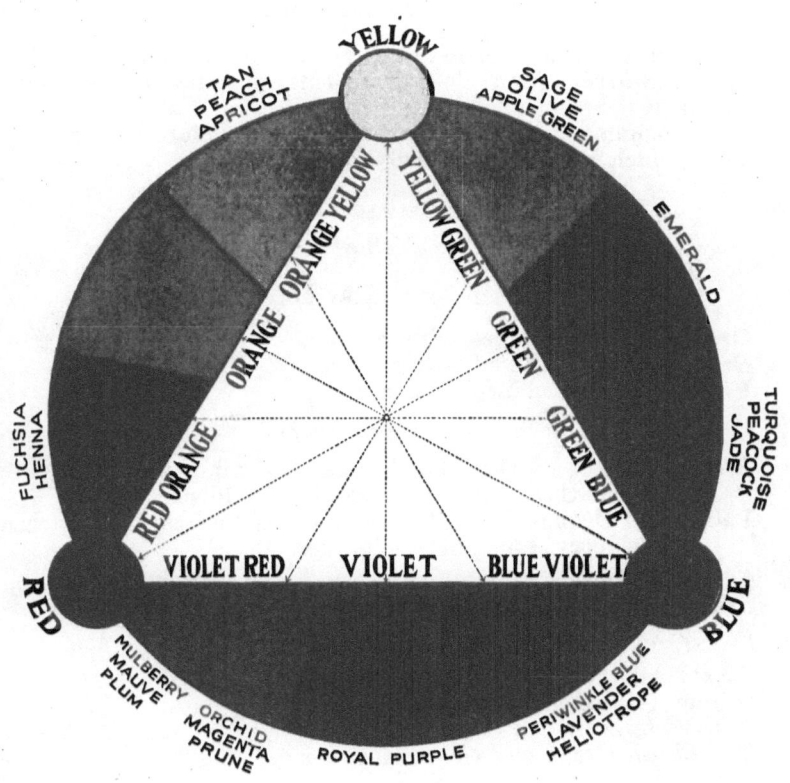

Color Plate No. 2—Color Chart

HOW TO USE COLOR

to violet, the complementary of yellow; or reversing the direction, the arrow from violet brings us to yellow as its complementary.

The summary below brings these facts before the eye in a form which makes them easily apprehended.

THE PRIMARY COLORS

Red Yellow Blue

THE SECONDARY COLORS

Orange: (Red combined with yellow).
Green: (Blue combined with yellow).
Violet: (Blue combined with red).

The Warm Colors

Red: In all of its shades and tints—including pink, rose, carmine and those browns which show reddish tones.
Yellow and Orange: In all their tints and shades, such as ecru, cream, ivory, tan, putty color, etc.
Yellow-Green.
Violet-Red: The mauves, orchids, mulberrys, plum, etc.

The Cool Colors

Blue: All the blues.
Green: All except yellow-green.
Blue-Violet.
The Bluish Grays and Greenish Grays.

THE NEUTRAL COLORS

Black White Pure Gray

THE COMPLEMENTARY COLORS

Green (composed of Blue and Yellow): Takes Red as its Complementary.
Violet (composed of Blue and Red): Takes Yellow as its Complementary.
Orange (composed of Yellow and red): Takes Blue as its Complementary.

CHARACTERISTICS OF COLOR

In addition to these relationships of color it is necessary to know something of the characteristics of color—concerning its effect on rooms, on other colors and on people. These characteristics are constant—they never change.

Red: The color of fire and blood. The warmest of all colors. Richness and hospitality, splendor and dignity are symbolized by it. Always aggressive and attention-compelling. Splendidly decorative when used in small quantities, but dangerous in large masses. Particularly appropriate for use in libraries and dining rooms. An advancing color. Used on walls makes rooms appear smaller. Pink is red lightened with white. Gayety, vivacity and animation are suggested by it; also the idea of youthfulness and daintiness. A tint of red that can safely be used in large masses. Best in bedrooms.

Yellow: The color of light. A warm color and the most luminous of all the colors. Expresses the idea of cheerfulness, sunshine, prosperity. The most adaptable of all colors; may be used freely in all of its tints and shades from cream, ivory, peach and ecru up to butter color and pure yellow.

Blue: The coldest color; associated in the mind with loftiness, spaciousness and tranquility of the sky. A noble color in decoration. Useful in almost any room except the breakfast room. Goes particularly well with the tans, orange and browns. Used in its lighter tones as a wall color it makes a room seem larger than it really is.

Orange: A product of Red and Yellow and partakes of the heat of red and the light of yellow. Of great decorative potency. Tan and golden brown are derivatives of orange.

Green: A quiet, restful color linked in human thought with the foliage tones of nature. A product of blue, a cold color, and yellow, a warm color. Yellow-green having a preponderance of yellow in its composition is a warm hue. All the other greens are reckoned as cold. Very useful in toning down over bright and too sunny rooms. Combines effectively with its constituents blue and yellow and with its complementary red.

Violet: Commonly called purple; the color of shadows, mystery and deep splendor. In its redder tones, such as mulberry, orchid, mauve and plum it tends toward warmth; the bluer tones, such as lavender and periwinkle-blue, are cool. Combines well with grays, gold, yellow, black and the greens. Lavender and orchid are most effective for use in bedroom decoration. Taffeta and silks may be used or chintzes with these colors in combination with others, using, if desired, an edging of lavender silk or taffeta.

Black and White and Gray: Are the neutral colors. Used in small quantities with the other colors, black and white set off and intensify the others through the effect of contrast. Mixing these two produces gray, a soft, unaggressive, background color. In room decoration pure neutral gray should rarely, if ever, be used; rather it should be tinged with the dominant hue of the room to key in with the furnishings of the room, as in the case of greenish gray, yellowish gray, creamy gray, blueish gray, lavender gray, etc. Such so-called grays, of course, are not, properly speaking, real grays, but rather are low-toned blues, greens, violets and yellows.

HUE, VALUE, INTENSITY

Before going on to discuss how to build a color scheme, I must briefly refer to three attributes of color which must be dwelt with whenever we undertake to use it. They are hue, value and intensity.

By *hue* is meant simply the name of the color—a means of designation, as for example, blue, orange, yellow, violet, red, yellow-green.

Value has to do with light and shade. We speak of medium values or tones, light values or tones, dark values or tones. A familiar use of the term is found in the rule "rooms should be decorated in an ascending scale of values," which means darker tones at the lowest part of the room—the floor; the lightest tones at the top—the ceiling; and medium tones in the spaces between —the walls.

The best synonym for *intensity* is intensity. The word is self-explanatory; we express different intensities of a hue by means of such adjectives as vivid, soft, glowing, dull, brilliant, etc.

INTERIOR FURNISHING AND DECORATION

HOW TO BUILD A COLOR SCHEME

The steps taken and the processes employed in building a color scheme are quite fully described in the story of the Six-Hundred-Dollar living room told in Chapter II. I would advise the reader to make frequent references to that story while studying this subject of color. The real purpose of that chapter is to present an object lesson which concretely illustrates as many home decorating principles and processes as possible; and it can be made particularly helpful in connection with the study of color.

You will recall that almost the first step was to decide on a dominant hue. Any successful scheme of color for home decoration will require the use of three colors—and as many as six may be used, if desired, but one of them must be used so much more freely than the others as to dominate the rest. No arrangement or composition of colors in decoration can be called satisfying or correct unless the dominant hue is readily apparent.

The factors which determine the selection of the dominant hue are:
1. The amount and quality of the light, and
2. The preferences of the occupants of the room.

Rooms in which the light is warm require the cool colors to tone down the warmth; those in which the quality of light is cold should be cheered up by the use of warm colors.

THE WALL COLOR THE PRIME CONSIDERATION

Here is a point that many decorators even, seem not to have grasped in its full significance: You may use warm colors if you like, in a south and west-facing room if you first cool the reflected light by toning down the walls by the use of cool tints of gray or gray-green—or vice versa, if you wish to employ the cool colors in the draperies, upholstery and floor coverings in a cold north room you may do so with satisfactory results provided you first warm the light of your room by putting warm colors in the large reflecting areas—the walls and ceiling; a cream-colored wall in a small room, or in large rooms even more intense hues of yellow might be used. One wonderful north dining room with walnut paneled wainscote has walls done in butter color; in that cheerful, almost sunny atmosphere the deep blue and gold draperies and Chinese blue rug produce a wholly charming effect.

Another expedient for tempering the cold light of a north room is to use warm color, such as cream, ecru, yellow or gold in the glass curtains, through which the daylight must filter.

After deciding on the dominant hue, and thus insuring unity, there arises the question of what other colors to use to provide diversity. One of the simplest and most practical ways to settle that question is the method adopted in decorating the six-hundred-dollar living room. A cretonne in which the dominating hue was charmingly combined with harmonizing colors was utilized as the source of the color scheme.

The color source might as well have been a picture—really that would be my first choice—or it might have been a fabric other than cretonne, such as striped material, or our color inspiration might have been taken from a breadth of upholstery tapestry, a roll of wallpaper, a rug or vase or from one of the infinite number of suggestions supplied on every hand by nature herself.

Not all color combinations found in fabrics are happily composed; unfortunately, many of them while inoffensive are commonplace in effect. But a very great number of patterns are available in which the highest type of artistic skill and feeling have been employed, both in color and design. The suitable one can be found if time enough is given to the search.

DISTRIBUTING THE COLORS IN THE ROOM

You have now, we will say, chosen the dominant hue and the colors to combine with it. At once you meet the problem of how to distribute it in the room: What colors and how intense in the rug?—the draperies?—the furniture?—the walls? What proportions shall be in the dominant hue, etc., etc.?

There is a fixed principle which governs the answer to part of that question, viz: "the larger the area the less intense the color" and "the smaller the object the more intense the color may be." This is undoubtedly the most important rule for the home decorator to grasp. It settles the matter of the walls once and forever. They and the ceilings comprise the largest areas of any room.

They form the background on which the artist paints his pictures. The most effective wall color is a tint or tinge of color that ties in with the dominant hue. The grays, such as green-grays and yellow-grays, cream, ivory, fawn, ecru, putty color, sand, café au lait, are successful wall colors.

For the more unusual rooms, such as sunrooms and breakfast rooms, more intense colors are very appropriate; a sunroom with a Venetian green wall would offer opportunities for charming color effects, as will be illustrated in one of the specimen color schemes outlined at the end of this chapter. Another principle which will be found always helpful is that relating to values. The darkest values or tones at or near the floor; the medium values in the walls and the lightest values in the ceiling.

The Furniture.—With these two principles in mind—one having to do with intensity of color and the other with the tone values—it is easy to see that the furniture with its upholstery, being next in area to the walls, will take colors of the next higher intensity, such as taupes, mulberry, plum, soft blue, dull green, maroon, old rose, mahogany.

The Rug.—The rug being of about equal area will take much the same coloring, and being at the lowest part of the room, will be dark in value. Light-toned rugs, especially in living rooms, libraries and dining rooms, throw the room out of tone and color balance. Such rugs as the Kermanshas, for instance, are best suited to delicately-toned drawing rooms and reception rooms, rather than to rooms devoted to the daily uses of the family.

The Draperies.—Above the furniture, both in the intensity of color and tone values, come the draperies. Being of smaller area than the furniture and rugs, they may display more intense colors; so we find in drapery materials the yellow-greens, the rose colors, burgundy, yellow, soft-blue, lavender, pink, henna and other hues of like purity and intensity. And because of their position toward the upper part of the room, they may be lighter in tone; some fabrics like the chintzes having backgrounds of cream, sand, ecru and even white.

HOW MUCH OF THE DOMINANT HUE

Enough of the dominant hue should be used to make it dominate. No mathematical ratio can be formulated, inasmuch as a small object in a brilliant hue may balance a much larger object in duller intensities; but the onlooker must never be left in doubt as to what color is intended to be dominant. The dominant hue must be distributed throughout the room generally, and, what is equally important, it should be used in different values and intensities.

A good example of this latter practise will be noted in the distribution of color in the Six-Hundred-Dollar living room, where the dominant hue—green—appears as a soft or medium blue-green in the draperies and cushion; a deep blue-green in the rug; a jade-green in the flower bowl. These are variations of hue and are absolutely essential to interest and diversity.

Differences in value in the colors of that small living room may be noted in the navy blue and black covering of the big upholstered chair (navy blue being blue with much black in it), the maroon of the other upholstered chair (maroon being a red-orange darkened by the admixture of black).

THREE CLASSES OF COLOR HARMONIES

Of the three types of color harmonies only two are practically useable. These two are harmonies of analogy and harmonies of complementaries or contrasts. In the first the only colors used are those that have a common color element—blood relations. In the second the contrasting hue or complementary is introduced to add snap, accent and interest. This is the type adopted in decorating the Six-Hundred-Dollar living room and produces the most pleasing and satisfying effects.

The clever artist who designed the cretonne which was used as the source of the color scheme in this room manifestly worked according to the complementary method of producing color harmony, as you will observe by lining up the colors in it: First, the analogous hues—green-blue, green, yellow-green and blue, forming a perfect harmony by analogy. Then red-orange, the complementary hue, in the pillow and interior part of the desk, and a duller shade of the same color—maroon in the upholstery of one chair.

The third class, known as triads, or trichromatic harmonies, calls for much experience in executing.

SOME SUGGESTIVE COLOR SCHEMES

The color schemes that follow are suggestions and provide illustrations of the practical application of the principles of

INTERIOR FURNISHING AND DECORATION

color that have just been set down. They will repay painstaking study and checking up. All of them have been executed either in my own practice or that of other decorators. All of them can be worked out in stock materials and most of them in materials of very moderate cost.

UNIFYING SCHEME FOR HALL AND DINING ROOM TO ACCOMPANY THE SIX-HUNDRED-DOLLAR LIVING ROOM

Colors: Blue-Green—Red-Orange—Black.

Walls of All: Sand-colored paper with pattern in greens, reds and blues—the general effect being that of a delicate gray-green.
Woodwork: Same as background of paper.
Floors: Dark walnut finish.

HALL

Rug: Small Chinese in black and buff.
Furniture: Black with appliqued stripe of blue or design in blue-green and red-orange.
Mirror: Dull gold frame with edging of blue-green.
Glass Curtains: Gold gauze.

LIVING ROOM

Rug: Dull blue-green linen or Axminster in small figure of green and black.
Draperies: Cretonne in blue-green, red-orange and black with small quantities of yellow-green on sand-colored background.
Furniture: Walnut or mahogany—two small pieces, blue-green with red-orange accent.
Upholstery: Cretonne, blue-green, blue, maroon.
Pillows: Blue-green, green, red-orange, black and one in stripe of black and red-orange.

DINING ROOM

Rug: Blue and Mulberry Axminster (or worsted Wilton).
Draperies: Striped sunfast weave in mulberry, yellow-green and fawn, lined with mulberry sateen or same material in solid mulberry, lined with yellow-green sateen, edging the

HOW TO USE COLOR

draperies with a two-inch band of the lining material, or, if preferred, a heavy cord in yellow-green.

Furniture: Walnut, dark oak or brown mahogany, or, if preferred, painted in blue-green with line and floral decorations in red-orange, black and yellow.

Upholstery: Chair seats and backs in mulberry and black striped velour or friezé.

Shades: Sand color with mulberry and yellow-green decorations.

Bowl for Fruit: Red-violet or red-orange.

In the dining room scheme, mulberry—which is red-violet, has been selected for the large areas, such as rugs, draperies, upholstery, instead of the more vivid hue of red-orange. The two colors are closely related, either one combining effectively with various hues of green. In a breakfast room or sunroom opening off from the above suite of rooms, the brilliant, gay red-orange would be chosen instead of the quieter, more demure mulberry.

A QUIET, LIVABLE LIVING ROOM
Colors: Brown—Blue—Buff.

Walls: Tan—or papered in two tones of tan.
Woodwork: Walnut, or a tone lighter than walls.
Floor: Dark brown.
Rug: Brown with dull buff in border.
Furniture: Walnut, brown mahogany or brown oak.
Upholstery: In browns, solid blues and striped material in brown and blue and blue and yellow.
Draperies: Sapphire-blue, tan-brown and dull pink.
Cushions: Same colors.
Pottery: Deeper blue.
Lamp Shades: Dull pink trimmed with pink. A quiet, reposeful and harmonious effect. Easy to do—easy to live with.

A LARGE, COLORFUL LIVING ROOM
Colors: Rose—Blue—Black.

Walls: Cream colored wallpaper—cream with ivory pattern.
Woodwork: Walnut.
Floor: Carpeted to baseboard in two-tone taupe.
Draperies: Block linen in black, rose and blue with large areas of light taupe and cream.

INTERIOR FURNISHING AND DECORATION

Curtains: Heavy sun-fast gauze—cream color.
Furniture: Walnut.
Upholstery: Davenport and one chair in rose. Love seat, block linen of drapery material. One chair, solid blue; one chair taupe; one chair, seat and back in black with needlework design in rose and blue.
Cushions: Black, blue, sage-green.
Wall Hangings: Painting over mantel in colors of room. Other smaller pictures in same. Large Chinese wall panel in rose and dull gold over davenport, mirror with dull gold frame in center.
Lamp: Ox-blood pottery base, cream-colored silk shade.
Shades: For other lamps and light fixtures sand color with decorations in dull rose and blue.
Books: In open bookcases. Rich color, comfortable looking —unusual.

AN INEXPENSIVE LIVING ROOM

Colors: Brown—Blue—Orange.

Walls: Wallpaper in a design of brown, blue and orange on tan background.
Woodwork: Like background of paper or walnut stain.
Rug: Tan with blue.
Draperies: Sun-fast weave in a stripe of blue and dull orange on sand-colored background; or cretonne in blue, orange and brown pattern on tan or ecru background.
Curtains: Ecru.
Furniture: Mahogany, dark oak or walnut.
Upholstery: Two pieces in blue (one of them a stripe in two tones of blue.) One piece in stripe of blue and dull orange. One in brown; one in tan with touch of blue.
Accessories: Cushions in soft blues and orange. Pottery and pictures showing same colors.
Lamp Shades: Sand color with same color lining and orange interlining. Easy to do in the less costly materials.

NORTH DINING ROOM

Colors: Red—Gold—Orange.

Walls: Paneled in walnut or brown oak; or wallpaper in deep tan.

HOW TO USE COLOR

Woodwork: Walnut or brown oak.
Ceiling: Antique ivory.
Rug: Henna with dull green-blue in border.
Draperies: Dull orange with dull green binding.
Curtains: Dull orange gauze or net.
Furniture: Walnut.
Upholstery: Old-red and gold damask.
Incidentals: Glass bowl in green-blue. A dining room of great cheerfulness and warmth.

DINING ROOM

Walls: Dull oak wainscoating; gray, brown, mulberry and green figured paper above.
Rug: Dull green-blue.
Draperies: Dull green, lined with mulberry.
Curtains: Mulberry-colored gauze.
Furniture: Dark oak or walnut.
Upholstery: Tapestry in dull blues, greens and reds.

SOUTH DINING ROOM
Colors: Old-Blue and Ivory.

Walls: Ivory or pearl-gray.
Woodwork: Same.
Rug: Old-blue domestic Wilton.
Draperies: Gay block linen or heavy cretonne in bird and branch pattern of red-violet, old-blue, yellow and other colors on ivory ground.
Curtains: White.
Valance: Same as draperies or dull blue rep edged with fringe or guimpe and finished with large, blue silk tassel.
Upholstery: Stripe in blue and dull orange or tapestry in blue with green and yellow.
Lamp Shades: Old ivory with dull blue and rose bindings. This cheerful dining room forms an appropriate setting for the cherished blue china, as well as for the family.

BREAKFAST ROOM
Colors: Green and Rose.

Walls: Soft shade of velvety green.
Woodwork: Rose putty color (very delicate rich tint of tan).

INTERIOR FURNISHING AND DECORATION

Floor: Tiles in dull green and dull red.
Draperies: Hand blocked linen or cretonne with design of rose and sage-green on ecru background, hanging on either side of the windows.
Curtains: Pongee edged with dull green moss trimming. (Casement windows overlook small but formal garden.)
Valance: Board or moulding painted to match woodwork and striped in green to match the trimming of the curtains.
Furniture: Soft ivory enamel and decorated in shades of dull green and rose.

BREAKFAST ROOM

Colors: Orange—Green—Red.

Walls: Warm gray.
Woodwork: Same with appliqued striping of orange and green.
Floor: Linoleum in tile effect or tile in red and green.
Draperies: Cretonne in green, orange and white.
Curtains: Ecru net with banding of orange.
Furniture: Painted in soft green, antiqued, and with decorations in red-orange.
Lamp Shades: Red-orange with yellow-green banding. This breakfast room will be filled with sunshine even on a rainy "Blue Monday."

SUNROOM

Colors: Green—Red—Black.

Walls: Soft green.
Woodwork: Blue-green.
Floor: Dull red tiles.
Rug: Dull green.
Draperies: Sun-fast weave in stripes of mulberry, yellow-green, tan and dull yellow.
Furniture: Black with red and green decorations. One piece in red-orange.
Upholstery: Cretonne in red-orange, green and yellow.
Lamps: Pottery base in red-orange or any warm red with parchment or paper shade in black, red, green and yellow.

HOW TO USE COLOR

UNUSUAL SUNROOM EFFECT

Colors: Old-Blue—Black—Lemon-Yellow.

Walls: Old rose.
Woodwork: Black.
Floor: Black.
Rug: Old-blue.
Draperies: Blue and black small stripe.
Curtains: Lemon-yellow gauze or net.
Furniture: Black.
Upholstery: Same as draperies.
Cushions: Old-blue, black and lemon-yellow in solid colors.
Lamp Base: Pottery in old-blue.
Lamp Shades: Lemon-yellow with orange interlining.

MUSIC ROOM

Colors: Green—Red—Gold.

Walls: Very soft antiqued green on paneled walls.
Ceiling: A tint lighter.
Woodwork: Same as walls including cabinets over radiators.
Floor Covering: Warm-toned Oriental rugs.
Draperies: Hand blocked linen in jade green, gray and bright red.
Curtains: Rose silk or warm gray gauze.
Furniture: Brown mahogany and walnut with small music cabinet and table in antique green with old-gold line decorations.
Upholstery: Couch in taupe, mohair friezé. One chair, damask in soft green, rose and gold. One chair, deep rose. One chair, needlework design on linen colored ground.
Lamp Shades: Sand colored silk.
Accessories: High vase on piano in green, Venetian red and gold. Antique gold mirror.

MUSIC ROOM

Built Around a Black Grand Piano.
Small Room—One Wide Lofty Window.

Colors: Black—White—Rose—Blue.

Draperies: (Chosen first because of the necessity for getting an agreeable pattern with black as a dominant element.) Block

INTERIOR FURNISHING AND DECORATION

linen in an architectural pattern in black, rose and bright blue on a background of white and light tan.
Walls: Creamy, light tan with subdued figure in broken tints of blue and rose—general tone light ecru.
Curtains: Heavy gauze in ecru like walls.
Floor: Stained midnight-blue (black with a hint of blue).
Rug: Black with violet border.
Wall Hanging: Large square of the drapery material, with an oval mirror in center, suspended on wall back of piano.
Furniture: Table in black and Chinese red lacquer (or painted). Music cabinet in black enamel. Chairs in deep black mahogany.
Upholstery: Settee in solid rose. One chair in black with needlework design in rose, blue and black on seat and back. One chair, peacock blue. One chair, in the block linen.
Floor Lamp: Black stand with dull blue striping.
Table Lamp: Black pottery base.
Shades: Striped silk in old-rose and pearl-gray; lining, sand color; interlining, deep rose.

BEDROOM FOR A MAN

Colors: Orange—Green—Black.

Walls: Tan and black striped wallpaper.
Floor: Dark brown.
Rug: Tan with black border.
Draperies: Block linen or heavy cretonne in orange, black and green; using the same for bedspreads.
Upholstery: Easy chair in black and yellow pin-striped velour.
Shades: Orange with green and black line decorations.

NORTH BEDROOM IN MAKE-BELIEVE SUNSHINE

Colors: Corn-Yellow—Blue.

Walls: Fine satin stripe paper in two tones of soft yellow.
Ceiling: A tint lighter.
Woodwork: Same tint as ceiling.
Rug: Golden-brown Wilton.
Draperies: Cretonne in floral design of yellow with touches of green and pale turquoise on ivory ground.
Curtains: Cream marquisette or fine quality of scrim.

HOW TO USE COLOR

Upholstery: One chair in drapery cretonne material. One chair in dull turquoise blue.
Lamp Shades: Yellow with ruffles of dull turqouise.

GUEST ROOM—SOUTH EXPOSURE
Colors: Black—Red-Violet—Yellow.

Walls: Sand color.
Rug: Dark gray with small all-over geometrical cross hatch figure in black.
Draperies: Chintz in quaint design in black, yellow and red-violet on white ground, with three-inch ruffle of mulberry taffeta.
Curtains: White marquisette.
Furniture: Four-poster bed with accompanying pieces painted black with decorations in yellow and red-violet. Ladder-back chair same as bed and dresser. New England candle table in red-orange. Rocker in chintz slip-cover.
Shades: Yellow with black edging.

CHILD'S ROOM OR NURSERY
Colors: Blue—Pink—Yellow.

Walls: Wallpaper showing Mother Goose scenes in soft blue, pink, green and yellow; eighteen-inch drop ceiling of plain cream paper above.
Floor: Light finish with large braided rug in all colors of the room with lots of black.
Draperies: Soft pink cotton rep.
Valance: Same as draperies.
Curtains: Ruffled curtains of unbleached muslin (or of pink and ivory banded scrim).
Furniture: Painted or enameled in ivory with colored decorations of flowers and birds.
Slip Covers: Rep same as used in draperies.

BEDROOM—SOUTH EXPOSURE
Colors: Green—Rose—Blue.

Walls: Warm French gray or papered in warm gray with pattern in soft green and very dull rose.
Woodwork: Warm French gray.

INTERIOR FURNISHING AND DECORATION

Rug: Patterned tan ground with soft green, old-rose and dull blue.
Draperies: Soft green damask, patterned in rose and blue.
Curtains: Silk gauze, color of walls.
Bed Covers: Changeable taffeta in lavender and blue.
Upholstery: Solid colors in old-rose and soft green blue.

BEDROOM FOR A GIRL (NORTH ROOM)
Colors: Pink—White.

Walls: Papered in delicately toned chintz design in pink, blue and greens on ivory ground; or ivory painted walls.
Woodwork: Ivory.
Rug: Soft gray-blue chenille or braided rug in pink, dull blues and greens.
Draperies: Pink and white chintz stripe.
Bed Cover: Same as draperies.
Furniture: Mahogany. Small table and chair in ivory with pink decorations.

BEDROOM FOR A GIRL—SOUTH EXPOSURE
Colors: Corn-Flower Blue—White—Buff.

Walls: Corn-flower blue, white and rose.
Woodwork: Ivory.
Rug: Cream color with border of blue, rose and buff.
Draperies: Chintz—corn-flower blue and white with blue tie backs.
Curtains: White ruffled muslin.
Bed Covering: Same as draperies.
Dressing Table: Dressed in chintz flounces same as draperies.
Lamp Shades: Rose with corn-flower blue border or ruffles.

BEDROOM—SOUTH AND WEST EXPOSURE

Walls: Delicate green.
Woodwork: Pearl gray-green.
Floor: Deep gray.
Rug: Dark gray-green.
Draperies: Violet colored linen banded with green.
Curtains: Marquisette dyed apple green; or white muslin with tie-backs of green similar to bands on draperies.

HOW TO USE COLOR

Valance: Pleated of cretonne in a pattern containing green, violet and gray.
Bed Coverings: Same as cretonne banded with violet linen or silk.

NORTH BEDROOM
Colors: Yellow—Violet—Black.

Walls: Ivory.
Woodwork: Pale yellow.
Floor: Gray with large braided rug containing all the colors used in the room with much black.
Draperies: Cretonne in which yellow predominates.
Curtains: Ruffled dotted swiss.
Valance: Bright yellow.
Furniture: Bed, bedside stand and dresser of pale yellow. Chair and couch, violet. Table lacquered black.
Lamp: Lacquered black.
Lamp Shades: Rose interlined with orange.
Picture Frames: Black.
Flower Jar: Rose.
Cushion: Rose.
Bedspread and Table Cover: Yellow linen with border of cretonne.

BEDROOM—FACING SOUTH, EAST AND WEST
(An experiment in cooling off a very warmly lighted and rather small room.)
Colors: Green-Blue—White—Red.

Walls: Painted and paneled in medium tone of gray.
Woodwork: Same as walls.
Draperies: Chintz in white with floral figure in blue, bright rose and green with a three-inch ruffled band of green-blue taffeta.
Rug: Small all-over figure in blue on gray ground with six-inch border of dark blue.
Bed Spreads: Green-blue taffeta to match band on draperies.
Furniture: Mahogany. One chair covered with chintz slip-cover.
Lamp: Small Japanese pottery figure in blues and greens.

Lamp Shade: Like the walls with ruffle of the green-blue taffeta. The effect is one of surprising sweetness, freshness and coolness. Two well chosen pictures emphasize the note of green blue.

BEDROOM FOR A BOY
Colors: Red-Orange—Black—Green-Blue.

Walls: Gray-green tone—either painted or in wallpaper in medium gray with soft tints of red, blue and green in an all-over, or floral design.
Woodwork: Black with red-orange striping.
Floor: Black.
Rug: Large, linen rug in a checker of black and red.
Draperies: Solid red-orange in linen or a sunfast weave with banding of green-blue.
Furniture: Dark oak or walnut with one piece painted black and one green-blue; the latter being the study table.
Upholstery: Couch or beds covered with sunfast mixed weave in stripes of soft red-orange and green on sand colored background. One chair in stripe of black and red-orange.
Lamp: On the study table a black pottery base.
Lamp Shade: Paper in sand color with line decoration in dull blue-green and red-violet.

BEDROOM—SOUTH EXPOSURE
Colors: Turquoise—Peach—Opalescent-Mauve.

Walls: Paneled and painted in antique ivory or papered in two tones of ivory.
Woodwork: Same as lighter tone in paper.
Rug: Chinese blue.
Draperies: Turquoise lined and banded in apricot. May be of taffeta, silk rep or mercerized poplin.
Curtains: Ivory gauze or silk.
Bed Covers: Turquoise with peach bandings and shirred mauve flounces.
Furniture: Painted in soft ivory with dull gold striping and medallions in green, rose and gold; or painted jade with green and gold decorations.
Upholstery: Solid colors in turquoise and apricot.
Lamp Shades: Apricot silk.

HOW TO USE COLOR

BEDROOM AND SITTING ROOM—SOUTH AND WEST EXPOSURE

Colors: White—Apple-Green—Pink.

Walls: Paper in small figure of apple-green, pink and lavender on pearl-gray ground.
Woodwork: Apple-green.
Draperies: Linen or chintz in apple-green and pink on white background.
Rug: Soft gray with dull green border.
Upholstery: One upholstered arm chair in the drapery material. One chair in pink.
Lamp Shades: Pink.
Pictures: Colors of the room, framed with white moulding.

KITCHEN—SOUTHERN EXPOSURE

Colors: Apple-Green—White—Pink.

Walls: White tile, or ivory white enamel wainscote. Wallpaper (the washable sort) above in floral, geometric or tile effect, in apple-green, white and pink.
Floor: Linoleum in tile effects of cream and green or black and green.
Curtains: Green and white gingham with appliqued band of deep red or cretonne in the three colors.
Cabinet and Shelves: Painted ivory white with floral designs of green, pink and blue.
Furniture: Table black with apple-green line decoration. Chair or stool the same.
Growing Plants.
Accessories: Cook books and small print on walls for incidentals.

A color scheme for a kitchen with northern exposure will be found in the chapter on "A One Woman-Power Kitchen." Chapter XIX.

COLOUR AND COLOUR VALUES

THERE is no need to dwell upon the importance to the decorator of a sound knowledge of colour and the ability to use it intelligently; no matter how fine a craftsman he may be or how great his technical skill in other respects, he cannot hope to be really successful—in the broadest sense of the word—unless he understands colour and can handle it effectively.

Colour is defined in the dictionary as " visual sensations produced upon the retina by light-waves of different length," and the first thing to remember about it is that it has no tangible form. From the decorator's point of view, it is an impression produced by the ability of a surface to reflect certain parts of a ray of white light and to absorb others. The existence of this impression depends upon the presence of light; where there is no light, there can be no colour.

The Theory of Colour

Sir Isaac Newton was the first to show, in 1666, that a ray of light passed through a prism of glass is broken up into a series of bands of the different colours which are the constituent parts of the ray. The image presented by this process is known as the spectrum. The colours of the spectrum, or main colours of these bands, are red, orange, yellow, green, blue, and violet, but these are only those most clearly visible; the limits of each are not sharply defined but merge imperceptibly into each other, and between them, but less discernible, are an indefinite number of intermediate colours.

The space occupied by the blue and violet bands is rather bigger than that taken up by any other adjacent pair, so that it is customary to include another colour—purple; these six (or seven) colours are popularly known as " the colours of the rainbow " for they can be seen, in varying intensity, when there is a rainbow in the sky, due to the refraction and reflection of the rays of the sun, witnessed through falling drops of rain.

Although colour cannot be seen without light, it is necessary to distinguish between the colour sensation which depends upon light alone (e.g. as when light rays are passed through a prism) and that which results when a ray of light is partially absorbed and reflected by a substance such as pigment; it is the latter form of colour with which the painter and decorator is chiefly, if not entirely, concerned.

It is indisputable that some people have a highly developed sense of colour which enables them instinctively, without any training, to select and combine colours so as to produce effects which are æsthetically pleasing. Those fortunate enough to possess this faculty in any marked degree are

Colour and Colour Values

few and far between, but the extent to which others, less gifted in this respect, can acquire a mastery of colour harmony is a matter upon which opinions differ. There exists a vast amount of literature on the subject in all its various aspects, but it may be said at once that the path of the student who seeks guidance on it is beset with difficulties, for much of the information available is vague and many of the theories advanced are contradictory.

There are numerous sets of rules formulated with the idea of assisting the beginner to devise colour harmonies on scientific lines. Such rules may be of some help to those concerned with designing textiles, wallpapers, and similar articles for which the scale of the work is usually small and constant and in which there are few variable factors to be taken into consideration. Even so, the value of these systems must be regarded as limited; it is true that they will indicate certain colours which harmonise with each other, but they can give no idea of the proportion in which each colour may be used and, in practice, the successful grouping and management of colours is largely a matter of proportions. In point of fact, a skilful and experienced designer will often employ in conjunction two or more colours which, according to the rules, ought never to be combined and he will, nevertheless, obtain a result which is perfectly satisfying and free from any suggestion of discord, simply because he knows just how much of each can safely be incorporated in his work.

It is hardly an exaggeration to say that no two jobs undertaken by the decorator in the course of his work are ever exactly alike; the aspect, the dimensions, and the shape of the various interiors with which he has to deal will differ substantially, and these and other factors mean that each room will present its own individual problems. It is obvious that no rules, however correctly or scientifically they have been drawn up, will provide a complete solution in such cases; they may, in fact, be more of a hindrance than a help to him, because they must inevitably exert a restrictive influence and thereby limit his scope.

Classification of Colours

It is, however, desirable that the decorator should understand the broad principles on which colours are usually classified and these will be stated as simply and succinctly as possible.

Speaking in terms of pigmentary colour (which, for this purpose, includes not only paints but stains and dyestuffs), there are three PRIMARY colours, so called because they cannot be obtained by combining any other hues. They are: red, yellow, and blue.

There are also three SECONDARY colours—orange, purple, and green—obtained by mixing equal parts of two of the primaries, thus:

>Red and yellow produce orange.
>Red and blue produce purple.
>Yellow and blue produce green.

Colour and Colour Values

Colour Circles

If we examine the accompanying diagram, we find that the circle is divided into six sectors, showing the three primaries and the three secondaries. The colours in sectors exactly opposite each other are known as COMPLEMENTARY colours (or colours which contrast most with each other). Diagrams of this kind are helpful to the beginner, for, in composing a colour scheme, a note of contrast is often of value in lending a note of strength to an arrangement which may otherwise seem weak and insipid.

If desired, the colour circle can be made more useful by the inclusion of intermediate colours; we can, for example, increase the number of sectors to twelve, as shown in Fig. 2. As in the case of Fig. 1, complementaries are directly opposite to one another; thus the complementary of blue-green is orange-red, and that of purple-blue is yellow-orange.

By mixing together two secondaries, we get a third group, known as TERTIARIES; these are russet, citron, and olive, obtained thus:

> Orange and purple produce russet.
> Orange and green produce citron.
> Purple and green produce olive.

From this it will be seen that each tertiary is compounded of two parts of one primary and one part of each of the other two.

It is worth while pointing out that confusion between what we may call "colour-light" (i.e. non-pigmentary colour) and pigmentary colour has given rise to some popular misconceptions. It is sometimes stated, for example, that the three primaries, if compounded in correct proportions, will give a white, whereas, so far as pigmentary colour is concerned, they will produce a grey. Again, it is often asserted that any colour can be obtained by mixing the primaries, plus—when necessary—black or white. In practice, because of the complex nature of pigments, there are distinct limitations to the range procurable in this way.

Factors which Influence Colour Mixtures

By blending two or more pigments, deepening them by the addition of some form of black, or softening them by the addition of white, we may obtain practically endless variations, both as regards character—that is to say, actual divergence or contrast of colour—or in degree. But in this connection we must note that it is not merely a matter of mingling any given colours, corresponding to a set of standards, by which changes are obtained. The nature of the pigments, of the mediums, and other substances with which they are ground up or mixed are factors that must be taken into account. We may, for instance, secure reds identical in appearance which are either metallic or organic, or a yellow derived from natural ochre or from an aniline base; but though exactly the same in appearance, on mixing with a white base they will give different results. This is sometimes due to

Colour and Colour Values

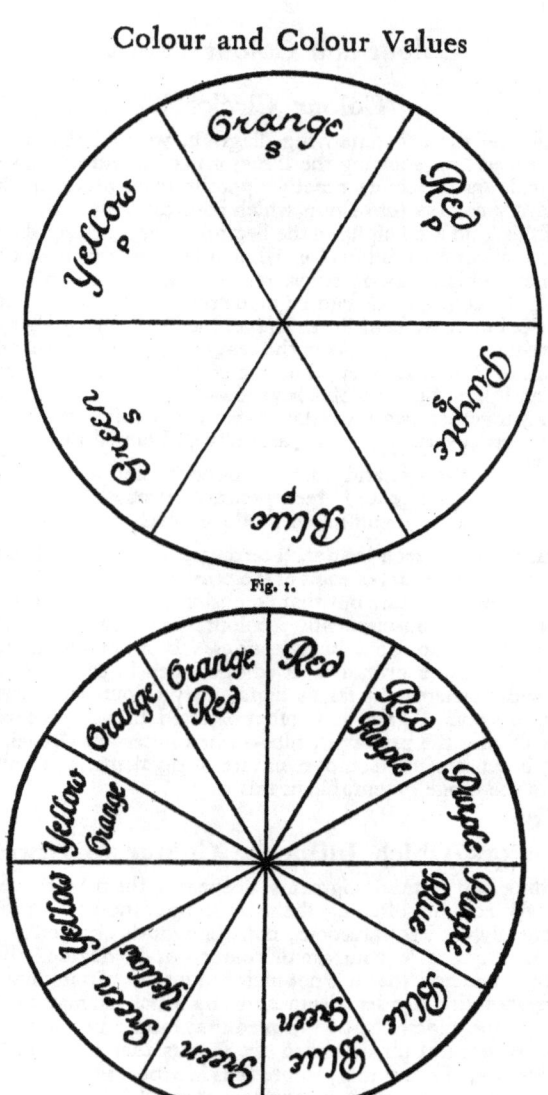

Fig. 1.

Fig. 2.

Colour and Colour Values

variations in physical structure (we may find diverse crystalline formations or amorphous masses), at other times to chemical reaction. The angle of refraction of light, and therefore the sensation of colour, varies with the character of crystallisation. Secondly there is more or less pronounced chemical influence under certain conditions between pigments themselves or the other compounds used in making up the paints. Materials containing iron or sulphur are among those setting up these changes. We obtain different results when there is merely mechanical combination, the minute particles of one colour being placed side by side with those of another pigment (as may be seen under an extremely powerful microscope, although to the eye apparently one colour is thoroughly amalgamated with the other), than when we secure chemical union by one substance absorbing or coalescing with another to form a new compound. It is not only the tinting pigment that is of importance in this connection, for the base or extender also has an influence. If vermilion is added in a given quantity respectively to an equal quantity of white lead and zinc white, there will be a difference in hue and tone and there will be a further difference if we employ a mixture of lead and zinc oxides. Other changes will supervene if the base is loaded with barytes, with barium carbonate, or china clay.

It is in the observance of these niceties (and they extend to the solvents and mediums) that the art of colour mixing resides.

Terminology

In addition to the terms already explained, there are certain others, used in connection with colour, which should be defined since they are frequently employed somewhat loosely and may thus cause some confusion. The most important are as follows:

Hue.—The predominant impression given by any particular colour, irrespective of its tint or shade. *Hue* may thus be regarded as being synonymous with *colour*.

Tint.—A modification of a colour, produced by diluting it with white.

Shade.—Sometimes used as a synonym of *tint*, but more properly, a dark gradation of a colour, obtained by adding black to it.

Tone.—The degree of lightness or darkness of a colour, in comparison with white or black.

Purity.—The relative *purity* of a colour depends on the extent to which it has been contaminated or greyed by the admixture of another colour.

Methods of Combining Colours

Colour schemes may be broadly classified under various headings, of which *mono-chromatic, analogous,* and *contrasting* treatments are the most important, so far as the beginner is concerned.

Mono-chromatic Colouring.—By this is meant treatment based on the use of a single hue, variations being procured by employing different

Colour and Colour Values

tones, obtained by adding white or black to the colour. There is no reason why a scheme of this kind should be in the least insipid or dull since the range of effects possible is very great. For example, the same shade of colour used on two surfaces of different texture will show a subtle variation, due to the fact that the reaction to light is dissimilar.

Analogous Colouring.—This implies harmony which is the result of combining colours which have close affinity to each other. We may, for instance, take a green and use it in conjunction with a green-blue and a green-yellow. The student will find the colour circle useful for creating schemes of this kind, employing colours adjacent to each other, as shown on a twelve-colour circle; the number of colours thus used should be limited to three or four at the most.

Contrasting Colouring.—One way of producing an effective scheme is by the introduction of a note of contrast. This can be done by using a complementary or contrasting colour. Here again, the colour circle, on which each colour is shown with its complementary in the sector directly opposite, will be helpful.

Colour Values

A factor of considerable practical importance in decoration is the relative value of colours. Certain colours, for example, are described as *advancing* colours, because they have the effect of giving prominence to surfaces and making them stand out. Reds, yellows, and orange usually possess this property and so, in a lesser degree, do the darker shades of most colours. Advancing colours must consequently be used with discretion in a small room, since if employed too lavishly, they may make it seem even smaller than it is.

Other colours have a contrary effect and are known as *receding* colours. They include the lighter tints, especially of blues and greens. If, therefore, we want to preserve a design on the same plane, there must be a careful balancing of colours. On the other hand, if it is desired to emphasise special features—as, for example, to give prominence to a projection, to deepen a recess or to correct faults in such projections, outlines or general composition, these properties of colours can be of the greatest assistance. The part which colour can play in concealing or minimising structural shortcomings is not, perhaps, sufficiently realised by the majority of decorators.

Another point which it is as well to bear in mind is that the appearance of most colours is affected in varying degrees by other colours which may surround them or be placed in juxtaposition to them. The same shade of yellow, for instance, placed against differently coloured backgrounds, will itself look slightly different in each case. Again, if two fairly bright colours are placed alongside each other, each will seem to be tinged with the complementary of the other. Thus, a green in juxtaposition to an orange will, in some degree, incline to blue, or again a yellow next to a red will assume a greenish cast.

Colour and Colour Values

Colour Harmonies

Colour harmony, as has already been pointed out, is mainly a matter of proportion, and the same combination of colours which appears discordant can often seem pleasing and harmonious if the proportions of one or more of them are skilfully adjusted. Because of this and because, also, in the absence of any generally accepted system of colour nomenclature, to refer to individual colours by name is an unsatisfactory form of identification, the value of any list of those which harmonise is doubtful. The following, abridged from a list compiled by Dr. G. A. Audsley, a well-known authority, is, however, included mainly as a basis for practical experiment by the student.

Blue harmonises with orange; with gold or bright yellow; with maize; straw colour; salmon; crimson; pink; lilac (weak); drab; stone colour; fawn (weak); grey (weak and cold); chestnut or chocolate; brown; white (strong and bright); black; orange and black; scarlet and purple or lilac; orange and green; brown, crimson, and yellow or gold; orange, black, and white.

Red harmonises with green (a pink and an apple green is one of the brightest); gold or yellow (strong and bright); blue; grey; white (very bright); yellow and black; yellow, or gold, black, and white.

Scarlet harmonises with blue-green; blue; purple or lilac (rather dull); violet (sombre); slate; blue and white; black and white; blue and grey blue, black, and yellow or gold.

Crimson harmonises with yellow-green; yellow or gold; orange; maize; purple; drab; brown; black.

Yellow harmonises with purple; blue; violet; deep crimson; lilac; chestnut or chocolate; brown; black (strong); white (bright); purple, scarlet and blue.

Green harmonises with red; scarlet; russet; if containing blue, tinge with orange; if deep, with a strong yellow or gold; black; white; scarlet and blue; crimson, blue, and bright yellow or gold.

Orange harmonises with blue, olive; violet; chestnut; deep brown; crimson and green; crimson and blue; purple and scarlet; blue, scarlet, and green; violet, scarlet, white, and green.

Purple harmonises with yellow; citrine; bright yellow or gold; maize; black (dull); white; scarlet and yellow or gold; scarlet and white; scarlet, blue, and orange; scarlet, blue, yellow (or gold), and black.

Lilac harmonises with bright yellow or gold; primrose; maize; cerise; crimson; grey; white; black; crimson and yellow or gold.

Violet harmonises with yellow or gold; orange; maize.

White harmonises with most colours and colour mixtures.

Black harmonises with white; bright yellow or gold; orange; maize; primrose; salmon; pink; scarlet; cerise; yellow-green; drab; fawn; buff; slate; grey; olive; citrine; scarlet and blue-green; crimson and lemon-yellow; crimson and yellow-green.

Colour and Colour Values

Choice of Colour Schemes

For most forms of domestic decoration, the keynote is—or should be—simplicity and it will generally be found that the most successful schemes are those built up with only a few colours. For the beginner, at any rate, it may be taken as an axiom that the more brilliant a hue, the more sparingly it should be used. Large masses of such colours as scarlet, orange, bright blue, or bright green need very careful handling and are best avoided, though these colours can be employed most effectively on a small scale for accessories, to lend a note of emphasis and interest to the scheme.

The largest surfaces in a room are provided by the walls, which should be regarded as backgrounds and treated accordingly. This suggests that their main areas should be decorated in neutral or greyed colours, but the lighter tints of almost any colour are no less effective for the purpose. A good principle to adopt is to make the floor darkest, the walls intermediate, and the ceiling lightest in tone. For many years it was the rule rather than the exception to finish the ceilings in plain white and, though of late there has been a tendency to introduce a little more colour in their treatment, this is still done with extreme caution in most cases, only the palest tints being employed. It is only fair to add that in more modern houses, ceilings are, almost invariably, much lower than in homes built at the beginning of the century, so that pale tints, which reflect more light, are almost essential if a feeling of oppression is to be avoided; nevertheless, a little more enterprise in ceiling treatment might well be shown.

Chief Considerations

In designing a colour scheme there are various factors—apart from the cost of the work—which the decorator must take into consideration. The most important are: (1) the client's preferences; (2) the aspect of the room; (3) its purpose, size, shape, and proportions; (4) nature and colour of the furniture, draperies, carpets, and accessories which are to be used.

1. The Client's Preferences.—Only on very rare occasions is the decorator given a completely free hand in the choice of colours for an interior, nor is it particularly desirable that he should be placed in this position. A room should, after all, reflect something of the personality of the person who lives in it, and unless the decorator is an unusually clever psychologist, a scheme devised by his own unaided efforts fails to do this; however satisfying it may be æsthetically, it generally has the slightly unreal atmosphere of an exhibition interior which is meant to be looked at, not lived in.

At the other end of the scale is the client who knows—or professes to know—exactly what she wants and looks upon the decorator as someone whose sole function is to carry out her wishes. This again is an unsatisfactory state of affairs, for instructions given in this way are rarely as definite

Colour and Colour Values

and free from ambiguity as they should be and are consequently liable to misinterpretation. Although they may have in their minds a very clear idea of the kind of effect they want to produce, few clients are able to visualise what the appearance of the finished room will be, and when, as often happens, it fails to come up to their expectations, it will, in most instances, be the decorator who is held responsible.

It is only logical that the person who is to live in or habitually use a room should decide upon the kind of treatment it should be given, more especially as regards colour, a subject on which most people have strong preferences or prejudices. A good decorator will not seek to impose his own tastes on a client against her inclinations, but he will not accept her own without question, if his experience indicates that the results will be disappointing. His aim should be to collaborate with her as fully as possible; he should try to ascertain her views and be prepared to put forward his own. Most householders welcome suggestions, provided the latter are based on sound knowledge of the subject, nor will they resent criticism if it is constructive and is made with tact.

For special jobs it will be a great help if water-colour sketches of the treatment to be given to the room in question can be submitted, but, needless to say, their preparation takes time and money and not every decorator has the ability to execute them. For ordinary purposes he can get a good deal of assistance from wallpaper pattern-books, many of which contain not only a range of matched fillings, ceiling papers, and borders, but also slips to indicate the colour of the paintwork; most of them include, also, coloured lithos of complete schemes which can often be adapted for a particular room. If the use of wallpaper is under consideration, it is always better, when possible, to pin a complete length on the wall for the client's inspection, rather than to rely on the necessarily small piece in the pattern-book.

Some of the leading firms of paint manufacturers issue literature illustrating colour schemes in paint and distemper, and these, too, can be very helpful. Colour cards have their uses but are sometimes misleading because colour, when seen in a small, isolated square on a card, is apt to look very different when employed in greater proportions and in conjunction with other hues on a wall surface. The influence of texture on colour should be borne in mind and if, for example, a plastic-paint finish is required, it is wise to show the client in advance a sample panel; specimen panels, which should be as large as possible, should also be submitted when scumble or other broken colour effects are being suggested.

2. Aspect of the Room.—The aspect of a room will play an important part in influencing the choice of colour scheme. Interiors which face north, and consequently get little sunlight, are apt to be cold and cheerless, but this condition can, to some extent, be corrected by the use of what are known as *warm* colours; these include reds, yellows, and orange, used in tints of varying strength according to the size and number of the windows and the amount of natural light which penetrates. A room with a northern aspect,

Colour and Colour Values

and with, for example, only one small window, is probably best decorated in pale tints of one or more of the warm colours.

Conversely, rooms which get a good deal of sunlight are better treated with *cool* colours, under which heading may be classed many of the blues and greens, the strength of the tints again being regulated, more or less, by the volume of light they receive. It is, however, a mistake to attempt to make too definite a classification of warm and cool colours; some blues, for example, which incline to purple, are by no means cold and can perfectly well be used in north rooms, while again, all yellows are not necessarily unsuitable for sunny interiors.

Colour and Illumination.—Quite apart from this, it must be remembered that the treatment of walls and ceilings can play an important part in the illumination of a room. A certain amount of misconception still exists on this subject; there is, for example, a fairly common illusion that the use of a high-gloss paint or other form of glossy finish will make a room lighter than will a mat paint (or other material) of exactly the same hue. In point of fact, each will reflect approximately the same amount of light, but with this difference.

When light strikes a surface, it is thrown back at various angles which depend on the texture of the surface. If the latter is perfectly smooth, as in the case of a mirror, or nearly smooth, as in a film of gloss paint or varnish, the light is reflected back in much the same direction from which it comes. In a mat or textured surface, on the other hand, the planes of the particles which it comprises lie at different angles, so that the light which falls on them is diffused and reflected back in many different directions.

Broadly speaking, therefore, in a room of which the wall and ceiling surfaces are finished in a smooth and lustrous material, there are highlights and glare on certain areas, while other parts are comparatively under-illuminated. With a flat surface the light is transmitted more evenly to every part of the interior, making for greater uniformity of illumination.

Relatively small differences in surface texture alone will make little or no difference, but a wide variation in the amount of light diffused can be brought about by the choice of colour treatment. Obviously, an interior decorated in white or pale tints will be much lighter than if it is finished in black or dark shades, but the extent of the difference in the volume of useful light obtained from a given light source, according to whether pale or dark colours are used for the decorative treatment, is much greater than most people imagine. A series of tests carried out some years ago to determine this difference gave the following set of variations, taking white ceilings and white walls as affording the maximum degree of light:

Ceiling	Walls	Degree of light
White	White	100
White	Pale green	70
White	Dark red	53
White	Dark blue	47
Black	White	50

Colour and Colour Values

Pale green, dark red, and dark blue are, however, indefinite terms capable of a wide range of interpretations. A more exact table, compiled by the Electric Lamp Manufacturers' Association Light Service Bureau, shows what proportion of the light of an ordinary gas-filled electric lamp differently coloured painted surfaces reflect. The colours in question are British Standard Colours for Ready-Mixed Paints, as shown on the shade-card issued by the British Standards Association (B.S.381; the figures in brackets after each name refer to the number on the shade card).

	Percentage		Percentage
White Paper	84	Lemon (55)	69
Portland Stone (64)	62	Golden Yellow (56)	80
Light Stone (61)	58	Orange (57)	42
Middle Stone (62)	37	Eau de Nil (16)	47
Dark Stone (63)	33	Sea Green (17)	38
Light Buff (58)	61	Grass Green (18)	18
Middle Buff (59)	54	Sage Green (19)	19
Deep Buff (60)	31	Sky Blue (1)	30
Silver Grey (28)	37	Turquoise Blue (2)	15
French Grey (30)	36	Peacock Blue (3)	11

It may be well here to point out that artificial lighting can play havoc with a scheme designed to be seen only by natural light. The ordinary household electric lamp gives a yellowish glow, so that, for example, red tints illuminated by it take on an orange tinge, while blues are inclined to look greenish. In interiors which are mostly lit artificially, as, for instance, in the case of theatres, cinemas, and many restaurants, allowances must be made for the change in devising the scheme.

3. Purpose, Size, and Proportions.—In building up a scheme, the purpose for which the room is to be used must be taken into consideration, for certain colours are capable, to some extent, of promoting different moods; this fact will influence the choice of treatment in a bedroom, for instance, where an atmosphere of restfulness should be the objective, or again, in a study, where the scheme should be of a nature to assist concentration. Admittedly, different people do not react in the same way to various colours, but with this reservation, the following list indicates the emotions generally associated with the main groups of colours:

Red.—A stimulating colour which must, however, be used with discretion since too much of it can prove over-exciting and induce restlessness.

Yellow.—Suggests sunlight and is consequently a cheerful and energising colour.

Blue.—A cooling and restful colour when employed with restraint, but one apt to be depressing used in large masses.

Orange.—Possesses in less degree the stimulating properties of red and can therefore be employed on a rather more generous scale.

Green.—A cool and tranquillising colour which aids concentration.

Colour and Colour Values

Purple.—If not too bright and used with discrimination, has a soothing and sedative effect.

Brown.—Dull and uninspiring in large masses but useful in combination with brighter colours, such as yellow and orange, to counteract any overstimulating effects they may produce.

White.—Suggests cleanliness and consequently valuable in such rooms as kitchens, bathrooms, etc., but too cold unless it is relieved by some brighter hue.

The importance of cheerful and invigorating colour schemes in schoolrooms is now more widely recognised than was the case at the beginning of the century, when the chief consideration in selecting colours for such interiors was that that they should be of a kind which would show the dirt as little as possible, hence the drab and dreary " institutional " schemes which were almost invariably the rule. It is worth while observing, too, that for hospitals, sanatoria, and nursing homes, the curative influence of colour deserves far more investigation than it has hitherto received. Experiments conducted in colour therapy suggest that the healing properties of colour in the case of certain diseases are greater than is commonly imagined.

We can use colour, too, to help to alter the apparent proportions of rooms and, in some measure, to correct those which are faulty. By means of either advancing or receding colours, areas can be made to look smaller or larger, and ceilings lower or higher, and structural shortcomings minimised in appearance. Dark interiors, as we have already seen, can be made lighter by the use of colours which reflect light, and rooms in which there is too much natural illumination—a condition seldom found in this country—can be given a more subdued atmosphere by employing colours which absorb light; it is sufficient here to emphasise that in planning a scheme, it is not enough merely to evolve pleasing combinations of colour harmony; the latter may look very attractive on paper, but if we fail to make allowances for the aspect, proportions, and other variable factors of individual rooms, the result, in practice, may be very different from what was intended.

4. Furnishings and Accessories.—Only on very rare occasions is the decorator able to plan an interior in its entirety and to choose, or collaborate in choosing, not only the colour treatment for the walls, woodwork, ceiling, and floor, but the furniture, carpet or rugs, draperies and accessories into the bargain. In the majority of cases he will have to adapt his ideas according to his client's taste in furnishings, and this will, needless to say, substantially restrict his scope. At times, however, this state of affairs is not necessarily a disadvantage for it means that he starts off with some insight into his client's preferences and he can often base his scheme on existing material. A picture hung in a focal position in the room—e.g. over the fireplace—may suggest a dominant colour for the wall treatment, and many successful schemes have, in fact, been composed in this manner.

A note of contrast is nearly always a necessity to redeem a colour treatment from insipidity, but it is worth while remarking that contrast should

Colour and Colour Values

not be confined only to colour. Texture should be offset by smooth surfaces, pattern by plain. Except in a very large room it is wisest to limit pattern to one surface, unless the same or a related pattern is used on others. If, therefore, the upholstery or carpet has a pronounced pattern, the use of a patterned wallpaper should be avoided. Similarly, a textured wall surface (as produced by plastic paint or certain types of wallpaper) is less effective than a smooth finish if the upholstery or draperies in the room are of coarse weave.

Exterior Colour Treatment.—In general, the main purpose of exterior painting is to preserve and consequently less thought is usually given to the choice of colour treatment, which is also influenced by such considerations as permanence to light; it must be conditioned, also, by the type of building and, to some extent, by its environment.

It is often urged that the relatively smooth and unbroken surfaces, which characterise so much modern architecture, provide an opportunity for a more liberal use of colour than was practicable in the older types of building. Certainly our streets are drab and unexciting as compared with many of those in southern countries, but while there is scope for more enterprise in the use of colour for external treatment, it should be tempered with discretion. The deciding factor is the amount of sunshine which each country enjoys. In England the reckless use of vivid colours tends to irritate, whereas, in warmer climates, the brightness of the sun and the depth of the shadows brings them into line.

In the older class of property, green, brown, white, or cream still retain their popularity, but in the more modern houses, particularly when they are cement-rendered, there are indications of a wider use of bright colours, especially for front doors or ornamental shutters, with attractive results. This tendency deserves to be encouraged, but it is important that all colours employed for the purpose should be reasonably proof against fading. If pale tints are required, it should be remembered also that some pigments, though fast to light in a pure state, do not retain this property when reduced with white or mixed with other pigments.

Colour in the Factory

A new trend in industry and one which holds great opportunities for the decorator is the movement, now gaining in force, to introduce more colour into the interior of factory buildings. This practice originated in the U.S.A. but is being adopted on an increasing scale in industrial establishments in this country. Experiments conducted over a number of years in plants of various kinds show that properly chosen colour schemes in factories increase efficiency and output, reduce the accident and sickness rate, and generally improve the morale of the workers.

The use of colour in this connection cannot be classed as interior decoration in the ordinary sense of the words, since the objective is not so much to produce an attractive interior as to enable the operatives to concentrate on

Colour and Colour Values

their work with a minimum of strain and distraction. Thus, it is recommended that, while for practical purposes the lower parts of walls should be relatively dark, the upper portions and the ceiling should be in pale tints, in order to reflect as much light as possible. The actual choice of colours must depend primarily on the nature of the work which is being carried out.

Colour can also prove an extremely valuable safety factor. Thus, it has long been common practice to paint various types of pipes and conduits in distinctive colours in order to make their identification easier, and a British Standard Specification lays down the colours which should be used for this purpose. A more recent innovation which is growing in favour is to paint benches and the moving parts of machinery in colours which, by contrast with that of the articles being produced, show up the latter more clearly.

There can be little doubt that as manufacturers appreciate the positive advantages of well-planned colour treatment in their establishments and realise the effect it can have on output, it will be employed on a much larger scale, so that this aspect of the subject is well worth the attention of the progressive decorator.

Colour Symbolism

For the benefit of those who may be called upon to undertake church decoration, we may add a note on the symbolic significance of colours employed in ecclesiastical work. Thus, white stands for light and purity; blue for contemplative faith; red for militant faith, fire, and charity; green for hope; black for mourning.

In addition, certain colours are traditionally associated with various saints, as follows: St. Matthew, green; St. Mark, purple; St. Luke, blue; St. John, red; St. Peter, blue; St. George, red and white; St. Paul, purple and white; St. Thomas, grey; St. Andrew, red; St. Mary, blue; St. Patrick, green and gold.

The sign writer should know the colours used in heraldry. These colours, known as *tinctures*, are as follows: *gules* (red); *azure* (blue); *vert* (green); *purpure* (purple); and *sable* (black). In addition, there are two metals, *argent* (silver) and *or* (gold). The colours should be as bright and pure as possible. White may be used for silver and yellow for gold.

Color ∽ Personality of Your House

*N*o matter how much money and time a woman spends on her clothes, if she dresses in a tiresome monotone—a repetition of one color in her dress, hat, gloves, bag, shoes—she presents an uninteresting appearance. However, if she uses an *accessory color* in trimming or jewelry, or wears a hat or gloves of contrasting color, her appearance is greatly enhanced and creates a more attractive impression on others.

THE PRINCIPLE OF COLOR IN HOME DECORATING IS THE SAME. Each time you enter a room you should get a fresh *lift* in spirits. The same *optimistic mood* should prevail throughout your house; it is thoughtless decorating to have even one drab room, as there is no necessity for it. The application of color, whether on the walls or in the furnishings, should not be left entirely to *intuition*. Of course the prime factor is to bring out your own tastes and personality; but there are also some intelligent rules of color which can be of great aid to you. There are considerations such as size of the room, its purpose, its exposure, all of which have a bearing on the selection of colors.

Is YOUR ROOM SUNNY? The background should be based on the *cool colors* such as green, blue, blue-green, or gray. With your choice of color you can combine other colors, which are pleasing to you and which blend harmoniously with a *cool blackground*.

Is Your Room Lacking In Sunlight? In such case the background is best when based on the *warm colors* which include pink, rose, dusty rose, yellow beige, orange. Of course you may be partial to some other colors which can be used in conjunction with the *warm* ones.

Consult The Color Wheel which shows the primary and secondary colors. This is the color method employed by the professional interior decorator, and it is wise to study this procedure in choosing your background and accessory colors.

Colors Have Personalities. Even though you follow the basic color rules, you do not have to be *tied down* to them in a hard and fast manner. Your own reactions must be taken into consideration, as you and the members of your family must be happy in your surroundings. *Never* use any color to which there is a personal objection. However, there are some definite *color personalities* which are interesting to observe: of the primary colors, *red* is vibrant and attracts attention, *yellow* is cheerful and refreshing, *blue* is cool and restful. Thus, if you wish to add interest to a dull corner, or if you wish to have one thing in the room stand out as the *high spot*, use a color in the *red family*. If you want to give a room a cheerful aspect, make use of one of the *yellow shades*. But if the effect of restfulness and coolness is desired, a dominant note of *blue, green, or gray* tones will produce that effect.

Where To Use Color. There is no set rule as to which part of the home should bear the greatest color accent. Floors, wall, draperies, furniture, lamps—all are strategic points on which color can be focused, depending on the individual room and its plan of decoration. Color can be emphasized in wallpaper or paint, in upholstery and drapery materials, in patterns of the floor covering. One color should not be utilized throughout—there should be contrasts or harmonious blendings of several colors, so that the room has an *interesting character* which makes itself felt. In the following chapters the subject of color relating to separate rooms and their furnishings is treated in more detail and should be considered carefully before you make your definite decisions.

Tricks With Color

Color can perform almost magical deeds in *camouflaging* and rejuvenating parts of the home, to bring out its best points. Here are some of the most usual problems which confront the home maker, and the ways in which to overcome them:

Must A Ceiling Be White? The ceiling is too large an area to be unrelieved white. A safe rule is to paint the ceiling to match the walls; but if the room is too low, a pale shade of the wall color gives height. However, when the room is too high, it is best to use a contrasting *deep color*.

How Can My Small Room Look Larger? By use of light-colored walls of the *cool shades*. Avoid sharp contrasts of color in woodwork and draperies.

How Can My Large Room Look More Compact? Walls can be of *warm color* or large wallpaper pattern. Color contrasts should be used.

How Can I Show My Furniture To Advantage? If your couch or chairs look too large for the room, have them covered or painted a color which blends with the wall. But if your furniture is small and you want to make it look larger, use light color or patterned covers, or a paint which is in contrast to the wall.

What Shall I Do With Uneven Spots Built Into The Room? If you have an unsightly fireplace or radiator, or irregularly spaced doors and windows, the best way to keep them in the background is to paint or paper them the same color as the walls. This helps to create an *optical illusion* of a disappearing act. But your room may have something outstanding which should be played up, such as an interesting mantel or a deep alcove. They should be *dramatized* by color which contrasts with the walls, to *emphasize* their effectiveness.

Do not *experiment* hastily with color schemes. It is often too late and too costly after your rooms are completed. Patiently plan your color combinations so there will be neither monotony nor harsh contrasts throughout the house. Above all else, do not be afraid of color—a wise combination of imagination and practical application of color will add *vitality* to your interior decoration.

Colour in the Small Home

F EW people seem to realize that colour schemes are intensely affected by their surroundings. The lighting conditions, the size and shape of the room, each one of these points will have a definite influence on the colours used for the scheme of decoration. Strong sunshine will dim seemingly brilliant hues, and climatic conditions will affect the same colour in different ways. A few reflections on the manner in which colours are used in various countries will explain what I mean. It will be found that strong colours such as red and purple are very prevalent in the decorative schemes carried out in southern parts of the Mediterranean, India, and the northern coasts of Africa. Here the intensity of the sunlight softens the harsh qualities of these colours and gives them an effect of harmony. Whereas if these same hues are used in great quantities in a mild climate such as England, they appear harsh and barbaric and create an atmosphere of restlessness and disquiet. In contrast, extreme northern countries like Russia, Norway, and Sweden, with their snow and ice, require the brilliance of these rich warm colours, and the peasant-craft of all these regions shows a great predilection for full colours such as red, orange, purple, and emerald-green. Similarly, it will be found that in a country like the United States, where the climate varies from extreme cold to intense heat, designers and architects are fond of employing many more vivid combinations of colour than are usually found in countries with a mild climate such as France and England.

Colour is closely related to light, and it is governed by the same laws which guide the harmonies of nature. Starting with Sir Isaac Newton, who discovered that light could be split up into a variety of hues by means of a glass prism, scientists followed up his theory and attempted to define a set of rules by which colour could be organized, and some explanation given why certain colours harmonized together whilst others placed against each other created a discord.

Colour in the Small Home

Goethe, Schopenhauer, Chevreul, Ostwald, all advanced theories about colour, in which its psychological and physiological qualities were analysed, but despite a great divergence of opinion, Newton's analysis of light still remains the basic formula on which the modern standardization of colours is formed.

Taking Newton's order of the colours in the spectrum, which gives us the following colours, yellow, orange, red, scarlet, crimson, purple, violet, ultramarine, blue, blue-green, green, and yellow-green, modern colour experts have arranged these shades into twelve main groups. An examination of the above list will show you that many colours are closely related to each other. In fact, if you made a diagram of the colours of the spectrum you would discover that certain colours definitely merge into each other. This is a very important discovery because it explains the laws of colour harmony and gives us the reason why certain shades harmonize together whilst others, being unrelated, create a sense of discord. This fact enabled Root to establish his table of the natural order of colours in which he indicates that yellow is the lightest of colours and violet the darkest. As Barrett Carpenter explains, Root's theory allows us to travel between these two extremes of colour by two roads; by way of red, or by way of blue, and by taking the natural order of colours we find that orange is deeper than yellow, red deeper than orange, purple deeper than red, and similarly starting the other way round, we discover that green is deeper than yellow, and blue is deeper than green, and so down to violet, the deepest colour of all.

Regarding colours in this way, it appears that the question of arranging or combining them should be quite simple, but, unfortunately, it has been found that even similar or closely related colours affect each other differently according to the quantities in which they are used. Light also affects colours in different ways, and this explains why tropical sunshine, containing as it does a large quantity of yellow, will neutralize the strength of strong colours such as red; whereas in milder climates the sunlight contains less yellow and, consequently, it does not affect other colours so strongly. Added to this fact is the discovery that certain colours attract light, whilst others are deadened by it. Consequently a knowledge of the reactions of colour to light is essential to anyone attempting interior decoration. It has been proved that colours also affect us physiologically —that is to say, that the human eye is affected by the colours it sees. Some colours, such as red and orange, make a greater demand on the eye than others, and because of this the eye soon wearies of the demands upon it, so it is best to avoid using large expanses of the two colours in the decoration of a room. On the other hand, the colours green and yellow please the eye and rest it. This explains the great popularity of these two colours in contemporary decoration, for unconsciously we are only obeying the laws of nature in using them. Blue, despite the fact that it is a cold colour, is very restful to the eye, and the lighter tones of this colour are much used in modern colour schemes.

It will be noticed that neither black nor white have been mentioned in the list of colours, and this is because they are a combination of other shades and are not pure natural colours in themselves. However, they play an important part in the arrangement of any colour scheme, and I will deal with their uses later on.

All colour schemes are based on arrangements derived from the three primary colours: red, yellow, and blue. By mixing these three together we obtain the three secondary colours. For example, blue mixed with yellow produces green. Purple is obtained by mixing blue with red, and yellow mixed with red gives us orange. This natural order of colours creates a circle ranging from yellow to violet, which provides a scale of colour harmonics very similar to the musical scale. As in music, colours, like musical notes, have a different relation to each other. Certain combinations of these notes provide a harmony, others produce a discord. The aim of every designer when creating a colour scheme is to try to evolve as many harmonies as possible, although discord has its place in decoration, as will be shown further on.

Harmonious colour schemes are achieved by using several colours which adjoin or are closely connected on the chromatic circle. Monotony is avoided by varying the intensity of each colour used according to the area covered. For instance, yellow is very satisfactory when used with green provided that less green is used than yellow. In all cases, the stronger colour should be employed in smaller quantities than the lighter shade used with it. Similarly, yellow used with red is an effective harmony, and this was frequently used by Chinese artists.

Other colour schemes can be obtained by contrasting the colours lying opposite each other on the colour circle, such as green and purple or blue-green and red-orange. But in employing contrasts one colour must dominate the other and two contrasting colours cannot be used in equal quantities. Frequently contrasting hues can be harmonized by mixing a little of each colour with the other.

Modern decoration has shown a tendency to break away from the use of simple harmonies and contrasts of natural colour. Instead, it favours the more subtle variations of colour obtained by mixing pure colours with black or white. The chief virtue of black is that it enables you to emphasize other colours in a room, and it brings out the richness of the colours placed beside it. Black mixed with any colour gives us shades, and these are also useful in creating a harmonious background of colour. White mixed with a colour gives us a tint of the same colour, and contemporary designers are fond of employing this device for their schemes. Many of the modern colour schemes are built up by using various shades and tints of the same colour. This system gives us the monochrome scheme and provides us with a colour arrangement which is always harmonious.

Studying the great English decorative styles of the past, it will be found that the majority of colour schemes incline towards a use of soft colours. Designers, like the Adam Brothers, particularly favoured pastel shades such as lilac, pea-green, dove-grey, straw-colour, and light-blue. Even to-day English architects and designers appear to favour light colour schemes. I have seen critics attack the use of light colours in this country as anaemic and lacking in strength, but surely the reason for this prevalence of soft colours is accounted for by the climate and by the soft character of the landscape? I have already pointed out that climate has a great influence on decorative styles, and there is no doubt that the warm passionate colours of the south appear out of place, except in small quantities, in the mild and slightly grey atmosphere of this country. Moreover, it is significant that the Chinese, who live in a climate somewhat similar to ours, and who are admitted to be amongst the most subtle colourists of all time, should favour soft clear colours. Perhaps this explains the great attraction Chinese art has always exercised over British art-lovers? However, the fact remains that Chinese colour arrangements are amongst the most suitable for use in modern decoration.

Chinese colour schemes are simple and achieve their effects by means of vivid contrasts. A room painted in Chinese yellow and white, the walls and ceiling being done in yellow, and the woodwork painted white with white curtains to match, will be enlivened by touches of lacquer-red or black. Celadon green will be used with lacquer-red. Chinese blue, which is a mixture of blue and green, will be used with green and black. Parchment coloured walls will often lend a harmonious background for Chinese yellow and white porcelain ornaments. All these schemes, with their use of pure colour, agree perfectly with the severe lines of modern furniture and the rough woven patterns of modern furnishing materials and, undoubtedly, Chinese art has proved a great inspiration to the best of modern designers.

We now come to the problem of colour as applied to the small room. It has been found that certain colours will make a room appear smaller than it really is. This is especially true of red. As Goethe comments: 'In looking steadfastly at a red surface, the colour seems actually to penetrate the eye. It produces an extreme excitement and still acts thus when somewhat darkened.' In consequence, this is a disturbing colour to use in covering a small space, and its use should be avoided in a small room except for accentuating touches. Orange is another strong colour, and this should be used sparingly. On the other hand, cool colours such as blue and green give an impression of space, and these two shades are ideal for decorating a small room. In fact, it will be discovered that all the lighter tones are satisfactory in a constricted space. The shape of any room will have a decided influence on the colour scheme used for its decoration. If the walls or ceiling fall at awkward angles, it is best to paint or distemper the whole room one colour. This will have a unifying effect and the best shades to use for such a scheme are light-blue, beige, light-yellow, apricot, or cream. Do not forget that the ceiling will have an important bearing on the colour scheme in a small room. A dead-white ceiling may emphasize the smallness of light-green walls. In such a case it is wiser to paint the ceiling a slightly lighter tone than the walls.

In a small room the proportion of the colours used for the scheme must be studied carefully, otherwise a wrong balance of colours will upset your whole scheme. Remember that a large mass of colour such as is provided by armchairs and a settee all upholstered in the same tone may upset the proportions of a room unless the covers are chosen to harmonize with the colour of the walls. For small rooms it is best to try to keep the colour scheme as simple as possible. Do not use more than one contrast in colour, or try to build up your scheme by employing shades and tints related to the main colour used in the room. Avoid using dirty colours. Clear colours are best for a small scheme. Combinations such as apple-green and beige, primrose-yellow and cream, light-blue and white, are all admirable for this purpose.

White is much used in contemporary decoration, particularly in its off-white tones. The advantage of white as a background is that it is luminous and provides an effective foil to any other colour placed against it. The danger of an all-white colour scheme is that unless it is relieved by other shades it tends to become monotonous, but white will always look well when placed against a coloured background.

When planning a colour scheme for a small room, bear in mind the consideration that apart from any colours you may be using, the wood and any metal used for the furnishing will also have its colour values. This also applies to any of the fabrics used in the room. As a rule it is a mistake to use large-patterned materials in a small room. Instead, choose woven materials or small-patterned fabrics. Strongly-patterned carpets should be avoided whenever possible and plain-coloured floor coverings used in such schemes. Sometimes it is possible to use a boldly decorated fabric against a very plain background, but when this is done attention must be paid to keeping the rest of the scheme as simple as possible; or the scheme must pick out the colours employed in the coloured pattern used for the curtain material.

Remember that colours used in large areas will appear darker than they do in small quantities. And a strong contrast in colour is preferable in a dark room.

Colour in the Small Home

Strongly lit rooms will always subdue the colours used in them, and for this reason it is best to choose light-attracting colours, such as yellow, for their decoration.

Colour can create an effect of light. This is especially true in a dark room. Colours which are unbearably bright in daylight become soft and attractive in a darkened atmosphere. This fact was known to the ancient Egyptians and accounts for the brilliant schemes of decoration found in all their tombs. Passing from the glare of the desert into the darkened subterranean passages which led to these deeply hidden rooms, the eye is still agreeably surprised and stimulated by the groups of richly-coloured figures which suddenly greet one after so much darkness. The Egyptians were fond of using strong reds, blues, greens, yellow, and white for the decoration of their burial places, and these tones, which would be unbearably bright in daylight, become soft and beautiful when revealed in the darkened atmosphere of their tombs. The Persians also practised this scheme of decoration. They were continually lighting up a darkened interior with brilliant schemes of decoration. Consider the rich groups of Persian tiles, with their intricate designs carried out in rose, white, gold, and flame on a turquoise-blue ground, and one soon realizes how lovely these gleaming masses of colour must have appeared set in a darkened church or an ill-lit stone palace. This principle, practised by the ancient Egyptians and Persians, still holds good to-day. A very dark room can be made to glow with colour and light provided that it is decorated in the correct manner. As a rule it is best to paint the walls and ceiling some clear light colour, such as yellow, pink, or golden-yellow. Then against this plain background you can place a richly coloured carpet on the floor or hang the dark window with a vividly patterned fabric. Lit by indirect methods of lighting, such a room, however small it may be, will appear alive and full of colour, and even more dramatic than a room which relies mainly on daylight for its lighting.

I have already mentioned the subject of discord in relation to colour. A discord is obtained when the natural order of colours are reversed. It is achieved by deliberately using a discordant colour in a scheme where the rest of the tones are harmoniously grouped together. Used in small touches a discord can be immensely effective, and in a colour scheme where the arrangement of the colours is simple a small discord will often enliven the whole effect. It throws the other colours into sharp relief and quickens what otherwise might be a monotonous colour harmony. Some simple examples of colour discords are red with purple and yellow-brown with pale-blue. However, the discord must be used discreetly in any colour scheme. It should never dominate any colour grouping, but it can be used for small touches of colours, such as in cushions on a settee, or in the design of a carpet. Both the Persian and the Japanese were fond of using discords in their decorative patterns, where they employed it as an emphasizing note, or as an opportunity to make a sudden change in the grouping of the colours. Discords are frequently found in nature, and the examination of certain fruits will show how it lays emphasis on any colour scheme. For example, the tip of a red cherry is pale-purple, and the high-light on a ripe orange will be a light-red and not yellow, as might be expected. This leads us to the discovery that all the most beautiful arrangements of colour are to be found in studying nature.

Admittedly, colour science is not easy. It is difficult for man to recapture the colour harmonies of nature. The knowledge of how to use colour is an instinct like good taste. It is significant that children have a far surer instinct for colour than their elders. But this does not mean that it is impossible for the average man and woman to obtain a working knowledge of how to understand and use colours. Most people have a natural preference for certain colours, and when you are decorating your home it is always wise to follow these preferences. Often a woman will design a beautifully coloured room although she is completely unaware of the laws of colour arrangement. Her natural instinct has guided her and the results are completely satisfactory. However, it does seem a pity that more attention is not given to this fascinating subject in the school curriculum, for frequently a little scientific knowledge will help to foster and guide natural taste.

In the past I have advocated the study of pictures as an inspiration for colour schemes. And indeed, all works of art will be found a continual source of new ideas for colour arrangement and show you the correct method of how to achieve colour harmony. A great painter or a fine decorative artist will have a natural understanding of how to blend and contrast colours; a colourist such as Van Gogh or Renoir will always be an excellent model to follow.

In creating a colour scheme it is helpful to have a central point of interest. A good painting or a coloured reproduction of a well-known landscape or a group of flowers will give you such a point, and then it is a simple matter to analyse the colours used in the picture and employ these as the basis for your scheme. Van Gogh's famous painting of 'Sunflowers' gives us an example of how to use this method. Here the artist has painted a group of sunflowers, glowing with warm oranges and yellows against a vivid light-blue background. The flowers themselves are placed in a simple, brownish-cream pottery vase. Thus in analysing the picture we have the following colours—light-blue, yellow, orange, brown and cream. Taking these shades as the inspiration for your colour scheme, the room should be decorated in the following manner. Paint or distemper the walls and ceiling the same light-blue as found in the painting.

Colour in the Small Home

Curtain the windows in a light-brown and cream woven fabric, and upholster the furniture in the same material. Cover the floor in a light-brown carpet and touches of light-yellow and orange can be introduced into the scheme for covering the cushions in these two shades. Light-coloured wooden furniture of pale oak or sycamore would look well in such a scheme and harmonize with the painting, which should be hung above the fireplace, thereby unifying the whole colour arrangement.

Other painters who offer interesting treatments of colour are J. M.W. Turner—who is undoubtedly one of the greatest of English colourists, with his melting reds and golds and those vast dreamy landscapes which seem to have been conjured up from another world—and the great masters of the Dutch school. There are Medici prints of Vermeer and Pieter de Hooch which give many interesting new combinations of colours, and any of these fine coloured reproductions would serve as models for new colour schemes.

When you are planning your colour schemes pay a visit to some of the great museums. Students in interior decoration do not pay enough attention to the great decorative styles of the past. The art of China and Persia still has many ideas to teach us in the way of using colour and how to treat decorative objects. An old Persian tile, the design on a Chinese vase, the gay designs on an Etruscan jar, the subtle colouring of old Sèvres porcelain, the rich glowing tones of Italian Primitives, each of these offer fresh ideas for decorative treatments. What a pity it is that more designers and would-be decorators will not avail themselves of the culture and the artistic knowledge of the past!

To summarize the whole difficult question of how to use colour, try to bear the following rules in mind: avoid using strong vivid shades of red, orange, and purple except in small quantities. Coldly-lit rooms can be made lighter by using a warm colour like yellow for the walls and ceiling. In rooms with a southern aspect employ cool colours such as light-green, buff, light tones of blue, and apricot. Many architects and designers favour neutral schemes combining neutral shades of white, black, and brown, but when using these combinations it is best to relieve the schemes with touches of colour like red, blue, or golden-yellow. Colours such as violet and orange should be used sparingly, although they are useful for the introduction of sharp colour discords. As a rule it is a mistake to mix black as a darkening medium for other colours. The correct way to lessen the brilliance of any colour is to mix it with a little of its contrasting hue. However, the range of mixed colours is so large that it is usually possible to obtain approximately the shade you desire, and if a softening of the colour is needed the painter can easily do this for you. Remember that the commercial names of colours are often misleading. If you want a specified colour, it is wisest to obtain a pattern of the exact shade you require and then ask the painter to match up his colour to this pattern. Often a plain-coloured fabric will give you the best colour pattern to work from as the colouring of modern textiles is particularly fine and sure. Many of the attractive pastel shades can be obtained by mixing white with the colour required and the proportion of colour added to the white will vary according to the depth or softness of the shade you require.

For the majority of colour schemes I would advise using a paint with a glossy finish, as this will attract more light than a plain surface paint. Study the lighting of your room before you plan the colour scheme, as a very light room can often be covered with a good clear distemper, whereas a dark room would need the lightening properties of oil paint.

Finally, remember that your colour scheme should be determined by the use of the room. A dining-room can stand a brilliant scheme of decoration which would be unsuitable in a living-room or bedroom. Do not be afraid of employing colour in your decorative schemes. Too many contemporary rooms have suffered from a lack of its livening influence. The human eye craves colour and decorative patterns, but do not imagine that an effect of colour is achieved by the use of many colours. Intensity of colour is achieved by contrast and not by a haphazard heap of colours thrown together. When choosing colours for your rooms allow your instinct to guide you, for most people instinctively choose the colours which provide them with the most harmonious and suitable background.

COLOUR SCHEMES

STUDY OF COLOUR AND ITS POSSIBILITIES. SIMPLE AND INTERMEDIATE HUES. COLOUR CIRCLES. COMPLEMENTARY AND CONTRASTING COLOURS. BUILDING COLOUR HARMONIES. PROFESSIONAL TERMS. PSYCHOLOGICAL GROUPINGS OF COLOUR. SELECTING COLOURS FOR DECORATION. PERIOD COLOURS. LIGHT-REFLECTION VALUES. SUGGESTIONS FOR VARIOUS ROOMS. EXTERIOR WORK.

PROBABLY no part of the decorator's training is more difficult to master than the study of colour. Innumerable books and articles dealing with the theoretical side of the subject almost invariably set down hard and fast rules which not only tend to hinder the student's natural colour sense but, in fact, prevent an interest being taken in what is really a fascinating and useful study.

It is not intended, therefore, in this chapter to give definite rules, but rather to offer suggestions which will help the student to explore the possibilities of colour design and to make experiments by which he can render his own colour sense more effective.

Colour Shades

Between the complete opposites of light and darkness there is an infinite gradation of colour shades or mixtures. The light diffused by the sun appears to be pure white, but it contains all the colours, as is demonstrated by passing a pure white ray of sunlight through a prism.

The resulting impressions, or sensations if you will, are registered by the eye as colours. It has been computed that between light and total darkness there are 30,000 or more shades of colour distinguishable by the average human eye.

It is not easy to define colour, for the definition would vary according to the occupation or outlook of the individual person attempting to define it. The chemist's description would differ from the physicist's, the optician's from that of the psychologist's; but our aim in this chapter is to consider colour as it concerns the decorator: his concern with colour is to study and use it as an artist.

Radiant Energy

In actual practice, the decorator is concerned with pigmentary or technical colour—colour bought from the manufacturer or pressed out of tubes, but to use these so as to produce an æsthetically pleasing result, he should have at least a working knowledge of colour from the point of view of the physicist, who considers colour as light or as radiant energy of various wavelengths and intensities.

He may be a "born colourist" and have an "eye for colour"; nevertheless, there are rules of harmony which the decorator should know as thoroughly as the alphabet or the rules of arithmetic.

It will be helpful in commencing any study of colour and its use simply to point out a few of the fundamental principles and to offer some practical suggestions that will make them serviceable to the purpose of the decorator. There are really only three main points to take into account, and to understand these clearly will help very materially in acquiring practice in the proper use of colour.

(1) The stimulus, or the source, or the conditions which the eye interprets as colour sensations.
(2) The reception and expression or interpretation of these conditions.
(3) The effects produced by the colour sensations.

Visible Phenomena

The essential extract from the dictionary's definition of colour is "a property of visible phenomena distinct from form and from light and shade, depending on the effect of light of different wave-lengths on the retina," or, put in a more simple way, we can say "colour is a visual sensation different from the sensation of form or shape and different from the sensation of light or shade."

To put it even more simply: "You see individuals or things first as definite forms or shapes; secondly, in different shades of light and dark areas and, lastly, in different colours."

It is easy to demonstrate the truism, "without light there can be no colour." Between the extremes of the positive and negative principles of pure light and total darkness, impressions represented in painting by the elementary colours of white and black, there exists an infinite gradation of shades or mixtures called greys. It should be noted here that the value of a colour is distinguished by its position in this scale of gradation from white down to black.

Again, it can easily be demonstrated and should always be borne in mind that white light is a mixture of a large number of coloured lights. In the arched solar spectrum of the rainbow the pure white light of the sun is deflected or refracted from the raindrops and the bow is seen in the atmosphere to consist of red, orange, yellow, green, blue, and violet.

The same six normal colours can be seen and, of course, in the same order, if a pure white ray of sunlight is passed through a triangular prism. The light is broken up into a band revealing *all* the colours of the spectrum, those immediately recognisable being red, orange, yellow, green, blue, and violet and in that order, symbolised by the letters R, O, Y, G, B, and V.

These six are called "simple hues," and the colours lying between them — red-orange and yellow-orange, yellow-green, blue-green, blue-purple and red-purple —"intermediate hues," designated by the symbols RO, YO, YG, BG, BP, and RP.

Though they are not used by experienced colourists and may tend to hinder a right development of the colour sense, nevertheless the student would find it helpful to familiarise himself with the relation of these primary and secondary colours by making a colour circle (as illustrated in Fig. 1) and two variants of such circles are given.

Colour Circles

It is not possible to secure pigments which correctly represent each of the spectrum colours, but to approximate these for the purpose of making a colour circle it is suggested to all those so interested that the following will be useful:

COMBINING COLOURS FOR HARMONY

	WATER COLOUR	OIL COLOUR
Red	Scarlet vermilion	Poppy red
Yellow	Chrome yellow	Chrome yellow
Orange	Chrome orange	Chrome orange
Green	Chrome green No. 2	Middle chrome green
Blue	Cobalt and a little ultramarine blue	Light ultramarine
Violet	Cobalt violet	Permanent purple

The three primary colours are approximated in Nature by the following—red by the geranium, yellow by the lemon, and blue by the sunny midsummer sky.

It will thus be seen that the following colours are complementary and contrast harmoniously:

Primaries: Yellow   Violet
          Red   Green
          Blue   Orange

Secondaries: Yellow-orange Blue-violet
            Orange-red   Green-blue
            Violet-red   Yellow-green

The colour circle illustrated in Fig. 2 demonstrates the foregoing principles.

Besides the *primaries* and the *secondaries*, which are obtained by mixing two of the primaries in about equal parts, there are the *tertiaries*, obtained by mixing two of the secondary colours; orange and green when mixed producing citrine, orange and violet producing russet, green and violet, slate.

The following tabulation shows quite clearly how the three main groups of colours—primary, secondary, and tertiary—are obtained.

It will be noticed from this tabulation that each tertiary colour contains the three primaries with one of them in greater amount than the other two, so that in russet there is a larger proportion of red, in citrine of yellow, and in slate of blue.

Building Colour Harmonies. There are two simple methods of providing harmony by combining colours which have something in common:

(1) Monochromatic or a one-hue scale.

(2) Adjacent or neighbouring colours.

Selecting Contrasts

There are two simple methods of selecting contrasted colours which harmonise:

(3) Complementary colours.

(4) Triads or triangular colour schemes.

The four small charts (Figs. 3–6) explain in a simple manner these four principal methods of using a colour or combining colours or hues for decorative schemes.

(1) *Monochromatic or one-hue schemes* (Fig. 3). Dominant harmony or a one-hue scheme is that worked out within one scale or around one colour. It is

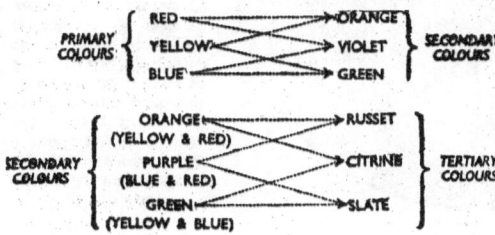

COLOUR SCHEMES

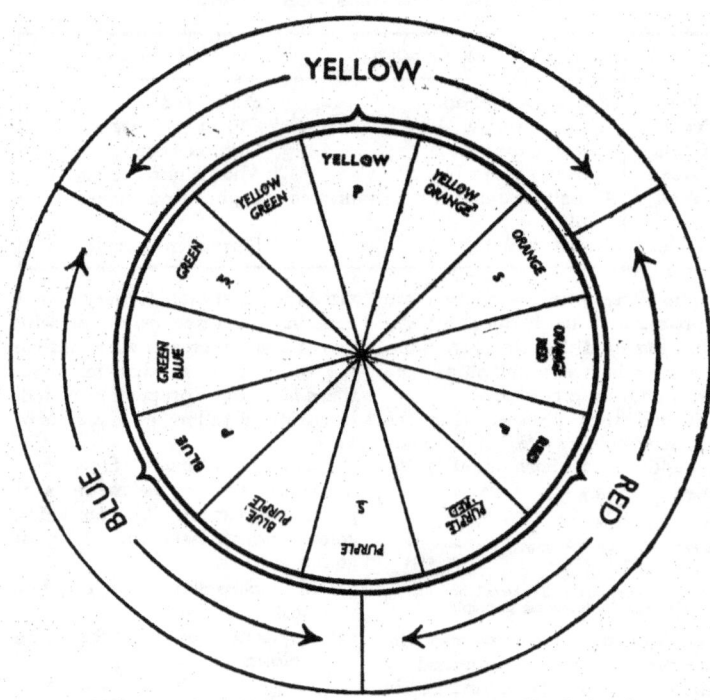

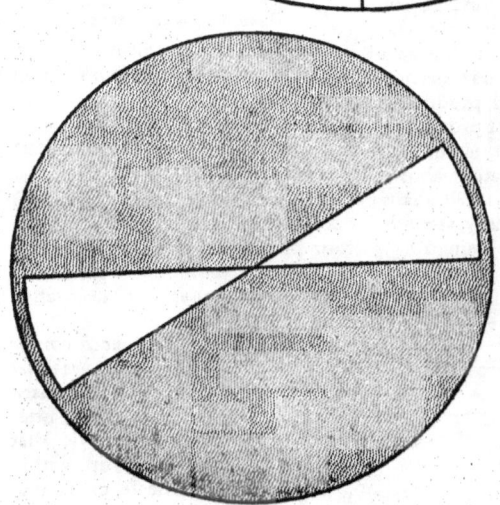

Fig. 1. In this chart the three primaries, red, yellow, and blue, are shown in the outer ring, and again in the subdivisions of the inner circle; midway between these are the secondaries — orange, green, and purple. This chart is particularly recommended to students for its simplicity: it is easy to colour and to make. If a slotted neutral grey disc is made and placed on to this circle, pivoted to it so that it can revolve, the user will be able to isolate the colour desired in one opening and at once obtain its complementary in the other opening.

RELATIONSHIP OF PRIMARY AND SECONDARY COLOURS

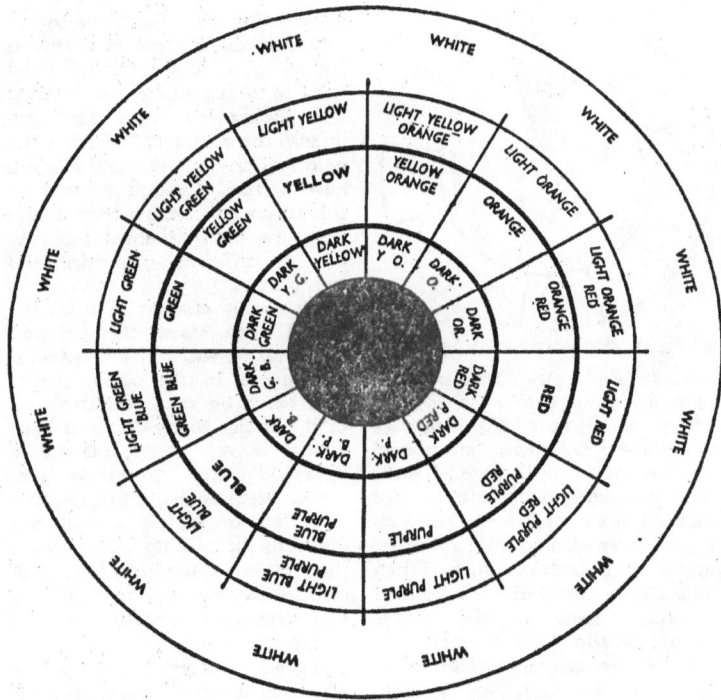

EXPERIMENTAL COLOUR CHART

Fig. 2. This is another chart which the student will find useful, and especially if he makes a coloured copy, as in the case of Fig. 1, with pigments. In the diagram shown above, only two gradations are given of each respective colour, but if, say, a series of six concentric circles is used and the gradations from dark to light clearly defined, not only will the chart prove even more useful for reference purposes, but the actual preparation of it will be of real practical value. It would further add to the usefulness of this chart if a series of slotted discs were made for each concentric circle. It is suggested that the chart should be enlarged up to at least 2 ft. in diameter, and made so that it will withstand frequent usage.

essential to remember that any hue or colour can be dark or light in value, dull or bright in intensity. Supposing the dominant hue to be blue, the shades of it may range from the palest of sky-blue to the deepest indigo. Grey-blue may range from a grey with only a comparatively small touch of blue in it to blue that is merely slightly grey.

All these are the possibilities of one hue and constitute a colour scale. For sky-blues and greens and greys to be considered of one scale they must swing around the same kind of blue. There are royal blues, blue-violets, and blue-greens, each of which is a different colour or hue and with its own scale.

(2) *Adjacent or neighbouring*

COLOUR SCHEMES

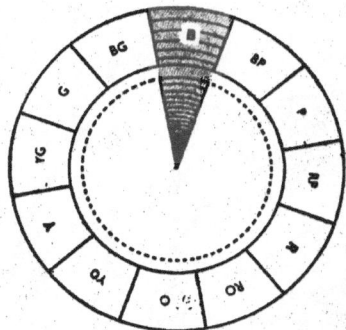

Fig. 3. Monochromatic schemes.

colours (Fig. 4). An analogous harmony is a colour scheme in which two or more adjacent hues plus their tints, shades, and greyed variants are used. Though adjacent hues occupying half the circle can be used, it will be safer to build up a decorative scheme from a smaller arc of neighbouring hues. When adjacent colours form the basis of a scheme, complementary accents should be added for contrast.

(3) *Complementary colours* (Fig. 5). Complementary colours are those directly opposite each other in the large charts illustrated in Figs. 1 and 2. The complementary of orange, for instance, is blue. If our orange tended toward the yellow rather than to the red, its complement would tend to the purple rather than to green. As with monochromatic or one-hue schemes so with complementary colours—a variety of dark and light values and of bright and dull tones adds immeasurably to a pleasing decorative effect.

Generally speaking, a complementary colour scheme is pleasing for a greater length of time to most people than either the monochromatic or analogous harmonies.

(4) *Triads or triangular colour schemes* (Fig. 6). For three-colour combinations, one colour is chosen and an equal-sided triangle formed from it to any other two colours. The longer the sides the more intense the contrast. Wherever the points of any one triangle fall you have a triad. Though these three colours are harmonious they should never be used in equal intensity but in different quantities and strengths.

Since this chapter is primarily intended to assist the practical decorator we will go back to Fig. 1, and suggest in turn colour groupings based on each colour shown in the circle. Many of the colours named have, of course, been "greyed." The groupings presented make no claim to completeness, but are merely offered as a guide to the placing of colours in their various categories. Individual colours may vary in hue, brilliance, and strength according to manufacturer.

Yellow. All yellows not greenish or of an orange cast, such as aureolin, banana, buttercup, cadmium yellow, champagne, canary yellow, ecru, lemon, original army khaki, maize, Naples yellow, straw,

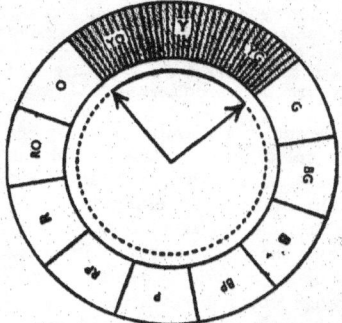

Fig. 4. Chart showing adjacent or neighbouring colours.

VARIOUS CATEGORIES OF COLOURS

primrose, satinwood, Spanish yellow, spectrum yellow, sulphur, yellow cream, etc.

Yellow-orange. All yellows containing red (until they arrive at the orange stage), such as apricot, beige, cadmium orange, chamois, Chinese orange, chrome orange, cinnamon, corn husk, cream, gamboge, middle stone, light tan, vanilla, natural wood, etc.

Orange. Colours specially representing yellow and red, such as golden brown, golden buff, warm cream, old ivory, natural leather, brown mahogany, oak, roman ochre, burnt orange, transparent gold ochre, russet, etc.

Orange-red. All reds containing yellow, such as copper, coral, cadmium scarlet, flesh, natural mahogany, transparent red ochre, mars orange, peach, brick red, light red, burnt russet, salmon, sienna, terra cotta, terra rosa, orange vermilion, scarlet vermilion, etc.

Red. All reds not bluish or of an orange cast, such as begonia, deep cadmium red, cardinal red, castilian red, red cherry, Chinese red, red mahogany, old rose, post office red, signal red, new deep spectrum red, Union Jack red, vermilion, etc.

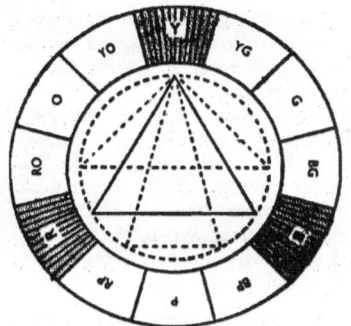

Fig. 6. Triads or triangular schemes.

Purple-red. Purples predominantly reddish, or reds purplish, such as alizarin purple, beetroot, cerise, crimson, garnet, magenta, purple lake, purple madder, raspberry, violet carmine, etc.

Purple. All violets not predominantly reddish or bluish such as heliotrope, lavender, lilac, mauve, pansy, petunia, royal purple, mineral violet, spectrum violet, wistaria, etc.

Blue-purple. Purplish-blues or bluish-purples, such as cornflower, iris, midnight blue, periwinkle, cobalt violet, parma violet, ultramarine violet, etc.

Blue. All blues not greenish or reddish, such as adonis blue, alice blue, cerulean blue, empire blue, forget-me-not, French ultramarine, garter blue, larkspur, mineral blue, new blue, oriental blue, salvia, saxe blue, smalt, sky blue, steel blue, etc.

Blue-green. All bluish-greens or greenish-blues, such as extra deep Brunswick green, chrome green No. 3, myrtle, reseda (or mignonette), etc.

Green. All colours balanced almost equally between blue and yellow, such as apple green, almond green, green beetle, bottle green, mid Brunswick green, cobalt green,

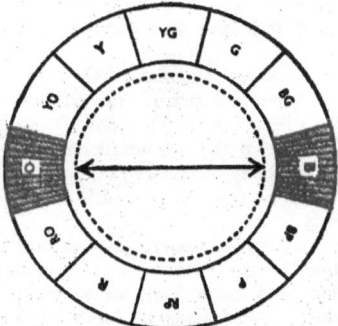

Fig. 5. Complementary colours.

COLOUR SCHEMES

emerald, evergreen, hunter's green, jade green, leaf green, malachite green, mistletoe, spectrum green, viridian, etc.

Yellow-green. All yellows predominantly greenish or greens noticeably yellowish, such as bronze green, pale Brunswick green, cedar green, chartreuse green, cadmium green, grass green, moss green, green muscat, olive green, pea green, etc.

Recognised Terms

Before proceeding to say something in detail concerning the basic colours representing the foregoing groupings or families, it is essential that the student should be quite clear in his mind as to what is meant by the recognised terms used by professional colourists. It is suggested that the student refers to Figs. 1 and 2.

Hue. The dominating characteristic content of a colour distinguishing one colour group from another, as a red from a yellow or a green from a blue, etc. It need not be a pure red, yellow, green or blue, etc. So long as it can clearly be included in the red, yellow, green or blue, etc., group, it is given the designation of its group, except that it is called a tint, shade or greyed form of the spectrum or pure colour.

The six "simple hues" are red, orange, yellow, green, blue, and purple, whilst the other six hues in the chart are called "intermediate hues"—orange-red, yellow-orange, yellow-green, green-blue, blue-purple, and purple-red.

Tints. The name given to light gradations of a colour, produced by mixing white with it.

Shades. The name given to dark gradations of a colour, produced by mixing black with it.

Value. Whether a colour is dark or light. If a colour is dark, its value is *low;* if light, *high.*

Chroma. Often called tonal value. Relative brilliance or dullness of colours when compared with white or black. If a colour is bright, its chroma would be high; if dull, its chroma would be low. Yellow, for example, has a light chroma; purple a dark chroma.

Balance. The qualitative use of colour in area, tone, and intensity.

Emphasis. The accentuation of a decorative feature or particular area achieved by making it either lighter or darker than its surroundings or background.

Accents. Those small touches of bright or contrasting colours introduced into a scheme to give it sparkle and life.

Warm Colours. The red-yellow-orange arc of the chromatic circle extending from yellow-green to red-purple; psychologically stimulating and warming and suggestive of fire and sunlight.

Cool Colours. The blue-violet arc of the chromatic circle extending from blue-green to blue-purple; psychologically restful and soothing, and suggestive of the colours of water, ice, foliage, and distance. Generally speaking, any colour is cool as it is blue and warm as it is red.

Neutralised Colours. "Greyed" or subdued colours or pure colours which have been "let down" by mixing with them a small amount of their complementary colour, or sobered by the addition of black or grey.

Advancing Colours. Sometimes called "near" colours, the reds and adjacent colours have an exciting influence, and seem to "come forward." This emotive influence

PSYCHOLOGICAL GROUPINGS OF COLOURS

extends through red-purple, crimson, scarlet, orange, and yellow, and is most powerful and fiercest with deep orange.

Psychological Groupings

Through association and usage colours have come to have specific attributes, and these must be taken into account in any study of colour and application of its use and power by the decorator. Sometimes called the "language of colours," these psychological effects, or associative usage of colours, may not all be fundamentally sound or consistent, nevertheless it is a recognised fact that certain colours have pronounced powers and can produce a definite mood.

The following are the five main groupings:—

(1) *Dark cool colours*, such as those in which blue is the dominating hue, suggest heaviness, weight, reserve, mystery, and even depression and foreboding melancholy.

(2) *Light cool colours*, on the other hand, suggest delicacy, expanse and freshness, solitude, rest, peace, and hope.

(3) *Dark warm colours*, such as those in which the reds predominate, suggest richness, vitality, power, and stability.

(4) *Bright warm colours*, such as orange, orange-yellows, vermilion, scarlet, etc., suggest strong sunlight, excitement, exhilaration, movement.

(5) *Light warm colours*, such as creams, pinks, etc., suggest loveliness, delicacy, femininity, cheer, delight, and hospitality.

From the foregoing it is at once evident that the effectiveness or otherwise of any decorative scheme will depend mainly on its colour appeal and the appropriateness of the colours for the particular room or scheme in hand. Practicability will of necessity have to be considered as well as many other factors, such as the room's source of light, its character, and the personality of its user.

Some of these considerations will be discussed in more detail later in the chapter, but meantime it will be helpful briefly to consider some of the fundamental characteristics of the principal colour groupings.

Fundamental Characteristics

Yellow. The brightest and most cheerful colour—"light of heart." It is the strongest contrast to black, and is used mostly for lightening dark rooms, but "glares" in those strongly lighted. Pure yellow as a pigment is easily debased by other colours. Note how in nature yellow flowers seem to sparkle amidst green foliage.

Orange. The most powerful colour; it has the potency of its two constituents; most pleasant in decoration when the yellow element is in excess of the red, giving the golden browns and tans. When the red predominates the colour is hot, aggressive, and unmanageable.

Red. The most vivid and pure colour; is exciting and stimulating; associated with the idea of fire, passion, fervour. It is fiercest when nearest yellow. Not suitable for walls of small rooms—gives a sense of imprisonment. It is most effective when used for accent; a red necktie has more appeal than a red suit! It gives a degree of warmth to all colours, especially yellow. Used sparingly by nature.

Green. The most varied of the colours and possibly the most used in decoration throughout the ages. With flowers, it is the general harmonising colour of the foliage and its realm in nature is almost boundless. The student should study the varied character of this colour in plant life and note the relationship between foliage and flowers. No matter what the colour of the flowers may be, there is always a prevailing hue or character in the green colour of the foliage by which it is harmonised with the colours of the flowers.

It is the colour of faith, hope, youth, life, and resurrection, and is a symbol of immortality.

Basically, it is a cool colour and has a tranquillising influence; though there are warm shades of green.

Blue. Is a receding colour, restful, and cool; associated with truth—hence the phrase "true blue"—dignity, divine contemplation. It is the dark element in all other colours. According to the amount of blue in it, so a colour is cold or otherwise. Pure blue is the coldest colour: "blue with cold" is not merely figurative language. The deeper blues are depressing. It is most powerful in strong light, but is neutralised by declining light.

Purple. The largest and most interesting group of colours and also the most retiring of positive colours, nearest in relation to black and shade. The name includes both red and blue purples. It is the colour of royalty, dignity, mystery and sadness, suffering and sacrifice; a colour rich with opportunities for decorators who will explore its possibilities.

Note.—The term *colour* is ambiguous when applied to the neutrals—white, greys, and black—yet the decorator must regard them as colours, for they are composed of and take in all colours.

White is the colour most extensively used in decoration and is the most advancing; harmonises with all colours, and is the contrast of black, and when mixed with it forms various greys. Especially useful when creamed and when used with grey. Is seriously cheerful, and for that reason is used to brighten without conveying gaiety.

There are as great a number of variations of white as any other colours; in fact, a most delightful scheme can be evolved using some of these variations, depending on small touches of intense colours for the accents.

Symbolises purity, innocence, peace, modesty, and delicacy.

Black. The most retiring of colours and one of the most powerful. In its purity is a cold colour and gives this quality to all light colours. Must be used with care where hue is of more importance than shade. At its best, it possesses endless depth. When used with discretion, it gives vigour and brilliance to other colours.

Symbolises death, mourning, tragedy, and silence, nothingness; but when used with white loses its severer meaning.

Pageant of Colour

These associations of ideas with colours are not by any means complete—the pageant of colour is spread out over all countries from the most primitive times to the present day. Standardised usage of colour is mostly confined to ecclesiastical symbolism, and significations are not all consistent or fundamentally sound.

History, literature, and daily life all provide the interested student

VALUE OF PRACTICAL EXPERIMENTATION

with opportunities to explore this aspect of colour usage.

Psychological reactions to colour are not only the outcome of innate colour preference, but because of an awareness to established usage and individual conception of the colour appropriateness for the particular scheme under consideration.

Different aspects of colour appeal strongly to different people: with some the attention is concerned with the colour itself and its qualities as a colour; with others its effect is the main consideration—it is either pleasing or displeasing, soothing or livening, cooling or warming. With some, colour preference is determined by æsthetic association of ideas such as truth, joy, sadness, death, fire, jealousy, superstition.

Sufficient has been said of the psychological effect of colour. Opie's statement is a proven fact: "Every passion and affection of the human mind has its appropriate tint; and colouring, if properly adapted, links its aid, with powerful effect, in the just discrimination and forcible expression of them; it heightens joy, warms love, inflames anger, deepens sadness, and adds coldness to the cheek of death itself."

In the building up of any colour scheme, knowledge of the elementary and simple theories of colour is essential, but only practical experimentation with actual colour will make the theories comprehensible.

Only a comparatively few people react to colour in the fullest degree and even then reaction is distinctly individual. A good colourist is mostly so by instinct and has what is colloquially known as "an eye for colour"; but a colour sense can be developed not only by continued practice *with* colour, but by noticing colour all around one.

Classify the colours seen, pick out and name the individual colours and tones of colour. Carefully analyse the decorative compositions of such artists as Frank Brangwyn, Charles Ricketts, Gerald Kelly; the theatrical sets of Gordon Craig and Oliver Messel.

Observe the contrasts in Nature's colourings of flowers and their foliage, of flowers themselves; of the plumage of birds; butterflies and shells; the rich silks and decorative brocades, particularly those of the Louis XV period, with their skilful blendings of light and elegant colours.

Note not only the general colouring but the individual hues, their value, intensity, and area. Colour science may produce certain recipes, but there are none that can be followed blindly in working out colour harmonies.

Source of Light

The first important factor to consider in selecting colours for decoration is the source of light or, in other words, the room's aspect. Rooms with sunlight, facing south or west, call for the use of the cool colours—those on the Chart in Fig. 1 in the arc from green through purple. Rooms with cold light, facing north or east, need sunny colours—that is, in the arc from orange through the yellow group. In some rooms, sunlight enters at different times of the day.

Depending on the time of the day when the room is most used, either cool or warm colours are suitable. It is not wise to use large areas of warm colours of great

COLOUR SCHEMES

intensity in a room which gets a great amount of sunlight; nor use cool colours in a room which gets a very small amount of natural light.

The next point for consideration is the use of the room—is it a bedroom or dining-room, formal or informal? Who uses it—a man, a woman, or a child? What is the type of the room—is a period predominant? What are the colour preferences of the individual using it? If the carpets and soft furnishings are previously selected, then these more or less dictate the colours for the walls and woodwork.

Do not attempt the extraordinary or unusual; within the boundary of the colour rules there is infinite variety without indulging in eccentricities. Resolve to memorise the colour chart, the position of the colours in it; the position of the three primaries and the three secondaries, for from these colours come all the shades, tints, and variations you have ever seen. Remembering this, the study and practice of colour becomes simple.

Another principle constantly to bear in mind is that related colours (colours from the same family) look well together. Complementary colours also, and different shades of the colour (varying in degree of intensity), look well together.

To Match Colours

If colours have to be matched, have a sample of the colour to be matched and do not "carry it in your head." Often room schemes are built up from the furnishing fabrics to be used in the room; the colours you suggest for the walls and woodwork must not only harmonise with existing furnishings, but have correct values, whether clear, bright colours or greyed tones are used.

Matching of colours should be done on the spot where the actual colour is ultimately to be used.

Period Colours

In each decorative period certain colours were most used. Decorators should know these and be able to recognise authentic period colours. Only those periods are mentioned here which are generally used in present-day decoration.

Louis XV. Feminine colours—dusty rose, soft blue, pale pink, fawn, grey, grey-green.

Louis XVI. Subtle colours, most of them from the cool side of the spectrum; delicate, affected and pretty colours, associated with Marie Antoinette. Also, the more formal colours derived from Greek sources, and influenced by the painter David.

French Provincial. Simple colours: Toile de Jouy tones of red and blue; russet colours.

Empire colours. For colour purposes linked with Directoire; heavy colours, red and green predominating. A study of authentic Aubusson carpets is a good source for the colours of this period.

Chippendale. Clear, livable colours, deep value, but soft tones of red and blue; clear yellow, reseda green.

Particular note should be taken of the rich wood colours used and, when possible, these should be introduced.

Hepplewhite and Sheraton. Clear, gay colours, more pastel than Chippendale colours.

Adam. Pastel tints; powder blue and soft yellow, dove grey and pink predominating.

Regency. Similar to Empire

colours, though lighter in value. Present-day interpretation of Regency leans toward softly greyed colours.

Victorian (the Mauve Decade). Deep, pompous colours, often in strong colour combinations with a leaning toward purple and violet shades. Thundery browns and bottle greens. Usually, white woodwork and mahogany or walnut.

Study and Experience

Chapter I has dealt fully with the various pigments used in the manufacture of paints, and likewise with the composition of the coats of paint for specified purposes; but all the information given is of no avail unless the young decorator will himself make experiments and familiarise himself with the various finishes and effects obtainable with pigmentary colours.

The results of such experiments should be carefully noted, and where the colours produced by different manufacturers are used, their variations should also be recorded, for just as the practising easel artist selects his colours from different makers because a particular colour is better from one source than another, so the wise decorator will exercise discrimination in selecting the sources for obtaining his pigments.

Paint is not "just paint"—something merely to cover a surface; purity and uniformity of colour are essential. If a job is to last and to stand a good deal of wear, then the colours must be fast, and pigment and binders be of the best quality. It is useless to expect good colour work with cheap and poor colours.

Also, it is not sufficient for the would-be master decorator to rely on a good foreman or a good colour mixer; he should have not only a technical or theoretical knowledge of colour and colour mixing, but should be able by practical experience to supervise the foreman or colour mixer in the exacting task of matching colours.

Colour matching should always be done in a good light, for as has already been pointed out, intensity of colour varies according to whether the colour is seen under natural or artificial lighting—the latter again varying according to the method of lighting used. Of course, natural light will vary also, according to the amount of sunlight during the day. All these factors must be considered.

The colour to be matched should be closely examined and its dominant hue decided; in other words, break up the colour by analysis and then experiment with very small touches of colour on a clean piece of glass with a palette knife, brushing out with a small fitch the result of the experiment on a similar ground to that on which the actual bulk colour will eventually be applied.

It seems almost superfluous to add that the colours should be mixed and decided in the room to be decorated, but there is nothing so valuable in ensuring success in colour matching as "trying it in position" and noting the effect.

Proven Makes

With regard to the various binders and ingredients which go to the mixing of paint, the reader will find detailed in another chapter information as to these, but just as with pigments, so it is essential that all the ingredients which go to the making of colours should be of the best quality, otherwise an

COLOUR SCHEMES

entire decorative scheme may eventually be ruined.

Apart from the mixing of pigments for straightforward work, experiments with glazing are essential if subtle colour effects are to be obtained. Differences in finishes, such as flat, eggshell gloss, etc., should all be noted as to their effect on the finished appearance of a given colour. The use of two finishes, such as a flat finish with a full gloss finish, even of the same colour, will often make all the difference to a fine decorative effect.

There are a hundred-and-one tricks of the trade which should be known to the qualified decorator, and only experiments and familiarisation with seemingly humdrum processes will gain for him knowledge and experience in these basic details of the painter's trade.

Further, unless the young decorator will make it his business to understand the elementary facts about colour harmony, he will find that he will never be esteemed as anything other than just a housepainter.

Training in colour mixing is absolutely essential for every decorator, and he should know how to combine colours to develop new tints, tones, and shades.

Study the Chart

And now just a word as to the handling of particular decorative problems. Bear in mind that the home which you have to decorate is your client's and not yours. You may know better, or think you do, than your client as to the type of decoration or colour scheme which will best suit his room or his personality. You will have opportunities to offer advice, and such advice will only be accepted if it is felt to be the outcome of knowledge and experience.

Whatever you do by way of colour scheme or wall treatment, remember it is the *background* for your clients; it must be a harmonious complement to the individuals in the house. Don't push the latest fad in decoration on to your client; often these eccentricities are things of the moment.

Familiarise yourself with good traditional work, and note the effect of certain colours with certain materials, such as woods and silks; the decorative value of various textures, and especially take into account the particular use to which the room you are to decorate is to be put.

You may be asked, for instance, whether the room will look best painted or papered, and be expected to give reasons for your decision. If it is a plain paint scheme, you may have to decide what its finish is to be and whether this is to be achieved by means of paint or distemper; if a paper is to be used, whether it is to be a patterned or a plain one.

If a wall-paper is to be used it will more or less govern the choice of colour for the woodwork. All these considerations will have their influence on the ultimate colour scheme for the room.

In the next chapter in this book, dealing with wall-paper and paperhanging, some useful hints are given on the selection of wallpapers for different apartments. The reader is advised to link the remarks in this next chapter with what is said here regarding the treatment of the various rooms in an average house.

To the decorator who appreciates good design, colour, and texture,

LIGHT-REFLECTION VALUES

	Per cent		Per cent		Per cent
White	89	Light grey	66	Eau-de-nil	54
Light ivory	81	Buff	66	Sky blue	52
Ivory	77	Opaline green	66	Fawn	43
Cream	75	Light tan	60	Gull grey	43
Ecru	68	Light sky green	59	Old rose	23
Shell pink	67	Hydrangea pink	55	Black	2

there is an opportunity with wall-paper to reveal his ability and to help his client to select the right wall-paper for the apartment to be decorated. With no other decorative material are there so many opportunities to introduce colour and design into a room, and at such comparatively low cost, and for this reason wall-paper must be reckoned as one of the decorative materials making the most important contribution to the æsthetic quality of a room.

The decorator should familiarise himself with the various types of wall-papers; he should know something of their light-reflection values, bearing in mind that the coarser the texture the more diffused is the reflection of light, the texture scattering the rays of light, diffusing them, and giving a quality essential to æsthetic pleasure.

The same remarks apply to the various types of paint, whether gloss, matt, or eggshell finish in oil paints, in the oil-bound water-thinned distempers, and in the plastic paints also.

Other Treatments

Not only is texture of importance as regards light reflection, but its very quality invites other decorative treatments, such as gradation of colour, glazing, scumbling, or decorative brushwork.

Appreciation of the value of appropriate textures should be much more cultivated by the decorator than is often the case at present, for in this there are almost unlimited opportunities.

Here a word of caution must be added that where plastic paints are used, whilst thickness of application depends on the type of texture desired, it is not necessary, neither is it desirable, to use these materials in a vulgar and coarse manner; the most beautiful textures are those worked in the lightest relief. So much depends on the ultimate scumbling and glazing of these light texture effects.

Light-reflection Values

In recent years attention has increasingly been given to the comparative reflection values of colours in gloss and textured surfaces and in varying materials. For our purpose here, reflection values are given for gloss paint only and on smooth surfaces; but it should prove valuable to the decorator to make his own tests.

As has already been said, consideration of texture is of the utmost importance, particularly to the interior decorator handling furniture and furnishing materials: oak, for example, is entirely different in texture to satinwood or mahogany, silks and damasks to reps and linens, and the varying textures of papers to paints whether glossy, eggshell finish, or matt.

The stepped list at the top of this page will be of some help in estimating the percentage of light

COLOUR SCHEMES

reflection of colours in everyday use.

As will be seen, white provides the maximum light reflection and black the minimum. Though the darker colours have less reflection value, they are, nevertheless, extremely useful in any decorative scheme when used in right proportions.

A few general suggestions are given which may help in the approach to the decoration of various apartments. Keep constantly in mind that in the creation of a colour scheme RESTRAINT should be your watchword, restraint in colour in dominant areas, reserving intensity of colour for the small accent notes.

An almost universal law of colour which should also be remembered is that: the larger the area, the more subdued should be the colours—the smaller the area, the more intense may be the colours.

Another useful precept to follow in selecting patterned wall-papers for colour in the background is: the proportion of patterned and plain areas should roughly be three parts plain surface and two parts patterned surface.

Stimulating Imagination

It is important to note that the schemes suggested may on first sight appear bizarre and unusual; they are, however, intended to stimulate the imagination and to get the decorator to break fresh ground.

Proportion and intensity of the colours specified will, of course, vary according to the size, shape, and lighting of the apartment. They are merely given as suggestions. The colours named are taken from the British Colour Council's Dictionary of Colour Standards. This work and its companion volume should be in the possession of all interior decorators.

Colours given for floor treatment refer to carpets or linoleum. Selection of fabrics for furniture will depend largely on the wood and its finish. Under "Accents" the colours given refer to the small intense notes such as cushions and lampshades and rugs.

Principal Rooms

The Bedroom. Determine the orientation of the room and the amount of sunlight it receives. If the room is dark, then bright colours are called for. Get the impression of brightness into the room, and some sparkle.

If a paper is chosen, consider the scale of the design in relation to the size of the room. Visualise the general colour effect of the paper with the wood of the furniture; there may be special pieces of furniture which need emphasis; if so, the background colours are of the utmost importance.

Woodwork already overloaded with mouldings needs, as a rule, self colours and no further emphasis by "picking out" with several colours.

Bedspreads are often the accent note or the most important colour note in the room; colour notes are provided as well by lamp-shades and cushions. The reflection in mirrors of the light from the windows will often give the sparkle needed to liven an otherwise dull room.

Strive for colourings that are restful yet not dull, and make a particular note of the colour of the window drapings, especially if a window netting is used, as window

SUGGESTIONS FOR VARIOUS ROOMS

TABLE I. Colour Schemes for Bedrooms

Walls	Ceiling	Woodwork	Floor	Furnishing Fabric	Curtains	Accents
Eau-de-nil	Light warm cream	Ivory white	Deep petunia	Light petunia	Amaranth pink	Blossom pink
Hydrangea pink	Light lichen green	Ivory white	Old rose	Opaline green	Old rose	Carnation
Oyster grey	Flesh	Light oyster grey	Saxe blue	Old rose	Alice blue	Amaranth pink
Honey-suckle	Honey-suckle	Pearl white	French grey	Old rose	Opaline green	Chartreuse yellow
Vanilla	Light warm cream	Light vanilla	Juniper	Light juniper	Old rose	Turquoise green

draperies such as gauzes, muslins, and silks all have their individual effect on the light which enters the room.

Have regard to the characteristics of the person or persons who are to occupy the room. Primary consideration should always be given to the personalities you are dealing with.

It may be that the colour scheme will have to be built around one or two key pieces of furniture or furnishings—if so, find out what these are.

The treatment of a man's bedroom should be different, say, from that of a young lady's bedroom, and the guest room, no longer looked on just as a "spare room," should convey a spirit of hospitality, enabling pleasant impressions of comfort to be carried away by the guest.

A few suggestions are given in Table I for bedrooms.

The Bathroom. Where porcelain fitments are installed, or tiles used, their colour will set the keynote for the colouring of the walls and woodwork, but pleasing contrasts can be made. Here, again, light tints are preferable, keeping the dark tones for the floor and skirtings. Keep the weight on the floor.

If the porcelain fitments are a light pink, for instance, there is no reason why the walls should not be a clean light green. Again, in some bathrooms there may be an alcove, which can be painted in a different colour from the rest of the bathroom.

Keep to clear, refreshing colours and light pleasing colour contrasts.

The Lounge or Living-Room. This room should be colourful, comfortable, and "livable" and express the joy of living, affording relief from the workaday round. If the room is formal, it should express graciousness; it should be unpretentious, with quiet, restful colourings. Study carefully the character of the particular room, for colour effects and design can have a psychological influence and inspire quiet relaxation or social activity.

Usually, this room is the "show" room of the house, and this distinction should be quietly obvious in the decorative scheme.

Table II gives a few suggestions for colour schemes for lounges or living-rooms.

The Dining-Room. Again the

COLOUR SCHEMES

TABLE II. Colour Schemes for Lounges or Living-Rooms

Walls	Ceiling	Woodwork	Floor	Furnishing Fabric	Curtains	Accents
Gull grey	Light salmon	Light gull grey	Mace	Black	Light golden brown	Amethyst
Light gull grey	Light coral	Gull grey	Brick red	Grebe	Olive green	Ivory Old rose
Shell pink	Pearl white	Shell pink	Wedgwood	Amethyst	Natural linen	White petunia
Banana	Light honey-suckle	Banana	Mastic	Chestnut	Smalt	White orange
Primrose	White	Light gull grey	Gunmetal	Oakwood	Rose pink	Silver White

orientation of the room will largely determine the choice of colours.

The dining-room should be pleasant, for it is here that meals are enjoyed and company entertained. What has been said with regard to the bedroom is equally applicable here as far as general principles are concerned. Unfortunately, colour of existing features in the room, such as fireplace tiles, for instance, may have to be considered; the woodwork of the furniture certainly must, so must the carpet if it already exists.

Aim to create an atmosphere of dignity and yet one of cheerfulness. Give consideration to the room's position in relation to adjoining rooms.

The treatment of the walls, that is, of the background of the room, is of great importance; too much insistence cannot be made on the creation of the background in attractive interiors. Wall-paper backgrounds, therefore, for dining-rooms should be conventional in design, bearing in mind the more or less formal character of the room.

Essential Background

If the student will bear in mind this simple little analogy it will help to drive home the emphasis placed in this chapter on the background. It is this: in a theatrical production it is the scenery which very often makes or mars a play; it is, in fact, the background for the action of the play, and the wise producer frequently grudges no time, labour or

TABLE III. Colour Schemes for Dining-Rooms

Walls	Ceiling	Woodwork	Floor	Furnishing Fabric	Curtains	Accents
Light apple green	Ivory	Deep ivory	Bottle green	Old gold	Gold	Bunting yellow
Old gold	Light gold	Ivory	Bronze	Chinese red	Grass green	Flame
Sage green	Light sage green	Sage green	Horse chestnut	Mace	Plum	Black Silver
Gold	Light murrey	Gold	Murrey	Carrot	Rust	Jade
Buff	Light olive green	Buff	Oakwood	Brick red	Terra cotta	Spectrum orange

PLATE VII

"BURR WALNUT" PAPER IN A LOUNGE

Realistic reproduction of the grain of burr walnut in a Sanderson wall-paper. The effect is obtained by quartering as with actual wood. The richness of this form of decoration creates an atmosphere of dignity and comfort.

PLATE VIII

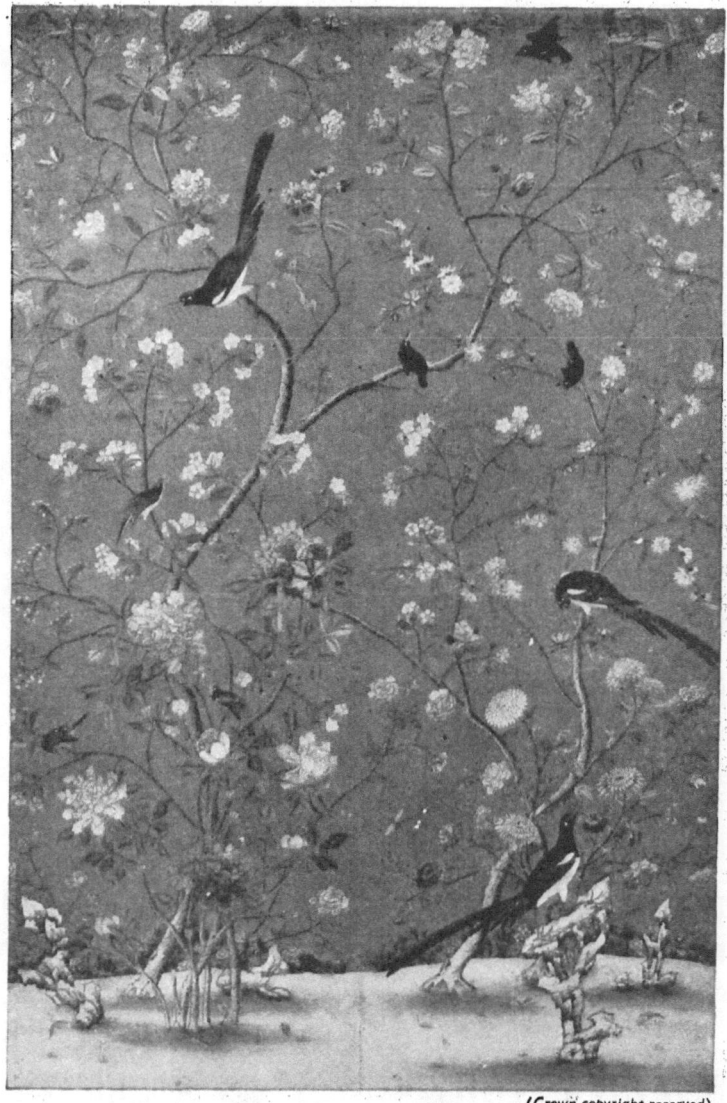

(Crown copyright reserved)

ARTISTIC WALL-PAPER FROM CHINA

Chinese designs have formed the basis of many patterns perfected for machine process by English paper designers. Above is a photo of some Chinese wall-paper of the middle eighteenth century at the Victoria and Albert Museum, London.

LIVING-ROOM, DINING-ROOM, AND KITCHEN

money in obtaining the setting most suitable for his cast.

One has only to consider the work of the leading theatrical scenic artists and to compare their work with the tawdry mediocre work to be seen in some of the cheap sets to realise the force of this illustration.

Table III provides a few suggestions for dining-room colourings.

The Kitchen. Here is the woman's workshop, and a good deal of the average woman's time is spent in her kitchen. Women nowadays are discovering the value of colour in their surroundings: therefore, make this room a pleasant one to work in. Clean, light, and cool colourings will help to refresh and inspire the housewife, and make the kitchen cheerful and gay and a pleasure to live in.

Washable Paints

A kitchen should always look clean and spotless, and gloss paints or washable water paints are, therefore, most suitable for kitchen work. Accent notes of colour can be obtained by painting the chairs or other furniture or even the kitchen cabinet fittings in contrasting colours; and the sales slogan for any decorator in connection with kitchen work should be: "Keep the kitchen clean and colourful."

Below are a few suggestions for kitchen colour schemes (Table IV).

The Entrance Hall and Staircase. Here first impressions of the house and its owners are received, and the hall is usually the connecting link between the different parts of the house. From it, when the doors are open, it is possible to see the decoration of the rooms leading out of it; therefore, the decorative treatment of the hall should link up with the rooms.

It is not necessary to have the same colour throughout: the lower floor should be a different colour or tone of colour from the staircase and the floor above. There should be harmony of colour, and special attention should be paid to the staircase treatment. Often the hall is darker than the rest of the house, and, therefore, the colourings used can be several tones lighter and more intense than the same colours would be if used in a light room where the sun is in evidence for many hours in the summer months.

Remember that if there is a half-landing, the woodwork round this half-landing and up to the second floor must be considered as part of the first floor. The finish of the stair rail, treads, and risers can, therefore, largely contribute to the complete decorative effect; often

TABLE IV. COLOUR SCHEMES FOR KITCHENS

WALLS	CEILING	WOODWORK	FLOOR	CURTAINS	ACCENTS
Lichen green	Lichen green	Chartreuse yellow	Moss green jaspe	Primrose	Grenadine red
Sky grey	Pearl white	Sky blue	Royal blue jaspe	Straw	Tangerine
Ivory white	White	Pompadour	Royal blue jaspe	Maize	Crushed strawberry
Champagne	Champagne	Verdigris	Apple green	Ecru	Azalea
Ecru	Light cream	Buff	Rust	Chartreuse yellow	Chartreuse green

COLOUR SCHEMES

the accent note of colour is concentrated in the finish of the handrail. Note, for instance, how smart and effective a polished black rail looks with the rest of the woodwork in pleasing tones of parchment.

Matching Carpet

Again, remember that the stair carpet will possibly dominate the scheme.

The hall is the part of the house which merits the decorator's closest attention, and he should make it his business to collaborate with the client in seeing that the decorative treatment makes the entire house appear attractive.

Above are a few suggestions for halls and staircases (Table V).

House Exteriors

Exterior Work. The best advice the decorator can give a client concerning this work is: "Be community-proud and neighbourly." Discourage eccentricity of treatment, employ colours which harmonise not only with the actual house to be decorated, but also with adjoining homes, and which fit into the general setting of the district.

The elevation and the type of the house must largely govern its colour treatment. Accent notes can be obtained by the special colour treatment of the front door. The right use of colour can help to overcome architectural problems; houses can be made to look larger or smaller, taller or wider, window openings emphasised or made less conspicuous.

Apart altogether from the fact that a well-painted house is a good investment, a colourful one makes for home pride. With the greater use of stucco and the large unbroken surface areas in present-day architecture, the decorator must think of large masses of colour, remembering that the door openings and window frames can make the accent note.

Some pleasing schemes with these large flat exteriors are obtained, for instance, with the stucco work painted white and the door, say, in brilliant green or blue; or the stucco painted a very light grey and the door and sashes in brilliant red; or, again, the stucco work in a light warm cream with the door and sashes in a strong blue and, possibly, ringing the changes with, say, the garage door in a post office

TABLE V. Colour Schemes for Halls and Staircases

Walls	Ceiling	Woodwork	Floor	Furnishing Fabric	Curtains	Accents
Deep parchment	Honeysuckle	Light parchment	Royal blue	Almond shell	Pea green	Tangerine
Nettle grey	Light lichen green	Ivory white	Almond green	Corn husk	Amethyst	Grenadine red
Maize	Light cream	Light cream and black	Amethyst	Crocus	Crocus	Begonia
Old ivory	Broken white	Old ivory (doors only beech brown)	Rust	Bronze green	Jade	Saffron Violet

red, which indeed would give a most pleasing contrast.

However, these suggestions are offered to start the decorator thinking along lines away from the ordinary orthodox methods in connection with painting house exteriors. Today there is a distinct trend toward use of brighter colour, and builders recognise this also in their choice of bricks and tiles.

Public Buildings

The use and effect of colour in public buildings such as places of amusement, offices, schools, hotels, stores, and hospitals are not dealt with here, as this chapter is primarily concerned with domestic decoration.

It is sufficient to stress the attractiveness of colour in public buildings as follows:

In stores it is of definite sales promotion value.

In hotels it is attractive.

In schools it brightens and cheers surroundings and can aid light-reflection.

In hospitals it can be of therapeutic value.

In offices and workrooms it is of proved psychological value; it can relieve monotony and contribute toward productiveness and contentment, with the added asset of increased good health.

Factors in Use of Colour

It is worth reiterating here that you may know about the properties of mediums and pigments, have a good working knowledge of building up a colour scheme, but you cannot put this knowledge into effect until you realise that:

Colour has a definite eye-appeal. If the right colours are selected, everyone who sees the scheme will derive pleasure from it, and be a potential new customer.

Colour has an emotional appeal. It pleases or displeases, and the feeling evoked when it pleases varies in degree of intensity from serenity of satisfaction to rapturous elation; or when displeasing, from irritable dissatisfaction to morbid depression.

Colour is the basis of decorative work.

Colour affects the size of the room. Light colours on walls and ceiling make small rooms seem larger. Dark colours on the walls "bring a room together."

Use a colour vocabulary. Know what you mean when you talk about colour to your client; keep abreast of the so-called fashion colours, so that when they are named by your client you understand what is meant.

Lastly, the use of colour should be governed by a great deal of practical common sense, keeping always in mind the fundamental principles of colour training. Good colour schemes are not the result of haphazard guesswork or accident. They are the product of careful study *and* experience.

To sum up, the craftsman must always remember that general colour and effect are more important than local brilliance. The most effective scheme of colour is one that is warm without being hot; grey or pearly, yet not cold; bright, but avoiding gaudiness; effective, without being blatant. The scheme in hand should have been discussed beforehand with the client, so it coincides with his personal wishes and the surroundings. It is also suggested that students should obtain from leading paint manufacturers a complete range of their colour cards.

COLOUR THEORY

Colour theory is not very useful when one is just going to do a room. The chief reason for including a reference to it in a book like this is that to some people colours are so many accidental visual phenomena, apt to get rather muddled up. This is unfair; colours behave rationally, rather like the scale in music, and they follow certain laws and behave in an orderly manner if rightly understood. The best way for the ordinary man to tackle colour-theory is to master very elementary diagrams like the accompanying one (Fig. 15), and then use the facts to supplement his instincts when they fail him.

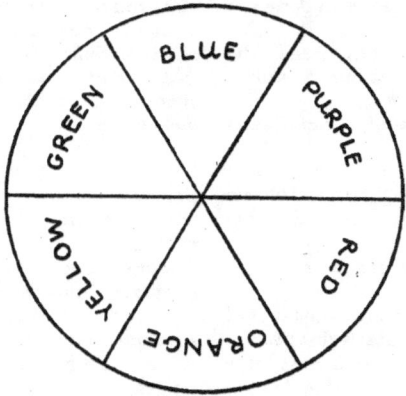

Fig. 15.
Simple colour chart, showing the three primary (pigment) colours, with the secondaries mixed from them in between. Opposites mixed so that there is an equal quantity of each primary form grey ; mixed in other proportions, neutral colours. Opposites are also each other's strongest contrast.

PRIMARY COLOURS.—Every school-child knows that there are three colours he cannot mix from others, red, blue and yellow. If we arrange these in a circle so that each occupies one-sixth, with one-sixth between each, the accompanying interesting diagram can be made which is as easy to remember as the

COLOUR THEORY

memory-stimulating "30 days hath September" or "many Latin nouns in -is".

SECONDARY COLOURS.—Most people have found at some time that they can mix orange. In this diagram, it comes between the two colours that make it—red and yellow. Green is mixed from, and goes between yellow and blue, and purple from and between blue and red. No one should try to mix these colours and then discard the theory because they look dull and wrong; getting a scientifically accurate diagram depends on having the right pigments. If anyone insists on making a coloured diagram, he can get coloured papers for the purpose.

TERTIARY COLOURS.—If in water colours one tries to mix red, blue and yellow together, one gets Thames mud colour or, more politely, grey. This is called a tertiary colour, the name given to colours which contain all three primaries, and which are on that account, a little grey. In the diagram it will be observed that diametrically opposite colours, if mixed, make grey because they each contain all three primaries, e.g., red (primary) and green (secondary, made of blue and yellow). These opposite colours are also, of course, visual opposites, that is, the greatest possible contrast to one another, as different as possible from one another. That this has a significance for our vision is demonstrated by the fact that if we stare hard enough at red, we see a green image where the red was if we shut our eyes, and if we look at a bright red blob on a white ground, a blue-green halo forms round it. We have also always used red and green to symbolise the opposing ideas of danger and safety, probably unconsciously to begin with.

CONTROVERSIES.—There are complicated controversies raging over colour theory, of which the writer is not unaware. The

COLOUR THEORY

above remarks may be scientific or they may not—experts are unlikely to be able to agree on that—but in so far as they are useful in an elementary way, it does not greatly matter. In the everyday handling of colour they do very often help to explain why a colour mixture is dull or unpleasant, and to correct it, or to suggest lines upon which a favourite colour can be played up to.

WAYS IN WHICH COLOUR THEORY CAN BE APPLIED. — (*a*) *The Primary Colours.*—In furnishing very few primary colours are used. A primary red is the colour that the post-office and the fire-brigade are so fond of, but in the home it usually appears in the form of lacquer red, a slightly more orange version than the primary, or as crimson, which is more plum-like. Both these have for some time been "out," but they are splendid robust colours and might well be used more. Primary blue is roughly the one that appears as French Ultramarine in the paint-box. A watered version is sometimes found in cheap textiles, bedspreads and quilts. Yellow is not supposed to be a furnishing colour, but in its more subtle versions it is one of the most satisfying and easily-lived-with of all the colours. It is normally represented in the furnishing textile trade as a kind of liverish tone applied to other colours, the browns, the fawns and the greens particularly. Cast out this tingle, and these debased colours return to richness and excellence of quality.

(*b*) *Secondary and Tertiary Colours.*—The circle diagram can be amplified by dividing it into infinitely small gradations of colour, to include all the peacock greens, all the tones of red and orange, all the apple greens and the lovely plums and violets. That circle, however, cannot be made to show the source of most of our furnishing and dress schemes, the colours with grey in them, or rather, the colours with some of

COLOUR THEORY

each primary in them, but grey is a convenient way of putting it. One of the things that the circle can teach is that the colours without grey are "pure" and are in a different *key* from those with grey in them. This is sometimes why a scheme looks wrong—a pure colour among tertiaries may throw the whole scheme out of gear. Replace the pure colour with a greyed version, and they fall into place, perhaps with the aid of pulling up one of the greyed colours a little further towards purity to stimulate contrast. One could do the opposite, of course, turn them all into pure colours, but a furnishing scheme is very seldom built up out of pure secondary colours, if only for the reason that cloth and dye find great difficulty in producing them, and if they are produced, the texture of the cloth or carpet introduces shadows and lights tending towards grey, one loses the brilliancy of the pure colours, without gaining the subtlety of an intentionally greyed scheme, and crudity supervenes.

DELUSIONS.—There is a widespread popular notion that a room in tones and shades of one colour has a colour scheme, and conversely, that to achieve a colour scheme, everything must match or "tone in." This extraordinary idea sometimes succeeds better than it deserves because of the brown furniture which custom so often decrees. It is seen at its worst, in fact, in rooms where the all-pervading colour is brown and the furniture offers no relief. This notion no doubt arises from the fact that a set of colours with one of the primaries common to all of them undoubtedly are related and can form the dominant theme in an interior. Contrast, however, is the basis of all satisfaction in colour as in things in general, but it must not merely be a contrast of tone, but a colour-contrast mainly; for example, orange is a tone contrast with dark brown, but not a colour-contrast and red is a colour-contrast with peacock

COLOUR THEORY

blue without being a tone contrast. Pale yellow and navy blue are both sorts of contrast. This brings us to another point which can be memorised from the circle; the most violent contrast for pale yellow would be dark purple, but these superlative contrasts are not too comfortable to look at. We, in our British way, prefer rather more of a compromise, and move round the circle to blue, thus reducing the distance between the two colours, but not so much as to do away with the contrast, as one would by coming into the same third of the circle as the yellow, that is, within the sphere of its influence. This distance idea is all very well when used with discretion; in the case of the navy and pale yellow, for example, which are a charming basis for a scheme, the discretion lies in choosing *dark* blue and *pale* yellow; blue and yellow the same tone can be extremely trite. In the same way, baby-pink and baby-blue, together though tolerable, are utterly insipid, while deep crimson and bluish peacock blue can be wonderfully rich, as one sees from Persian carpets, which usually, however, have a dull brown framework underlying the design to bring the two together.

THE BALANCE OF CONTRAST.—The foundation law governing the use of contrast is that there shall not be equal quantities of contrasting elements. Contrast is most telling either in *large* areas of neutral pale colour—for example, French grey walls with our navy and yellow scheme, or very pale green with copper and fawn, or in *small* areas of fierce, strong colour, for example, touches of red or crimson in cushions or pipings in a grey-green room.

A further point has so far only been touched upon, the subject of neutrals. Neutrals never are quite neutral, as they cannot help following the ordinary law of colour, which is that each colour affects its neighbour, however pale they both are.

COLOUR THEORY

In a sensitive scheme the exact shade of some neutral becomes as important as the dominant note in a bold, theatrical scheme, because of the action of complementary colours.

THE INFLUENCE OF COMPLEMENTARIES. — The reader will remember that she was told that a blob of red, if stared at, would produce its complementary, blue-green, as a halo round it. What happens, then, if the red blob is on a ground which is not improved by having blue-green added to it? Mud-colour results, more particularly if the ground is a fairly subtle warm neutral. If it is grey, it simply becomes greener, and is all right. Then again, some well-meaning person does a weave composed of red and green threads. At a short distance away these *mix* and turn khaki or some such tint. But what happens if the red and green blobs are so big that they can't mix? One can work it out. The red throws green on the green and it becomes brighter, and the green red on the red, and there they are, actually acting according to plan, and being each other's most powerful contrast. This, of course, happens in a minor way with duller colours, and is, in fact, happening all the time, so that is why no colour can be trusted to be what one thinks it is, till it is seen with its intended companions.

OTHER REFERENCE TO COLOUR IN THE BOOK. — Notes on colour samples for decoration are found in Chapter 4, and on colour with different woods in Chapter 6; there are a few remarks on quality of colour in Chapter 2, while Chapter 15 deals with Colour in practice. These taken together will serve to suggest to the reader that contriving successful colour arrangement is no easy matter. It is, however, not surprising that people are inept with colouring. They have never been taught to compare colours, which is, of course, the whole basis of colour-understanding.

COLOUR IN PRACTICE

Every person, whether they know it or not, has natural colour predilections and these colours they can handle well, while almost every person, however gifted, has certain colours to which they are insentitive and which they handle badly. The untrained person seldom can exploit her own special gift, and hardly gets beyond, "I do love that green," and the trained person may fail to recognise her own limitations.

With these facts in view, to advise people on colour hardly seems very useful. There are, however, in furnishing certain factors which depend on circumstance, not on personal taste, and these may be briefly outlined.

THE INFLUENCE OF REFLECTION.—This is hardly ever taken into consideration, because to do so is difficult. Even a curtaining with a red stripe on a cream ground will show a reddish reflection in the folds, and one has therefore to reckon with a warmer effect than would appear from the flat sample. Any strong colour will reflect on to other surfaces if brightly lit, for example, a red carpet with the sun shining on it will tinge a low ceiling with red, particularly if it is shiny, and similarly any other shiny surface within range.

UNUSUAL COLOURS.—By way of general remarks upon colour, the most noticeable thing about popular taste in this country is its timidity, which nevertheless does not imply any subtlety of effect—rather the reverse. The timidity is often expressed by a willingness to accept any commonplace colour, however crude, and by a recoiling from any unusual colour, however excellent its quality.

There is absolutely no need for people to cling obstinately to buff, green, gold, brown and cream. Enterprising people whose pockets will only run to medium-priced materials may, however, have to look long and hard before they get any of their fancy, except perhaps in carpets. First-class colours have appeared in plain Axminsters in the middle price ranges, probably a sign that textiles will not be far behind. On the assumption that people of taste must possess something of good quality, however small a proportion of the whole, one might suggest that they avail themselves of the very excellent neutral oyster and fawn shades in which artificial silk damasks of inoffensive design, appear. An example is the simple ripple damask (see Furnishing Budget No. 2, living-room). They can then buy small cuts of quite expensive material for cushions and pelmets.

Colours obtainable at the "upper end" of the trade, and seldom in "popular" lines are the following, stated under their British Colour Council 1939 name, and then by a common descriptive name:—

  B.C.C. Sky Green (lime green, a green nearly yellow).
  B.C.C. Mermaid (a strong sky-blue, rather greenish).
  B.C.C. Harrow Blue (dark navy).
  B.C.C. Zigeuner (mulberry or dark reddish purple).
  B.C.C. Bengal Red (claret, or dark red plum).
  B.C.C. Hawthorn-berry (a light, rich crimson).
  B.C.C. Chinese Lacquer (a piercing slightly orange red).
  B.C.C. Imari Red (the colour of new barge sails, or darker).
  B.C.C. Rose Dawn (grey, but very pinkish).
  B.C.C. Pink Beige (mushroom).
  B.C.C. Earth Brown (very dark nigger, without the yellow tinge).
  B.C.C. Fudge (the colour of well-baked pie crust).

These colours are most likely to be found in the shops which do a trade in contemporary furnishings. There are a number of these firms all over England, and their aim is to produce at popular prices, goods of the character until now peculiar to the exclusive trade. They are relying for custom upon that large class of persons with discriminating taste, but smallish incomes.

COLOUR IN PRACTICE

THE USE OF EXHIBITIONS.—The above list of colours are, indeed, some of those which have been put upon the market in small quantities primarily in response to the demands of professional decorators. These and the "public colours", as they might be called, show a marked difference in character. The new ranges of stuffs and carpets in which these interesting colours appear will be found at the trade exhibitions and at the British Industries Fair. In the evening, enterprising members of the public can gain a very good idea of what has newly been put out to tempt the decorators from the dressing of the stands. The "bread and butter" lines, what the public will find later in its own stores, are inside in bunches. The numbers of the exclusive stuffs can be taken and local furnishers asked to obtain them. For short lengths, however, a retailer, and therefore his customer, pays a few pence a yard more.

"COLOUR SCHEMES".—It is a mistake to determine upon a colour scheme which must be closely adhered to ("That dress does look awful in this room, Mother"), especially in a living-room where a good deal goes on. Not only does one tire more quickly of the chosen colours, but the room is bound to have a pretentiousness which may become burdensome. This is perfectly all right in a formal room, whether in a formal house or merely one room set aside for formal living, and it is here that an architect or decorator is in his right place. For the informal home life of the majority of citizens, the most successful colourings base themselves on a satisfactory relationship between walls, floor and paintwork, into which the furnishings can break as accents or supporting elements in a friendly, informal way. Mellowness is a very pleasing characteristic in the colouring of a living-room, but it is seldom attained by rigid adherence to rule or system.

COLOUR IN PRACTICE

FURTHER POPULAR ERRORS.—There is a great deal of nonsense talked about north rooms, for example, that they must have warm, pale colours. What they need is clear positive colour, whether cold or warm, according to whether the rooms are bleak in character or not. Then again, people say they must have light colours in a dark room, but if they do they will have no colour at all. It is best to have strong bold colour, numerous bright accessories and put the artificial light on as needed. Again, the models upon which many people base their colour schemes (and they might do worse) are often the specimen rooms that shops produce to show their wares in. Now only too often the decoration of the room has been chosen so " safe " that for the next year it can be a pleasant setting for any amount of stock furniture. On these lines it is almost an impossibility to do those entertaining things which a person can in their own home, picking out the paintwork with thin coloured lines, decorating a plywood pelment with an amusing design, hanging pictures with coloured cord, using edgings and pipings which are only for that particular *décor* of that room, pinning up things that take their fancy but which would look mad in a shop, arranging flowers and plants, using little bits of odd stuff and patchworks for cushions, lining cabinets with patterned papers, and setting up backgrounds for favourite objects, framing a print or poster amusingly, breaking up the solemnity of a painted fireplace with a stipple or marbling, edging cotton curtains with woollen braid, using roller towelling or sun-blind canvas for curtains in order to get the stripes, making decorative roller blinds, or waisbelts for curtains—all the things, in fact, that people used to know how to do in the days when people got their own things made quite cheaply.

All these are factors in the success of the chosen colour scheme. Some readers may feel that in a book of this sort they should be told once and for all that just *that* blue goes with

COLOUR IN PRACTICE

that copper-colour, but this sort of thing is impossible, or rather useless, because even if that were incontrovertibly established, it would not help anyone to do a successful room. The only thing that can possibly help them is to stimulate them to look about and see colours together, in dress shops, in antique shops, on the stage, in plants and animals, at exhibitions, till their heads are full of colours and they positively dream of them at night. After that they will not need to listen to anyone talking colour.

For those, however, who feel that all this is very thin, here are some notes on the more or less common factors in most rooms, the woods:—

Natural Oak. Pinks make it look drab by contrast. Greens, blues, greenish blues bring out its colour. Browns need to be dark and rich to afford tone contrast. Room wants accent. Wood warms in time like a biscuit baking.

Dark Oak. Its chief virtue is that one can hardly go wrong, so long as one *does* use *colour.* Take a Persian rug as a start.

Walnut. If gingery, all the greens, greys and grey-blues. If greyish, as is most usual, then pinks as well, and crimson and peacock blue. Not fawns and buffs but pale yellow.

Mahogany. If dark polished and reddish, all the traditional colours such as Adam (sage) green, French and dove grey even slate grey and grey-blue. Crimson and yellow, but not rust, or crude greens, or any very thin shrill colour. Plum-purple (cold), any rich not too bright blue. If waxed and brownish, much the same without the crimson, plum-purple and slate-grey.

Sycamore, and with it, *Birch.* All the bright delicate colours such as peach, apricot, pink, pale turquoise. Dark brown, navy blue. Not yellow unless, fairly strong and greenish. Tan and rust. Very easy. Birch might be used a great deal more.

ARTIFICIAL LIGHT AND COLOUR.—Everyone dislikes choosing coloured things by artificial light, and, obsessed with this dislike, they fail even to test out colours by electric light, if they are pleased with their daytime appearance. All the greens

COLOUR IN PRACTICE

and blues suffer badly, but the strong greenish blues less than the grey-blues. Many greyish colours do not alter but become dull and heavy. Crimsons become almost like rusts, and have great potency. Yellows look much milder. Brown and dull purple are indistinguishable, and dark blue and black. Tans and light browns hardly alter, and this applies also to the coppery pinks, and to the rusts. Blue is the factor that tends to weaken and disappear, while the orange colour of the light itself comes brilliantly forth. The brighter the electric light, the whiter it becomes, and the nearer daylight, an argument for fully lighted rooms where the cold colours are desired. A large number of small sources of light, however, do not total up to make as white a light as one efficient opal fitting. Two colours the same by day do not necessarily seem the same at night, owing to a difference in their chemical composition.

THE ELEMENTS OF COLOR

HUE, VALUE, CHROMA

MANY PEOPLE maintain that inasmuch as color is a thing to which we react emotionally, it should be used emotionally. They do not approve of color study or any phase of a scientific approach to color. True, there are hundreds of gifted people using color in every field from portrait painting to cosmetic merchandising who depend entirely on a natural flair in using it. But to claim this to be the only approach would exclude everyone else from using color with confidence or success.

Many people play by ear, but the fine musician knows all there is to know about the technique of music, and hundreds of thousands learn to play by learning to read music and by studying its technical details. No one would dream of suggesting that if one wishes to play the piano he needs only to get a piano and try it out. But people will continually suggest that one has only to dash some colors together to learn all about color. Of course, by putting enough combinations together and by judging the results accurately, one would eventually know all there is to know about it. But the trial and error method is expensive when it involves gallons of paint, yards of material, and labor, as it is likely to when one is decorating a house.

Science has found and proved that there are something like a million color variations. About a thousand are in use. In addition to this, fashion promotion has further complicated the problem by inventing at least ten names for each one of them. Ten thousand is a lot of anything, and when we add to it the statement that only the eye can measure or judge these, it places an overwhelming burden on the individual—a burden which frightens most people. Actually

Decorating Your Home

there are only ten basic hues from which these thousands are made.

A working knowledge of color may be gained by learning to recognize its measurements and distinguishing features. Color has three dimensions: hue, value, and chroma. The word "color" embraces all three dimensions. When you say a color is blue, you have named its "hue." When you say it is light or dark blue, you have given its "value." When you add that it is brilliant or dull, you have called attention to its saturation or color strength—its "chroma."

The ten basic hues are illustrated on the color wheel. An additional ten hues might be created by designating the in-between hues

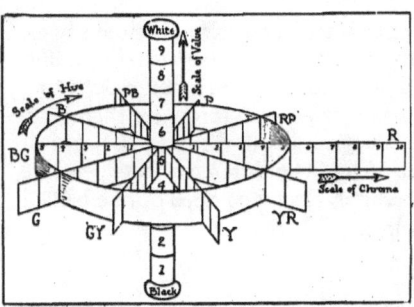

This color tree shows hue, value, and chroma in relation to one another. The hues are shown in the circular band, which is similar to the color wheel. The scale of values is the upright center axis. The branches of the tree represent the chroma dimension. (Courtesy Munsell Color Company, Baltimore, Maryland.)

as yellow yellow green, red red purple, blue blue green, and so on, thus making twenty hues. Knowing the hue, however, does not tell what to expect of the actual appearance of the color. Red, for example, ranges from a near black to almost a clear white, and yet still remains the hue red. Virtually all nail polish preparations are red, but the variations seem to be limitless.

Different values are achieved by adding white to raise, and black to lower, the normal value of any hue. The natural appearance point, or normal value, of each hue does not necessarily occur in the exact center of the value scale, nor does the normal value of one hue coincide on the value scale with the normal value of another hue. Red is low in value at its natural appearance point, and most

The Elements of Color

of its variations in value are achieved by adding white. On the other hand, yellow is high in value to begin with and most of its variations result by adding black.

The third dimension, chroma, measures the degree of intensity, or strength, of the value of any hue. The strength of a hue is dulled or neutralized most effectively by adding its opposite, or complement; thus, when red and its complement blue green are mixed together in equal amounts, gray is produced. When more blue green is present, a cool gray results, and as more and more blue green is added, the chroma is best described as a neutral blue green. Reversing the procedure produces the same variations in red. Each hue has as many values in any of its neutralized stages as it has in its full strength.

Learn to recognize the ten basic hues, then the in-between hues, so that you are able to detect the difference, say, between green and green blue, or between blue and purple blue. Then practice detecting the different values of each hue so that you can recognize them anywhere up and down the scale. Lastly, learn to distinguish between intense and neutralized values. When the difference between hue changes and chroma changes becomes clear, you need not be baffled by the names stylists give to colors.

COLOR CONTRASTS

White mixed with black produces gray, but white appearing in juxtaposition with black looks whiter, and the black blacker. Each hue and its opposite, as different pigmentally as black and white, react the same way.

Striking color effects are usually found to consist of complementary colors. But striking effects depend more on value contrasts than on hue contrasts. The eye registers a difference in value first. Differences in value can be seen farther than differences in hue. At a distance, blue and red of exactly the same value and chroma could look exactly alike, but a very high value of blue and a very low value of blue would register their difference for several city blocks.

Again, just as tone is the most important of the design elements, value is the most important of the color dimensions and becomes

Decorating Your Home

the controlling characteristic of tone. In making the sofa disappear into the wall (see Chapter V), tone was used to overcome line and mass difficulties, but it was the elimination of value differences throughout that accomplished each step.

COLOR SCHEMES

Looking at Munsell's color wheel, we can chart definite color schemes which are safe to follow. The most used and easily handled are those known as complementary; they involve two hues directly opposite each other on a line through the center—for example, red and blue green.

The color scheme for a room with a southern or warm exposure might have high-value blue-green walls and a low-value, slightly neutral blue-green rug. The draperies could contain large amounts of blue green of several values, with smaller areas in values of red. Red, it must be remembered, embraces all the values and chromas of red which bear such names as rose, pink, wine, and countless others. The name red is not confined to stop-light red, it is restricted only to red which is not the slightest bit yellow or purple in its hue. This room could have a red sofa, low in value, and possibly a chair or two in the same hue. The other upholstery material might be blue green of a value higher than the rug. The smaller objects—lamp bases, books, pillows, and ash trays—could carry the red theme around the room. The pictures and wall ornaments should contain small notes of red also.

To build a complementary color scheme does not require the exclusion of every other hue from the room. It requires only that the complementary colors be dominant. Subordinate hues may be introduced. Choosing the hues for the subordinate scheme may be done in innumerable ways. A safe plan is to consult the color wheel and select them from either side of one of the dominant hues in the particular color scheme you have chosen. Thus, in the red and blue-green scheme, yellow red in values and chromas known as gold, and blue in low values, could be introduced to vary the dominant scheme. These two hues will be recognized on the color wheel as complementary to each other also. Therefore, they are good in combination

The Elements of Color

with each other and are closely related to the main complementary scheme.

The complementary scheme of blue and yellow red is best when the yellow red is neutral. Neutral yellow reds are fashion's tans and beiges. Oriental rugs frequently appear in the soft high values of neutral yellow red with a deep blue border. Blue is a very agreeable hue and gets along with every other hue on the color wheel, but it is

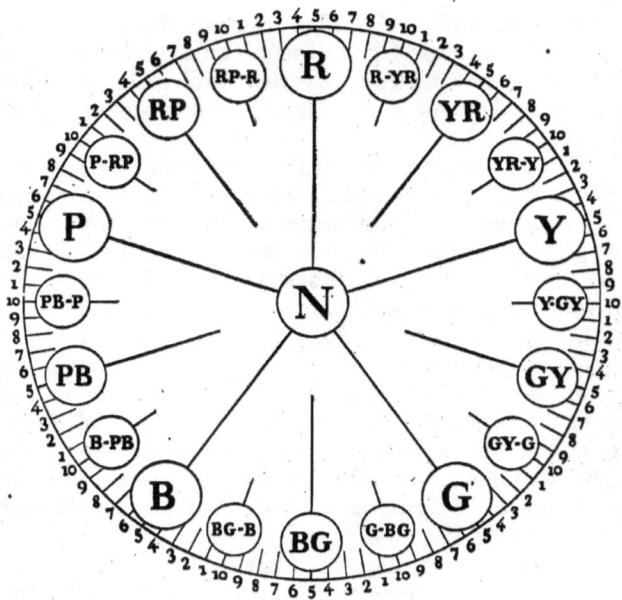

The color wheel (Courtesy Munsell Color Company, Baltimore, Maryland).

the coolest hue and quickly cools any area to which it is applied. On walls, blue may create a hard unflattering light for a room.

What is likely to be called blue is really purple blue. True blue is difficult to produce in dyes and pigment matter generally and has always been rare. The robes of the Madonna were painted blue in

Decorating Your Home

early Renaissance pictures to pay her honor, as the paint was expensive and difficult to obtain.

Other safe color schemes are those known as analogous, or neighboring. As the name implies, they are found next to each other on the color wheel. One may begin anywhere on the color wheel to choose analogous colors, being careful to select those which are composed of the same two primary hues, but they must not include one which contains any fraction of a third hue. For example, red, red purple, purple, and purple blue are analogous because they are all made of the same two primary hues: red and blue. Blue itself may be included, but this stretches the arrangement a little too far for unity. Blue green is not analogous with these as it contains a fraction of yellow.

The very hot analogous group is short, consisting of red, yellow red, and yellow. Red purple is not analogous with it, nor is green yellow, because they introduce other hues. The hot colors, like all hot objects, are difficult to handle, but when neutralized, that is, when the complement has been added, they are naturally cooled off and become manageable.

All the greens—yellow greens and blue greens—are good background color, especially when used as nature uses them in somewhat neutral tones. They provide the best background for man's nervous system, and the best background for all other hues. True green is neither warm nor cold, as it is composed of equal parts of yellow and blue, and this balances the warm and cold content.

Black and white are not considered hues and may be introduced into any color scheme to provide value contrast, which heightens color effects. In interior decoration, the most satisfactory color schemes, whether complementary or analogous, use large amounts or areas of one hue in combination with smaller amounts of the remainder of the selected color scheme. This statement is based on the accepted theory that two things of equal importance create a division in any situation. Large areas of any hue should be on the neutral side of its chroma measure, leaving the small areas for the intense hues. Nature, for example, has made the elephant completely neutral in tone, while butterflies are luminous in intensity.

Color has a definite effect on man's physical and emotional makeup. It is always a part of the study of psychology and must be regarded as the most important medium of the decorator's craft.

THE USE OF COLOUR IN INTERIOR DECORATION

THE selection of a colour scheme must always conform to definite existing requirements, viz., general fitness for purpose, according to the character and uses of the room and building. A church will require sober and restful treatment quite different from a dance hall, which may be very stimulating and attractive in both colour and ornament, whilst a cinema, seen only in artificial light, needs special care to avoid undue loss of colour values.

In domestic interiors, the architectural character, aspect, furnishings and personal taste of the client must also be considered, and the really successful scheme will not dominate, but will be subservient to all these conditions. Modern lighting arrangements can do much in producing an effect of unity, but conditions of daylight are usually of equal importance.

The interesting and subtle scheme, whilst making use of a variety of warm greys for the large areas, can gain sufficient contrast of tone and colour by the introduction of carefully selected and related hues.

This relationship may be one of simple harmony, as when two or three adjacent colours are selected from the chromatic circle; or may be that of contrast or true complementary relationship. Monochromatic schemes illustrate contrast of tone only, and these are not usually satisfying to the eye, which prefers the presence in one form or another of all three primaries, red, yellow and blue.

The use of pure white is not to be commended for

large areas, but unity with a scheme may be produced by adding a touch of the dominant hue.

A study of the colourings of flowers, birds, and other natural forms, will provide an endless variety of contrasts of tone, hue, and purity, with equally numerous examples of balanced harmonies, which offer ideas and inspiration for decorative schemes of colour.

Certain broad principles must be observed in their application to interior work. Pure bright colour must be reserved for small areas, or reduced by the addition of broken white or warm grey for the larger areas.

Contrast of luminosity or tone is always desirable, and the whole scheme should be of a dominating hue, with a small proportion of its true complementary colour for contrast. All three primaries are thus represented.

Assuming for example that orange is chosen as the dominating hue, this could be broken by admixture with its complementary, blue violet, to produce a range of related greys. These in turn may be reduced with black and broken white to form numerous tints and shades, definitely related to the original keynote of colour. A good scheme of almost any degree of purity can be selected from hues prepared in this manner.

Discord is often used in small quantities to impart additional interest and contrast to an otherwise harmonious scheme. This effect is achieved by a reversal of the natural tone value of some particular colour in the scheme, and according to the extent of this reversal, harsh or subtle discord may be produced and controlled.

The natural tone value, or natural order of colours, is clearly illustrated in the student's box of water-colour paints. A comparison of these colours will show that considerable difference of strength or tone value exists: yellow being the lightest and violet the darkest of colours.

The relative positions of remaining hues are indicated on the chart, beginning with the lightest tone at the top and gradually increasing in strength towards the base where the deepest tone is placed. True complementaries are also arranged as diametrical opposites in the same chart.

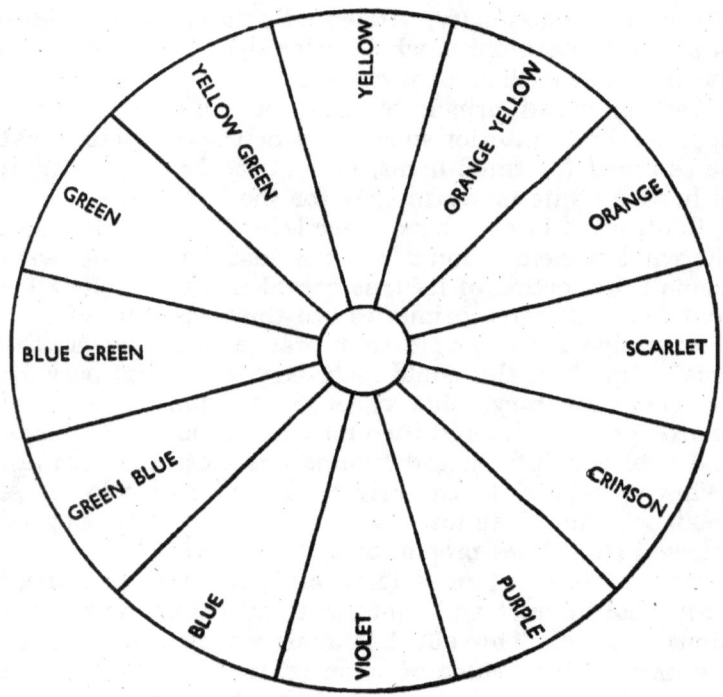

THE CHROMATIC CIRCLE

Fig. 0

Simple harmony is produced by using any three adjacent colours in their natural order, as for example yellow, yellow-green and green, the green being the deepest in tone and yellow the lightest. A discord could be produced by adding white to the green and thus forming a tint paler in effect than the yellow or yellow-green.

Care is therefore necessary to avoid the production of accidental discord when altering the natural tone value of any colour, and an effort must be made to work in conformity with this order, irrespective of the purity of the colours being used.

COLOR

WHAT IS IT?

THE creation of a home has been one of the chief preoccupations of woman for centuries. In this work of creation an understanding of color and design is of more importance than the mere possession of money, important as that is. And yet woman, generally, has been taught little about the principles of color. It is often a source of wonderment to me how successful the majority of untutored women are in using color; possibly through intelligent observation; perhaps through unconscious psychological and retinal nerve reactions. It is well known that it is not necessary to study color harmony to be influenced by it, since color sensation is instinctive. Color harmony is in our eyes and this has its psychological effect upon us. How closely color affects our everyday life is being more and more clearly demonstrated by physicists and psychologists.

In creating a home, a woman expresses and discloses herself. It is her selection and arrangement of what goes into it that give it beauty and charm, not the amount of money she spends in its embellishment. A limitless bank account may permit her only to demonstrate bad and confused judgment. No home should be a slavish copy of another; neither should it look like a shopwindow. It should be a setting for those who dwell in it—a background reflecting but not overshadowing them. It should be a place in which they can relax and be themselves. Even vibrant people have difficulty competing with strong colors all the time, so the home should not be decorated like a night club or a stage setting. It should have a personal quality about it that reflects the woman particularly but that will be expressive of the entire family. And at the basis of this personal quality will be the color scheme.

It is not possible in a small section of a book such as this to discuss color and its uses in the detailed manner the subject demands. However, I shall attempt to give the fundamentals underlying the use of color, and if an interest is aroused, the reader will find many books listed in the Bibliography for further study.

Great strides have been made since the seventeenth century when Sir Isaac Newton demonstrated that sunlight passed through a prism could be broken up into a continuous gradation of color called the spectrum. Since then many color theories and color systems have been proclaimed. Hermann L.F. Helmholtz (1821-94) made many studies regarding the nature of light, and these led to more comprehensive systems. Many of the color theories disagreed with one another. The physicist who sees color as light uses a system based on one set of primaries and secondaries; whereas the chemist, who considers color as pigment, uses a system based on pigment colors.

In 1905 Albert H. Munsell developed a workable color system with three color dimensions—hue, value, and chroma. This system is based on ten hues—yellow, yellow-green, green, blue-green, blue, blue-purple, purple, red-purple, red, yellow-red—and ten gradations of each hue, and is widely used today. It enables decorators and manufacturers to name definite colors in a way that is readily understood by all. Many decorators and manufacturers use beautiful words to designate different colors, such as "shocking pink" or "fuchsia," but since these names mean at least slightly different shades or tints to different people, the situation becomes more and more complicated for the bewildered home decorator.

One of the latest contributions to the study of color has been made by Louis Cheskin, technical director of the Color Research Institute of America and the author of two books on color. He confirms that there have always been disagreements about the primary colors and maintains that the latest studies made since the breaking down of the atom prove that the true primary colors are green-blue, magenta-red, and yellow. He claims that with these three primaries plus white and black it is possible to mix 1,296 colors, and that anyone with a formula and these five colors will be able to mix any desired color.

To make the approach to the understanding of color and its use in the home as simple as possible I shall resort to definitions that will give a concise meaning to the terms generally used. I would suggest that everyone buy a color wheel, as this will be of the greatest help in the assembling of color combinations.

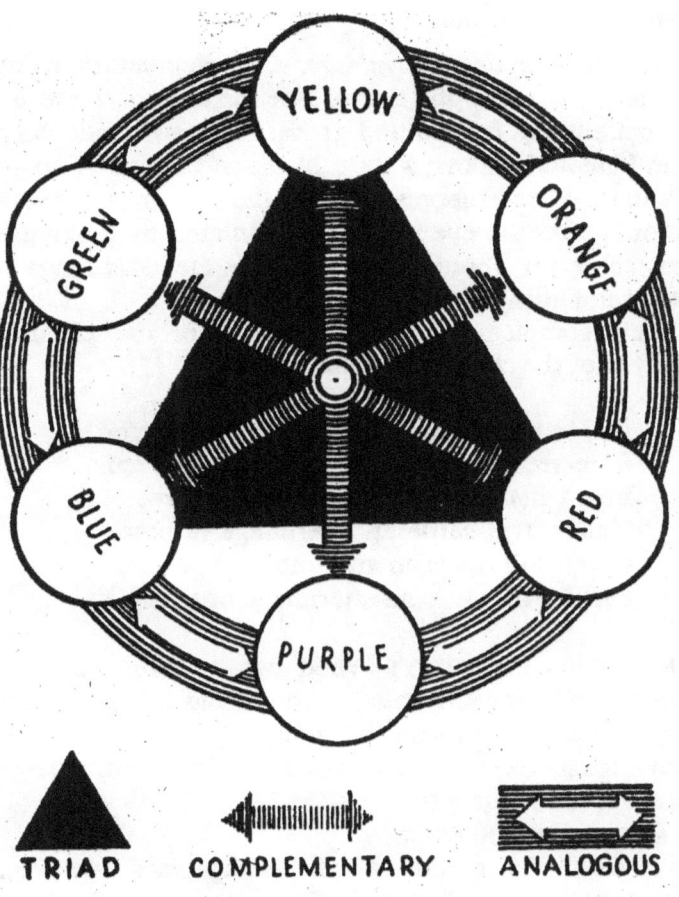

PRIMARY COLORS: Red, blue, yellow. SECONDARY COLORS: Orange, purple, green. ANALOGOUS HARMONY: Colors which adjoin one another on the spectrum. COMPLEMENTARY HARMONY: The color obtained from mixing two primaries. TRIAD: A balanced group of three colors selected at equal intervals on the color wheel.

AND WITH ANTIQUES

Afterimage or Aftermirage: Complementary colors are seen by one optic nerve. For instance, the eye has an optic nerve for red and green. A second optic nerve sees blue and yellow; a third black and white. A co-ordination of two nerves enables the eye to see mixed colors. After the eye has been stimulated by looking at one color for about thirty seconds, the afterimage in the complementary color is seen.

This complementary color is that of the physicist and not of the chemist. For instance:

> Red will cause an afterimage of blue-green.
> Blue-green will cause an afterimage of red.
> Blue will cause an afterimage of yellow.
> Yellow will cause an afterimage of blue.
> Green will cause an afterimage of purple.
> Purple will cause an afterimage of green.

ANALOGOUS HARMONY: When two or more consecutive colors of the spectrum, such as blue and green, are used, we call it analogous harmony.

ADVANCING OR ACTIVE COLORS: Yellow, red, orange. Green is moderately so.

COLOR DIMENSIONS:

1. *Hue.* The quality which distinguishes one color from another is called hue. Each section of the color wheel is a hue. It is easiest understood as the name of a color, such as red.

2. *Value.* The lightness or darkness of a color—the amount of light it reflects—is called its value. When white is added to a color it becomes a *tint*, a color higher in value than its spectrum value. When black is added, it becomes a *shade*, a color lower in value than its spectrum value.

3. *Chroma.* The strength or weakness—intensity—of a color is called chroma. Chroma represents the amount of purity or fullness of a hue.

COMPLEMENTARY COLOR. By mixing any two primary colors, a color is obtained which is complementary to the third primary pigment.

PIGMENT COMPLEMENTARIES. Red and green; yellow and purple; blue and orange.

COMPLEMENTARY HARMONY. This is obtained when a color and its complementary are used, such as green and red.

COOL COLORS. *See* receding and passive.

MONOCHROMATIC OR DOMINATE HARMONY. When one color is used throughout its shades and tints it is called monochromatic or dominant harmony.

PRIMARY COLORS. A primary color is a basic color. Every known color is obtained from these three. By mixing all three pigment primaries, a gray is obtained. Pigment primaries are red, blue, and yellow.

RECEDING OR PASSIVE COLORS. Blue and purple. Green is moderately advancing.

RELATED COLORS. Those colors which adjoin one another on the spectrum are related colors.

RETINAL STIMULATION. Physiologists have discovered that there are four primary colors known as the physiological primaries: red, green, blue, and yellow. In our eyes we have three sets of retinal nerves. One set is sensitive to the red-green rays, one to the blue-yellow rays, and the third controls the sight of black and white. These nerves co-ordinate in seeing other color mixtures.

SECONDARY COLOR. A color that results from the mixing of two primaries is called a secondary color.

SPECTRUM. When the colors in light are broken up

so that they fall upon a background in their fullest intensity, the result is known as a spectrum. The six colors are purple, blue, green, yellow, orange, and red.

A TERTIARY COLOR. When a primary color is mixed with a secondary color, the resulting color is called a tertiary. It will vary in accordance with the proportions used.

A TRIAD. A balanced group of three colors selected at equal intervals on the color wheel is a triad. This can be easily seen if it is noted that the first color forms a triad with those two colors into which its complementary may be split.

WARM COLORS. *See* advancing and active.

COLORS—HOW THEY AFFECT YOU

Can you picture living in a world devoid of color, where everything appears as it does in a gray-and-white photograph? If this were so, people themselves would be as colorless and as alike as so many clams. Only within a short period of time has it been proven by scientists that colors have a definite effect upon our nervous system. The art of primitive people employs pure colors, for primitive people and children are not attracted by tints and shades. Up to five or six years of age the normal child prefers red to any other color and is not at all attracted by pastels.

Most people find the warm, active colors stimulating and the cool, passive colors relaxing. Many believe that each color awakens a particular emotion in our minds. Others contend that memory, through an association of ideas, sometimes quite unconsciously, causes us to like certain colors and to dislike others. Tests have shown that this psychological reaction can often be traced to some early experience. In any event, certain colors have a definite emotional association for most people. In literature, in art, and in our everyday thoughts white is the symbol of innocence and joy; black of mourning and wickedness. We often link yellow with meanness and treason, as when we say that someone has a "yellow streak." Blue stands for constancy, as "true blue," while red is the most ardent of all the colors, standing in its worst sense for cruelty and sin. We have all read Hawthorne's *Scarlet Letter*, and most of us, I am sure, have sung the old hymn "Though Your Sins Be as Scarlet." Green is closely akin to blue and may signify hope, but is more often used to express jealousy, as "green with envy." Purple is a symbol of royalty, "born to the purple," but it may also be reminiscent of a decadent period—the "mauve decade."

One not especially sensitive to color may not realize the peculiarly irritating properties of certain colors and color combinations to some people. Normal people react to color stimulation as to other stimuli and unconsciously surround themselves with both cold and warm hues; this combination gives a balanced stimulation. Depressed persons will invariably yearn for the warm, stimulating colors and will be more depressed if surrounded by a predominance of cool colors. They will feel better if their homes are decorated with colors from the red and yellow family with contrasts and accents only from the blue-green family. In like manner, very active people, who lead a stimulating existence, will tend to build their decorating schemes around the cool colors with accents from the red-yellow family.

Beatrice Irwin in *The New Science of Color* says that people demand one color or another in their surroundings, depending upon their state of being. She also says that colors are either physically, mentally, or spiritually stimulating, sedative or recuperative. Miss Irwin is of the opinion that the soul, the body, and the mind demand in the colors surrounding them the complement of their own state.

Today this idea is being followed in hospitals, in schools, in business, and in advertising as well as in homes. In mental hospitals depressed patients are put in rooms that are stimulating and manic patients in rooms done in the cool colors. A surgeon no longer works in a glaring septic white operating room, his eyes soon fatigued by the brightness of light reflected from tiled walls to shining instruments. Many operating rooms today are done in grayed green, a color soft and soothing to surgeons and nurses. If medical science has found the use of color schemes desirable, how important it is for homemakers to have some understanding of the value of color in the decorating of their homes.

COLOR—HOW TO USE IT

In selecting color for a home, the first two questions to be asked are "What decorating style trend do I wish to follow?" and "What color scheme is most suitable for a particular room and for those who will occupy it?"

In decorating a home as a background for antiques, a particular group of colors is indicated in each of the four general periods: Early American, Colonial, Federal, and Victorian. Today's style trends and inclinations have affected the use of these groups of colors but the colors themselves are still indicated. Since nothing would be accomplished by going into a discussion of these period colors in the present chapter, we shall discuss them in detail within each period section.

Before the home decorator reaches the question of a color scheme, she has, I am sure, made a decision as to which period style she will follow. Then she may study the different colors that have proven most suitable for that period and select those she prefers.

Since the living room will be used not only by the family but by visitors it is best to have it done in a complementary color scheme, or it may be desirable to use three or more colors. As these schemes combine both warm and cool colors, they will prove most satisfying to everyone. Bedrooms should be as restful and relaxing as possible. For this reason a color scheme not too brilliant and not too complex is desirable. Nowhere in the house will the individuality and personality of the occupant be so apparent as here. If desired, the dining room may be more formal than the other rooms, always remembering that the table should be the focal point of the room. A study or library should be decorated in a manner conducive to study. The books will be a strong focal point of color.

Each room created will have a definite personality. With thought and care the desired effect can usually be achieved. Each room should reflect in a greater or lesser degree those who occupy it. Often one will hear a homeowner complain that he does not like his home which has been done with great care and at much expense by a trained decorator. It is beautiful and follows all the decorating rules but it expresses the decorator and not the homeowner. The colors may be intriguing but they may be the wrong colors for him. The furnishings and accessories may be perfect in every way but not at all suitable for those who live in the rooms.

AND WITH ANTIQUES

In using colors for decorating, pure colors are exciting; gray colors give a sophisticated effect; warm colors are stimulating; cool colors relaxing; dark colors stately and formal; light colors gay; related colors either warm or cool.

Decorating schemes are worked out by means of various color harmonies. The three most used are monochromatic or dominant harmony, analogous harmony, and complementary harmony. In dominant harmony, different tones of the same color are used, as in a room done in beige, tan, and brown. Analogous harmony is one that uses two or more consecutive colors on the color wheel, such as blue, green, et cetera. Both monochromatic and analogous color schemes may prove lacking in an interesting contrast of color qualities. Complementary harmony is obtained by combining a color and its complement, as red and green.

Probably more rooms are done in complementary colors than in the other harmonies, as they make for a balanced retinal stimulation and for an interesting variety and contrast. A room all warm or all cool, all active or all passive, unless done with the utmost skill, eventually becomes annoying. If two primary colors of equal value are used together in a scheme, the result may be confusing, since the contrast will be so sharp as to fatigue all the nerve endings. Hence there should be the right proportion of each color and its shades and tints. Generally, receding colors should be used for the large masses of background with active advancing colors for the small areas. Tints should be used generally for large masses of colors except when a dark background (shade) is used advisedly to achieve a certain desired effect.

If the background is light, there should be dark

notes in the furnishings for interesting contrast. If the background is dark, furnishings and accessories in high value (tints) will effect a suitable contrast. Always remember that the proportions of contrast must be subtle and not equal. A light color will appear lighter against a dark background and a dark color will appear darker against a light background.

In general a room should progress from dark floors to somewhat lighter walls to lighter ceiling. It is becoming popular to have the ceiling—even in period decoration—a paler tint of the wall color rather than white. Unless desirable as a shock spot of color, accent colors should be repeated more than once at different levels. Occasionally it is interesting to have one spot of analogous color in a complementary color scheme if the accent is worthy of the job it has to do and sufficiently important for the job. For instance, in a living room done in reds and greens one might have a very simple, very beautiful turquoise-blue lamp of adequate size with a dark red shade. Or the shock accent could well be a proper-sized picture or wall hanging. Do not, however, have shock accents throughout the entire house. They may seem interesting at first but eventually become irritating.

In combining shades and tints of a color with other colors, it is well to remember that bright or pure colors on a dull ground of the same hue or of any hue not complementary—for example, a bright green on a dull green, on a dull blue, or on a dull yellow—will deaden the dull color. The dull color will also affect the brightness of the pure color. This reaction of colors is owing to the fact that the bright color throws its complementary color into the dull color. Thus a red will throw its complementary green into the green background, making it brighter, but a green thrown into a blue or yellow background would make it duller.

If a room is too large it can be made to appear smaller by using warm, intimate advancing colors. If it is desirable to make a room look larger, use the cool receding colors. If the ceiling is too high, use a warm advancing color, the value of the color depending upon how much the ceiling is to be brought down. If it is desirable to make the ceiling look higher without the use of striped paper or other mechanical trick, use a very high value of a receding color, such as blue. Avoid glossy finish on woodwork, walls, and furniture. In the kitchen especially, where walls of white glossy paint or enamel are apt to be found, the reflection of bright lights on these shining surfaces causes quick eye fatigue and may lead to cuts and burns.

In color, as in other features of home decoration, there should be unity in the entire house, particularly if the rooms are connected by open doorways. This color unity is not so necessary between one floor and another except that the hall decorating scheme on the first floor will undoubtedly be carried up to the second floor. Because of this there will be color transition. In the small house or apartment the use of the same color or slightly varying tones of the same color as backgrounds will give unity. An effect of monotony is avoided through the use of different colors in the accessories of adjoining rooms. Sometimes it is advisable to reverse the color schemes, that is, have the background color of one room as the accent color in the adjoining room, using different values of the colors for contrasting interest.

Graying colors is one of the simplest methods of keying. The transition from a room done in complementary colors with the warm color dominant to a room done in the same complementary colors with the cool color predominating is interesting and good decorating. For instance, the living room could have a background of grayed red of a very high value—practically a warm gray—with accessories in shades of blue-green background with yellow and mauve contrasts. The kitchen could have grayed-blue walls with red and yellow contrasts. A hall paper could pick up all these colors of blue-green, blue, red, yellow, mauve, and warm gray. A color scheme, however, should never be carried out so perfectly that it becomes monotonous and too studied; neither should it be so haphazard that it is confusing and irritating.

If a room is dark, it can be made to appear sunny by using a pale, warm yellow. If it is filled with sunshine in the summertime, it can be made to seem cooler by the use of grayed green. With a judicious use of color you can make your home do what you want it to do. Color is your servant. Make it work for you.

SUGGESTIVE COLOR SCHEMES

"The timid flower that decks the fragrant field,
The daring star that tints the solemn dome
From one propulsive force to being reeled,
Both keep one law and have a single home."

Good color schemes are the most important factors in good home making.

Much research has recently been devoted to experiments demonstrating the immense effect of color, and different degrees of light on all forms of organic life. In the case of human beings the effect produced mentally exceeds, if anything, the physical effect. Therefore, it would be hard to overrate the importance of color schemes in decoration, as affecting the health and happiness of those who may be exposed to its influence. A good rule to remember in selecting color is, "Choose that which is cheerful without being gaudy, and quiet without being sombre."

In suggesting color schemes I wish to emphasize the importance of not attempting to

HOME DECORATION

have schemes of many color combinations unless we have a good natural or trained eye for color, for one shade just the least bit off color will make a discord, just as one wrong note will do in music. But to the man or woman with a good color eye all things are possible, for there are no two colors that will not go together if certain shades and degrees of color are rightly blended.

How seldom do we see unusual color schemes unless perchance we go to the home of an artist, yet nature every day is offering us suggestions.

"Come forth into the light of things,
Let nature be your teacher."—*Wordsworth.*

Watch the setting sun. After it has set behind the western hills see how wonderfully the pink and purple tints are blended with the grey of evening. Or wander in the woods and feel the peacefulness of the green trees, the silvery stream and the blue sky above. Or see in the turning leaf the rich warm beauty of the red and copper tones. Our homes would be more harmonious and restful if we would but bring the teachings of nature into them.

Proportion in color must be carefully considered in order to secure a successful room.

SUGGESTIVE COLOR SCHEMES

Some tones are strong and massive, and a little goes a long way, while others require a considerable amount of space to make themselves felt. We should try to make the colors seem to balance, so as not to feel any one tone too strongly, but rather to feel them all in one perfect harmony.

There are a few facts upon which rests the whole science of color harmony, and these it may be well to understand if one has not naturally a trained eye for color.

There are three colors, known as primary colors, from which all other shades are made. They are red, blue and yellow. Purple, orange and green are called binary because made up of two primary colors, orange is made of red and yellow, green of yellow and blue, purple of blue and red.

Harmony is obtained by putting together colors that are related. Blue and green are related through blue, but if the blue and green are mixed together the result will be a bluish green that will harmonize better with either the blue or the green than the colors themselves will harmonize. Harmony in color, as in music, depends on a certain blending of tone, rather than upon startling distinctions. Complementary colors are those that have not

HOME DECORATION

a color in common. Two complementary colors may be made harmonious, because there is a harmony of opposites based on the law of contrasts. For instance, if red and green are mixed together gray will be obtained. Therefore a red with much green, and a green with much red will harmonize well because both are near to the neutral gray.

It is important to consider colors by artificial light because they often look different, and in fact are different. A blue paper will look greenish at night because the yellow rays of the light are absorbed by the paper and the combination of yellow and blue make green. In the same way something that is red by day may appear orange at night.

Not only must we strive to have beautiful color schemes in every room, but we must take care that each room blends well with the one into which it opens. In a small house it is best to let one color predominate in the hall and the room seen from it, as this tends to give a feeling of spaciousness.

A house I know in England which was decorated by a well-known London artist, although handsomer and more costly than most of us can afford, is full of suggestive color schemes.

A charming vista, an Abnakee rug, and portieres in dull green, biscuit color and old rose, matching the paper

SUGGESTIVE COLOR SCHEMES

The woodwork of the hall is oak, without varnish, and the walls are divided by strips of wood with panels as high as the tops of the doors. Between the panels the walls were left in the rough plaster and painted brown, the color of the oak. Above the panelling the walls are stenciled. They were first stenciled in outline in blue and brown on a white ground, and were afterwards filled in with red and green. The furniture is large and massive and covered in bright leather. The simple but effective mantelpiece is made of gray Hopton stone, unpolished, the metal work of burnished iron and polished brass. The thick heavy rugs carry out the color scheme of the walls.

The drawing-room is very large and is carried out in cream, dead pink, plum color and green, all perfectly blended. The walls are panelled in small oblong panels and painted ivory-white like the rest of the woodwork. At each end of the room is a tapestry panel of bright silk flowers on an iridescent purple background, which gives one of the most beautiful color effects imaginable. The ceiling and frieze are cream, but a very faint stencil design in old rose on the frieze seems to bring the walls and ceiling into closer harmony. Some of the chairs are ivory-white, with loose cushions made of the same tapestry as used in the panels on the wall, while the rest of the furniture is mahogany.

The feature of the room is the mantelpiece, which is made of cream marble unpolished. Over the chimney-place a panel of mosaics glows with color and adds a delightful touch to the room. In the morning room the ceiling, frieze and woodwork are all white. The panels on the wall are filled with blue linen and are stenciled with a very pretty design in green, purple and white which makes a delightful color scheme.

The smoking-room is very original and strikingly beautiful. The woodwork is English oak without any finish whatever, not even a wax finish. The mouldings are heavy and give support to a rich frieze. The dado is filled with Japanese matting. Above this the rough plastered walls are painted a deep cream. Then the frieze is stenciled with heavy colors, but its chief charm is its daring introduction of metal. Small pieces of polished iron are hammered into the wall and smaller pieces of brass are introduced at regular intervals giving it a jeweled effect. The bright fire burn-

SUGGESTIVE COLOR SCHEMES

ing in the grate throws a reflection making it rich and lustrous in its appearance.

This house should be seen to be fully appreciated for the color schemes are so unusual they are hard to imagine. Although the treatment of the various rooms is bold and the colors strong the house is very restful, so skillfully are the colors blended. Had the effects not been carefully planned and the harmony of the whole house studied by an artist it might have been garish, but instead it is a masterpiece in decoration.

I am afraid a good many of us get into ruts about color schemes, judging from the sameness there is in the houses about us. How many libraries have we seen that were not carried out in either red, green or tan?

One of the most beautiful rooms I know has a color scheme of blue, green and silver gray. The woodwork is a light gray, the fittings that are usually of brass are of steel and pewter. The room has a wainscoting of gray, and above this a beautiful figured paper of green and blue. The green is a rich, warm olive, and the blue a queer cadet blue. The chairs, which are gray, are for the most part upholstered in plain olive green, with one or two easy-chairs covered with green and blue tapestry. The curtains are of plain blue, and the portieres are green, with a border of blue and gray. Other touches of the green and blue are introduced in the pottery. In this room the olive green gives richness and warmth; the blue sufficient brightness of color and the soft silvery gray gently draws the two colors together.

Another pretty and unusual color scheme can be carried out in a rich plum color, with green and touches of tan to give relief. The walls could be covered with a plain plum-colored felt, of not too dark a shade. There are one or two good ones on the market; but if the right shade cannot be obtained, it is better to use plain tan.

The portieres and curtains could be of plum-colored velour, and the chairs upholstered with a tapestry in plum, green or tan. The carpet or rug could be a neutral green. The inside curtains could be of Arabian colored scrim, and stenciled with a design in grapes and leaves. The tablecloths and pillows could be carried out in the same colors, and the room would be delightfully rich and restful.

The only drawback to an unusual room is the difficulty of obtaining the right shades;

SUGGESTIVE COLOR SCHEMES

but these can usually be found with perseverance, and, if not, they can be had by dyeing. The woman who is clever at home dyeing can save a lot of money and get excellent results. Often cheap material, when dyed a beautiful color, looks quite costly. For instance, I have seen unbleached muslin dyed a beautiful golden yellow, which, when held against the light, so that its rough weave could be seen, looked exactly like the shikii silk which is in such high favor, but too expensive for most of us.

Unless a person has a well-trained eye for color and a sense of proportion it is dangerous to use novel schemes and treatments. The safest plan is to copy what is best in the things we see around us, and to use only a few colors in each room, so there will be as little danger as possible of colors clashing. The walls of a pretty dining room I know have a white wainscoting with a deep red paper above it. The portieres are a two-toned red, and look rich and warm against the ivory-white woodwork. The rug is red, with touches of white. This makes a most cheery room. The disadvantage of red, generally, is that if it is a bright red it is too glaring, and if it is a dull, deep red it makes the room too dark; but this treatment with the white woodwork overcomes these obstacles and makes a most delightful room.

Another pretty room is carried out in green and white. This also has white woodwork and a white wainscoting. Above this is a soft green felt paper. Most of the chairs are of wicker, painted green, to match the rest of the room, not the vivid emerald green that is often sold, but a soft moss green. Touches of yellow and old rose are introduced in the chair coverings, cushions, etc., but the general effect is of green and white, which is delightfully fresh and pretty.

Rooms furnished with heavy mission furniture should not have white paint. The fumed or weathered oak is more suitable. Rooms of this sort should have a bold treatment. Those carried out in brown and tan, or tan and red, can be made most effective. Such a room should be simple almost to severity. They are usually spoilt by being overcrowded with a lot of little things that are quite unnecessary.

In a bedroom there is less danger of our going wrong than in the downstairs rooms. But generally they show lack of thought. Often a person gets as far as carrying a room out in certain colors, such as pink and green,

SUGGESTIVE COLOR SCHEMES

but will have a rose paper on the wall, a poppy chintz on the chairs, and cretonne with pink chrysanthemums for the curtains. This not only introduces alien shades of pink, but also too much variety. It would be infinitely prettier carried out as a rose bedroom, so that wherever flowers appeared they were roses or rosebuds. Such a room would show at once that thought had been spent on it. A charming green and pink room is carried out in the following manner: The wall paper has a pretty all-over design of poppies and leaves, some of the poppies being light pink, others dark. The floor is covered with a plain green carpet rug. The woodwork and furniture is stained green, while the inside curtains are white with a cretonne border of green and pink. The little rocking chair has a slip cover of chintz with a poppy design. This room hits a happy medium by being pretty and dainty, without being too perishable.

Bedroom schemes can be carried out with painted furniture to match. This is really economical, as cheap furniture can be ordered in the unfinished state, and this can easily be stained or painted at home. Very pretty effects can be had with a blue and green room if the chairs, etc., are painted the right shade of blue. In such a room there should be plenty of green to balance. The rug could be green and the inside curtains could be of plain green denim to give relief to the eye.

Anyone who thoroughly plans and carries out a good simple color scheme will be more than repaid, and will wonder how she could ever have been content to huddle things into a room without any thought of the "whys" and the "wherefores" of color harmonies. A disordered house may prove very annoying, but a discolored house may be positively injurious.

To-day in the hustle and bustle of civilization, restfulness in the home is more needed than ever before. For where are we to find that health giving quality, if not in our homes? Since experiments have shown the remarkable effect that color has upon human beings, both physically and mentally, it becomes the duty of a home-maker to consider the colorings of her home in relation to cheerfulness and repose.

We often hear it said that "so and so" is sensitive to color, but do we understand it literally or consider it but a figure of speech? Color, like music, is a question of vibration, and affects certain nerves, one nerve, the epi-

SUGGESTIVE COLOR SCHEMES

gastic, being particularly sensitive. This nerve is sometimes so affected by the vibrations of distasteful color, that it causes a feeling of repugnance, and even of sickness.

Yellow is the color that gives cheerfulness, it is sunny, joyous, and jubilant, and at the same time giving a feeling of quiet reserve.

Red should be used with great discretion. It is an unhealthy color for wall treatment, and has many disadvantages. It contracts a room, causes dark shadows at night, and is both tiring and depressing in large quantities. It is usually used to give a feeling of warmth and coziness, but it is not necessary to bring red into a room to create such an impression. Red, however, used in the furnishing of a room is delightful, but even here it should be used sparingly.

Pink is pretty when used with white woodwork, and gives a feeling of daintiness, and even of gayety; it should be used sparingly, however, in downstair rooms.

Green is the most restful of all colors; and the most satisfactory for use as a background. Dark olive green is the richest and most harmonious shade, and gives a feeling of warmth. In contrast to this is the gray green which gives the impression of coolness.

HOME DECORATION

Repose in a room depends greatly upon a certain evenness of color. Sharp contrasts shock and startle, so it is important that there should be a careful blending of colors.

When we realize the effect color has upon our senses, we see the necessity of taking advantage of the most restful and refreshing schemes, so that our home may be a peaceful retreat, where we may rest after the labors of a busy day. "This," as Ruskin says, " is the true nature of home; it is the place of Peace."

THE SECRET OF COLOUR

THE secret of how to use colour is subtle and elusive, for colour, besides being a science, is also, like sound, taste, and smell, a physical sensation.

For centuries it has been the aim of man to imitate the colour harmonies of Nature. But how is it possible to recapture the fugitive beauty of the world around us? Can we pluck 'the blue of the unattainable flower of the sky,' as Richard Jefferies called it, or can the art of man recreate the ever-changing colour of the sea, with those mysterious gradations of shade that turn it from a mournful grey to a shimmering turquoise in the setting sun?

Can art steal the secret of the waxen loveliness of the magnolia flower, or of the white peony, with its imperceptible tinges of yellow that only serve to intensify the tones of white?

Can we repeat the miraculous harmony of light falling on a dazzling white building that shades it to tones of grey and purple?

Fortunately we can. For Sir Isaac Newton, by his discoveries concerning light, gave us the key to the rules that govern these natural harmonies. Before then the science of colour was little understood. Even the Greeks and Romans knew little concerning the treatment and ideas associated with colour, and as Dr. Oswald points out: 'The older

THE SECRET OF COLOUR

writers name only *White*, *Black*, *Yellow*, and *Red* as distinct colours.' He goes on to say: 'Just as the history of Ancient Music is characterized by the fact that one or another performer added a fresh note to the original five, so also in the history of practical colour-science do we find an extension of resources by the discovery or invention of new colouring matters. In innumerable instances indeed we find attempts to utilize the colours of flowers for technical purposes wrecked by the extreme instability of the majority of pigments derived from this source. Nevertheless, in this way a few colouring matters satisfying higher requirements were, in course of time, obtained from the vegetable and animal kingdom. The discovery of the *Purple* colour in certain gasteropods was made in the days of antiquity. The Middle Ages brought with them the *Yellow* from *Persian Berries*, and the *Lakes* (crimson lake) from *Yellow*, *Red*, and *Violet* Woods (under which heading *Madder* root is included), *Kermes*, and *Saffron*. *Verdigris* and the *Blue* colours from *Cobalt* were also added in the Middle Ages.'

It was not until the eighteenth century, when the rise of chemistry began, that colour became a proper study and science. Sir Isaac Newton is really the father of this whole science, for when he made his momentous discovery that white light could be spilt up into a variety of colours by means of a simple glass prism he opened up a whole new avenue of colour and light. The story runs that Newton's analysis of light was accomplished two years after the Great Plague in 1666. Driven from Cambridge University by threats of the plague, he had retired to the country, and it was at Stourbridge Fair that he bought the prism with which he carried out his celebrated experiments.

Newton's discovery, unlike many scientific facts, is comparatively easy to understand. Although past generations of great painters had used colours with wonderful harmony and

THE SECRET OF COLOUR

precision, it needed the scientist to discover a formula by which some form of classification could be made. Newton's analysis of light gave us this formula. Briefly, his theory is that all colour is contained in light, and he proved this by showing that when light is reflected through a prism it breaks up into certain colours; and it is from this range of natural colours that the modern range of decorative colours springs. Newton's discovery enabled later-day scientists to work out a standardization of colours. To-day these colours for practical purposes have been regulated into twelve main groups:

YELLOW, or chrome yellow as it is called by the decorating trade.
ORANGE, or chrome orange.
RED, or poppy red.
SCARLET, or spectrum red.
CRIMSON, or purple lake.
PURPLE, or mauve blue.
VIOLET, or a mixture of deep ultramarine and mauve blue.
BLUE VIOLET, or deep ultramarine.
BLUE, or oriental blue.
BLUE GREEN, or turquoise blue.
GREEN, or poster green.
YELLOW GREEN, or light green.

You will notice that neither *Black* nor *White* is mentioned in this list, and this is because they are a combination of other colours and not pure colours in themselves. But we shall deal with the problem of black and white later on. Meanwhile, if you read through the above list of colours you will notice that many colours are closely related to each other. In fact, if you inspected a diagram of the colours of the spectrum you would see that certain colours definitely merge into each other. This is a very important discovery, because it explains the laws of colour harmony and gives us the clue why certain colours look well together in a room, whilst others, being inharmonious, create an atmosphere of distaste and unrest.

The laws of Nature also allow us certain natural combina- of colours. For example, *Blue* mixed with *Yellow* produces *Green*. Similarly, *Purple* is obtained by mixing *Blue* with *Red*, and *Yellow* mixed with *Red* gives us *Orange*. These established facts about the production of the primary and secondary colours should make the use of colour compara- tively simple, but unfortunately, as colour can be created out of light it is also strongly influenced by the light thrown upon it. Moreover, it was discovered that certain colours attract light, whilst others are deadened by it. Consequently, a knowledge of the reactions of colour to light is essential to anyone attempting interior decoration.

Past scientists have proved that colours affect us physiolog- ically—that is to say that the human eye is physically affected by the colours it sees. Some colours make a greater demand on the eye than others, and for this reason the eye soon wearies of the demands made upon it. Consequently, the eye instinctively demands restful colours or a harmonious grouping of colours that rests the eyesight because of its natural harmony.

Amongst the strongest colours are *Red* and *Orange*, and these two shades soon tire the eye, and so it is best to avoid using large expanses of these two colours in the decoration of a room. On the other hand, colours such as *Green* and *Yellow* please the eye and rest it, and so by the laws of Nature they are admirable colours to use for colour schemes. This explains the enormous popularity of all tones of green and yellow in contemporary decoration.

We now come to one of the most important and in- teresting facts about colour—its psychological value. Goethe was one of the first men to realize the psychological values of colour, and devoted a large portion of his book, *The Theory of Colour*, to describing this aspect of the study. Goethe's work was very valuable and prepared the way for the nineteenth-century scientists. It may be interesting to recall some of his observations on the psychology of colour.

Speaking of colour in general, he remarks: 'People experience a great delight in colour generally, the eye requires it as much as it requires light. We have only to remember the refreshing sensation we experience if on a cloudy day the sun illumines a single portion of the scene before us, and displays its colours. That healing powers were ascribed to coloured gems may have arisen from the experience of this indescribable pleasure.' He then goes on to analyse the psychological values of each colour. Discussing *Yellow*, he says: 'This is the colour nearest the light . . . in its highest purity it always carries with it the nature of brightness, and has a serene, gay, softly exciting character. In this state applied to dress, hangings, carpeting, etc., it is agreeable . . . we find from experience that yellow excites a warm and agreeable impression. . . . This impression of warmth may be experienced in a very lively manner if we look at a landscape through a yellow glass, particularly on a grey winter's day. The eye is gladdened, the heart expanded and cheered, a glow seems at once to breathe towards us.' Discussing *Blue*, he goes on to say: 'As Yellow is always accompanied with light, so it may be said that Blue still brings a principle of darkness with it. This colour has a peculiar and almost indescribable effect on the eye. As a hue it is powerful, but it is on the negative side, and in its highest purity is, as it were, a stimulating negation. Its appearance then is a kind of contradiction between excitement and repose. As the upper sky and the distant mounts appear blue, so a blue surface seems to retire from us. But as we readily follow an agreeable object that flies from us, so we love to contemplate blue, not because it advances to us, but because it draws us after it. Blue gives us an impression of cold and this again, reminds us of shade.' Finally, commenting on tne properties of *Red*, he says: 'The active side is here in its highest energy, and it is not to be wondered at that impetuous, robust, uneducated men should be especially pleased with this colour. Among savage nations the inclination for it has been universally remarked, and children when left to themselves begin to use tints they never spare vermilion and minium. In looking steadfastly at a red surface, the colour seems actually to penetrate the eye. It produces an extreme excitement, and still acts thus when somewhat darkened. A red cloth disturbs and enrages animals. I have known men of education on whom its effect was intolerable if they chanced to see a person dressed in a scarlet cloak on a grey, cloudy day.'

To-day it is not advisable to take Goethe's pronouncements too literally. His book was published in 1810, and since then a revolution has taken place in the production of colours. The discovery of dyes from the constituents of coal-tar in the second half of the nineteenth century gave the world a whole new range of colours hitherto unknown, and modern science and machinery have enabled us to extract more subtle and elusive gradations of colour than was possible in Goethe's time. For instance, whereas it is still an established fact that red is a dangerous colour to use in any quantity in a scheme of decoration, yet the dilution of this colour with white can give us a whole range of soft tones of pink that are admirably suited for a modern setting. In fact, the chief tendency in interior decoration in the twentieth century is to avoid so-called warm and restless colours, such as red and orange, and to prefer the use of cool and restful colours such as light blue and light green. I have already attempted to explain the attraction that the colours of

THE SECRET OF COLOUR

Nature exercise over our eyes, so it is quite understandable that all shades of green should exert a fascination. Green being closely related to blue, is not a jarring colour like red, and being a predominant shade in Nature, contains so many restful harmonies that it will always remain paramount among colours. It has been said that 'the palette of the decorator is quite different from the painter's palette. The painter may form new colours and shades by the simple process of mixing, whilst the decorator must combine set colours with interesting textiles and surfaces in order to produce these harmonies of contrast. From the decorator's point of view, each colour has its own range. This range depends mainly upon the colours he is able to add to a given colour.'

This question of the ranges of colours available, and the possible contrasts of colours that can be used, is now the next point to be examined.

The architect and the interior decorator have only a limited number of colours and colour contrasts at their command, and the success of their work depends largely on how they combine and use them. Undoubtedly, the art of contrast is one of the secrets of successful interior decoration.

The modern decorator is all in favour of sharp contrasts in colour. The sharpest colour contrast is black and white, and one of the reasons for the preference as well as for grey and silver is the fact that these colours are neutral, in that they do not appear in the list of primary colours. Consequently, they lend themselves to combinations with other colours. White, being closely related to all colours, is strongly affected by colours placed beside it. This should be remembered when white is being used as a principal shade in a room—naturally, this also applies to cream.

Because black and white is such an effective contrast, this particular combination has enjoyed great popularity in recent years; but it is likely to become monotonous unless

D

relieved by other colours. The chief virtue of black is that it enables one to emphasize other colours in a room, and it brings out the richness in colours placed beside it. It forms an admirable background for colour, but in wide areas black paintwork should be avoided, as black tends to absorb light rather than reflect it. This also applies to colours related to black, such as purple. Certain colours are successful when contrasted in this scheme, for instance, blue contrasts admirably with black or white. Similarly, red contrasts with white, brown, yellow or orange, but it has been proved that scarlet is an unhappy contrast with violet, and orange-yellow is bad with green. In fact, it is as well to avoid using too much contrast when planning a scheme and to rely mainly on harmonious groupings of colours. A student of colour soon discovers for himself that the most beautiful arrangements of colour are usually achieved by a gradual gradation of the colours used. All colour in Nature relies on the gradual merging of colours, and this can be seen when studying the colour of a flower, where the effect of colour is achieved, not by one level colour but by a series of varying tints that together create the illusion of one main colour.

Similarly, some of the most effective modern interiors have been created out of the monochrome scheme. A scheme of this kind is achieved by taking one main colour, and then building up the decoration of the room around this one shade, using the various tints of shades closely related to it. For instance, supposing you paint the walls of your room beige, a monochrome scheme can be built up by covering the furniture with brown fabric relieved with touches of cream, and curtaining the windows in some material that links up with cream, beige, and brown. The result will be very harmonious, because each colour is a division of brown. Again, an all-green scheme can be evolved by using olive green and chartreuse green against apple-green walls.

Recently, contemporary decoration has shown a tendency to use more and more pastel shades when planning colour schemes, and these pastel shades are easily obtained by merely mixing the basic colour such as red, blue or yellow with white until you obtain the softness of colour that you desire.

The advantage of pastel colours is that they are unobtrusive and restful, and form an effective background for decorative detail and furniture.

To summarize the whole difficult question of how to use colour, it is best to bear the following rules in mind: avoid using strong colours such as red, orange, and purple, and wherever possible try and use the softer shades of green and yellow, and such combinations of blue as turquoise, dark or navy blue, can look well as long as they are not used for the main colour of the room. Remember, however, that all-blue schemes are apt to appear cold. The architect and the interior decorator of to-day favour neutral schemes combining neutral shades of white, black, and brown, but when using these combinations it is best to relieve the schemes with touches of colour such as red, green, and yellow. Violet, although a lovely colour in itself, does not lend itself to successful colour schemes and should be avoided except in small touches.

Finally, try to use light-attracting colours such as yellow and green as opposed to purple or blue. As a rule it is a mistake to mix black as a darkening medium for other colours. The correct way to lessen the brilliance of any colour is to mix it with a little of its contrasting colour. The range of mixed colours is so large that it is usually possible to obtain approximately the colour you desire, and if a softening of the shade is desired the painter can easily do this for you.

THE SECRET OF COLOUR

One last note about painting: when you are choosing your colours try to achieve as much harmony as possible, but do not worry too much about how to mix the colours you desire. For the majority of colour schemes I would advise using a paint with a glossy finish, as this will attract more light than a plain surface paint.

The science of colour may at first appear very baffling and complicated, but its study brings its own reward. You will be happiest if when choosing your colours you allow your instinct to guide you, for most people instinctively choose the colours that provide them with the most suitable background. However, try to keep your colour schemes as simple as possible, for as Richard Jefferies discovered: 'Pure colour is rest of heart.'

COLOUR

Colour exerts such a great influence in our lives that our first impressions are largely dominated by it. When we enter a room for the first time, or look at a new dress or a picture, we experience a sensation of pleasure or otherwise, depending on whether the colour is to our liking or not.

Everyone with normal vision is colour conscious, though not by any means to the same degree; children and primitive peoples, for instance, show a marked preference for strong, bright colour and vigorous combinations which may appear gaudy and unpleasant to more cultured tastes. Some people are so extremely sensitive to colour that they may suffer acute mental discomfort in the presence of clashing or incongruous colours, whilst others may be quite undisturbed in similar surroundings.

The decorator should be able to discuss colour problems in a knowledgeable and convincing manner, especially as it is sometimes necessary to warn a client against an unsatisfactory choice of colour. This may require some diplomacy to avoid any appearance of running counter to the client's wishes, but if the decorator has a sound practical and theoretical knowledge of colour he will generally inspire confidence in his opinions.

COLOUR THEORIES

Colour has been the subject of a great number of textbooks and the student is often bewildered by apparently conflicting and misleading theories. The chief cause of confusion is probably due to the totally different results obtained by mixing coloured *lights* as compared with *pigment* mixtures, and we shall therefore attempt to make this distinction clear, as well as to offer suggestions for the practical application of colour to buildings.

The advanced student should acquaint himself with the "three-dimensional" conceptions of colour as expounded by Ostwald, Munsell, and Lawrence, and also with the works of such authorities as Rood, and Luckeish (see Bibliography, page 436). As an introduction to the subject, however, the beginner cannot do better than to read "Colour" by H. Barrett Carpenter, followed by "Colour in Interior Decoration" by John M. Holmes, both of which are extremely lucid and well illustrated in colour. Mr Holmes' book is, in our opinion, the most practical contribution to the subject of colour as applied to interior decoration. But the student should not only *read* about colour; actual experiments should be carried out so that he gains in practical experience as well as in theoretical knowledge.

COLOUR TERMS

Before we can begin to discuss colour we must define the expressions used, to ensure that reader and writer are thinking alike. Much confusion is caused by the absence of any commonly accepted terminology; in America, for instance, some of the terms are quite different from ours and since these have been adopted by certain writers in this country, we include them here.

Hue is simply another name for "colour". We speak of a "reddish hue", a "yellow-green hue", and so on.

Purity refers to the strength of colour, i.e., its intensity or, as the scientist calls it, "saturation". The colours of the rainbow, for instance, are of maximum purity. When a pigmentary colour is mixed with another, or with white, black or grey, its purity value is reduced or weakened. In the U.S.A., the term *Chroma* (the Greek word for colour) is generally used instead of purity.

Tone value refers to the lightness or darkness of a colour. When white is added to a colour a lighter tone is produced, whilst the addition of black produces a darker tone. Thus a colour may be raised or lowered in tone value. In America the word *value* is used by itself to express the same meaning.

When a colour is lightened or reduced with white it is referred to as a *tint*. When it is darkened by the addition of black it becomes a *shade*. The term *shade* is often loosely applied, as in "Shade Card" (meaning Colour Card), or a "light shade" (when a light *tint* or pale colour is meant).

The Chromatic Scale refers to the whole range of colour which, for convenience, is arranged in the familiar colour circle. Ideally the colour circle would be a continuous band of colour graduating or blending from yellow, through green, blue, violet, purple, red and orange, back to yellow, but it is generally shown stepped in separate distinct hues, the number of which varies with different authorities. Carpenter, for instance, shows *fourteen*, Holmes *twelve*, Munsell *ten* and Ostwald *eight* basic hues.

Harmony — Colours, such as yellow, orange and red; yellow-green, green and blue-green, etc., which lie adjacent or fairly close to each other on the colour circle are said to be *harmonious* or *analogous* colours, since, in combination, they are pleasing to the eye.

Contrast — Colours which lie directly opposite or nearly opposite on the colour circle are *contrasting* colours. Carpenter defines contrasting colours as being "those which when placed side by side intensify each other but do not change".

The contrast gained by the juxtaposition of two complementary colours is said to be a *true* contrast. These pairs of colours are termed "complementary" because, when added together as coloured lights, they produce *white light;* thus yellow and blue, purple (or Magenta) and green, red and blue-green are pairs which produce white light and are therefore true contrasts or complementaries. Colour circles which show such pairs lying directly opposite are therefore based essentially on the intermixture of coloured light.

PAINTING AND DECORATING

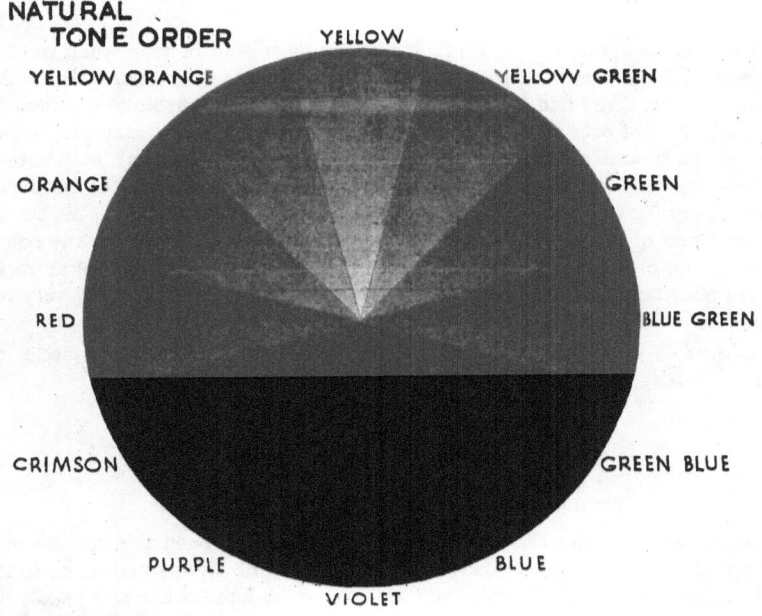

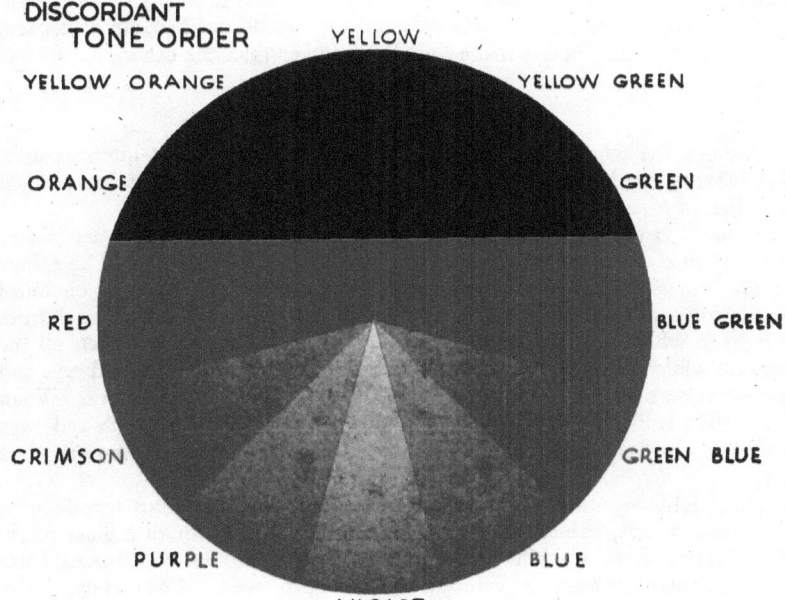

Fig. 189. Harmony and discord

The normal colour circle shows hues arranged in natural tone order, i.e., a progressive deepening of tone from yellow to violet. When this tone order is reversed (i.e. when yellow is made the darkest and violet the lightest tone) a circle of discords is produced

Contrast as applied to *pigmentary* mixtures is said to be true when the two pigments mixed together produce a *dark neutral grey;* thus yellow and violet, orange and blue, red and blue-green are pairs which are capable of producing a neutral grey, *but only when the hues are correctly related.* For example, to find the true contrast to a particular scarlet it is necessary to make trials with various blue-greens until one is found that will, when mixed with the scarlet, produce a neutral grey (i.e., a grey which inclines neither to red nor green). This applies to every pair of true pigment contrasts and, if the opposite hues on any colour circle do not produce a neutral grey when mixed together, they are not correctly related according to the principles of pigment mixture. (Incidentally, very few published colour circles are satisfactory in this respect.)

Discord — When colours of maximum purity are arranged in a circle, we find an orderly progression from light to dark in this order —

Yellow (lightest colour, nearest to White)

Orange	Green
Red	Blue-green
Purple	Blue

Violet (darkest colour, nearest to Black)

Rood has called this "the natural order of colour". When this natural tone order is reversed, i.e., when black is added to the light colours and white to the dark, we get a circle of *discords*, with violet now the lightest hue and yellow the darkest. It will be noticed that red and blue-green, being mid-way between light and dark, retain their natural tone relationship and do not become discordant with each other until one is made lighter or darker than the other.

LIGHT AND PIGMENT

Although the painter and decorator is dealing with pigment intermixtures, it is desirable that he should understand the differences between coloured *light* and coloured *pigment.*

"Colour" is the effect produced on the eye by the different wavelengths of light. When there is no light there is no colour — only blackness. The colour of pigments (and of all "coloured" matter) is determined by their chemical composition and their capacity to absorb or reflect certain coloured rays from the light in which they are seen. A white surface, for instance, *reflects* all the light rays whilst black *absorbs* them all. A red surface reflects only red rays and absorbs the rest; similarly a green surface reflects only green, and so on. When a red surface is illumined solely by blue light or green light (in which red rays are absent), the light rays are totally absorbed and the surface therefore appears *black.*

White light, or sunlight, is made up of innumerable different wavelengths or, in other words, colours of light; when it is passed through a glass prism and projected on to a white screen, it is split up into its constituent parts and the familiar *spectrum* or "rainbow band" is produced. Conversely, white light may be reconstituted by adding together the spectrum colours as lights.

It is not necessary, however, to use the whole of the spectral band since the three light primaries, i.e., red, green and blue, will suffice. When these three light primaries are projected separately on to a white screen and allowed to converge until the beams overlap, *white light* is reproduced. When only two light primaries are mixed, a *secondary* colour is produced; thus red and green produce yellow; red and blue produce purple (or magenta); green and blue produce blue-green (see Fig. 190). It is important to note that light *secondaries*

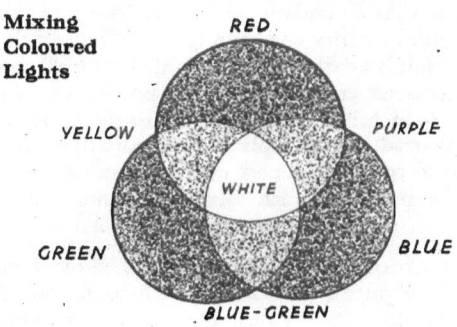

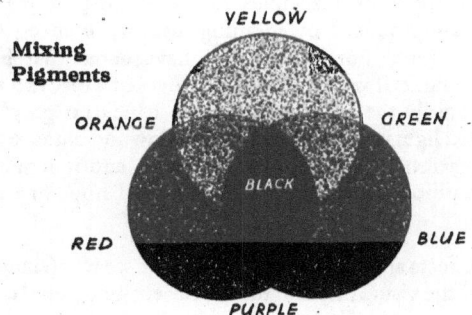

Fig. 190. Lights and pigments
Showing the "additive" effect of mixing the three light primaries (producing white light) compared with the "subtractive" effect of mixing the three pigment primaries (producing black, or near black)

are of higher luminosity (i.e., nearer to white light) than the *primaries* which produce them; this is due to the "additive" effect of mixing coloured lights. When a light primary is mixed with its contrasting secondary the result is *white light* again because all three primaries are then involved. Thus projected light combinations of blue and yellow, red and blue-green, green and purple, all produce *white light*.

When we consider the effects of *pigment* mixture, however, we find many important differences. Firstly, the pigment primaries are red, blue and yellow;

these are the three basic colours which cannot be produced from any other combination, but which, in theory, are capable of producing all other colours. A mixture of two primaries produces a *secondary*, thus — red and yellow produce orange; yellow and blue produce green; blue and red produce purple. Two secondaries produce a *tertiary* colour; thus green and orange produce citron or citrine; orange and purple produce russet; purple and green produce olive. When coloured pigments are mixed together, a certain amount of darkening and loss of purity occurs; thus secondary colours are less pure than primaries and tertiaries are lower still in purity and tone value. When all three primaries are mixed together the result is a dark neutral grey (almost black) and the same occurs when two complementaries are mixed as noted previously. This darkening or "subtractive" effect (which is directly opposite to the lightening or "additive" effect of mixing coloured lights) explains the limitations of the three-colour theory, for, while it is true that almost every hue can be produced from red, yellow and blue, the results of such mixtures cannot compare in purity or brilliance with those of available manufactured pigments.

It will be seen from the foregoing that failure to distinguish between the mixing of lights and of pigments can lead to much confusion. Some authorities base their theories on the optical effects obtained by spinning coloured discs and whilst this method is extremely interesting, it can also be very misleading if one attempts to apply its principles to the mixing of pigments, because the *visual intermixture* produced by spinning discs is, in effect, the intermixing of *reflected* coloured light. For instance, we have noted that blue and yellow lights produce white light; if we paint the two halves of a disc in a similar blue and yellow and spin it rapidly the effect produced is a neutral grey*. Thus, when projected or reflected light is being considered, yellow and blue are complementary. Yellow and blue *pigments*, however, produce *green*, and it requires a mixture of yellow and *violet* to produce a neutral grey. These distinctions must always be borne in mind.

Optical colour effects are highly important to the weaver (since he can usefully exploit the effects of the visual intermixture of closely juxtaposed coloured threads) but to the decorator their chief interest probably lies in the production of sponge-stipple, spray-spatter and colour combing effects in all of which visual intermixture plays its part in providing a more "vibrant" quality than is possible with plain colour. The main concern of the painter, however, is with the *actual* mixing of pigments and he therefore requires to study colour theory mostly from that angle. The method advocated by Mr Holmes is, we repeat, the most practical that we have found so far. By selecting twelve basic coloured pigments of maximum available purity (as he advocates), adjusting each pair of contrasts until they produce a neutral grey when mixed, the colour circle becomes of great practical value instead merely of theoretical interest.

---

* By spinning *pale* blue and yellow together, a greyish "white" is produced. Pure white cannot be obtained with disc mixtures because *reflected* light is never as brilliant as *projected* light.

THE USE OF COLOUR CIRCLES*

It is often pointed out that a knowledge of colour theory does not necessarily make a colourist, and that, in fact, many fine colourists have no knowledge whatever of scientific colour theories. This is true enough and it is readily conceded. On the other hand, born colourists are few and far between, while the number of people requiring colour guidance is indeed great. If knowledge of colour theory alone cannot make a colourist, it will at least be of great assistance in helping one to avoid unsatisfactory colour combinations.

If colour theory is to be of any practical use to the painter and decorator, he must be able to apply it to his everyday work. The colour circle showing only twelve hues of maximum purity seems totally unrelated to the dull common pigments of the paint bench — the ochres, siennas, umbers, red oxides and Brunswick greens, etc. The first step then is to find out how these common pigments fit in with the general scheme of things and we propose to outline the preparation of two colour circles that will enable the student to "place" not only his common stainers but also those subtle pastel hues shown on most paint manufacturers' colour cards.

One may either purchase twelve "Spectrum" poster colours to make up the colour circle, or, alternatively, use oil colour in tubes; the latter are probably the best for our purpose because we are going to compare them later with our ordinary stainers in oil. Quite a useful circle can be produced from a minimum of six oil colours — two yellows, two reds and two blues, viz., lemon chrome, mid chrome, vermilion, crimson, ultramarine, and Antwerp blue (a greener blue than Prussian). These are mixed in pairs to produce yellow-orange and orange (from mid chrome and vermilion), purple and violet (from crimson and ultramarine) and yellow-green, green and blue-green (from lemon chrome and Antwerp blue). A circle produced from such intermixtures will not be of maximum purity, of course, but it will be of practical value in that it enables the student to test out the red-yellow-blue pigment theory for himself.

Before the twelve colours are arranged in a circle (as in Fig. 191) each opposite pair should be tested to ensure that they are true contrasts. Thus lemon chrome and violet are mixed to produce neutral grey; if the grey inclines towards red, add more ultramarine to the violet; if it inclines to blue, add more crimson to the violet, until a neutral grey is obtained. Only in this way can a violet be found which is a true complementary to the lemon chrome. Having established the first pair of true contrasts, paint a small patch of each on knotted paper and put the remaining colour in a small screw-top jar for further use (about an ounce of each colour should be sufficient).

---

* It is regretted that, owing to the great difficulty in reproducing colour circles to show correct colour and tone relationships, and the subtle differences of tertiary hues, we are reluctantly compelled to illustrate these in monochrome. It is hoped, however, that the student will produce his own colour circles on the lines indicated by the author, because, apart from being a useful exercise in colour, the circles will form valuable reference charts.

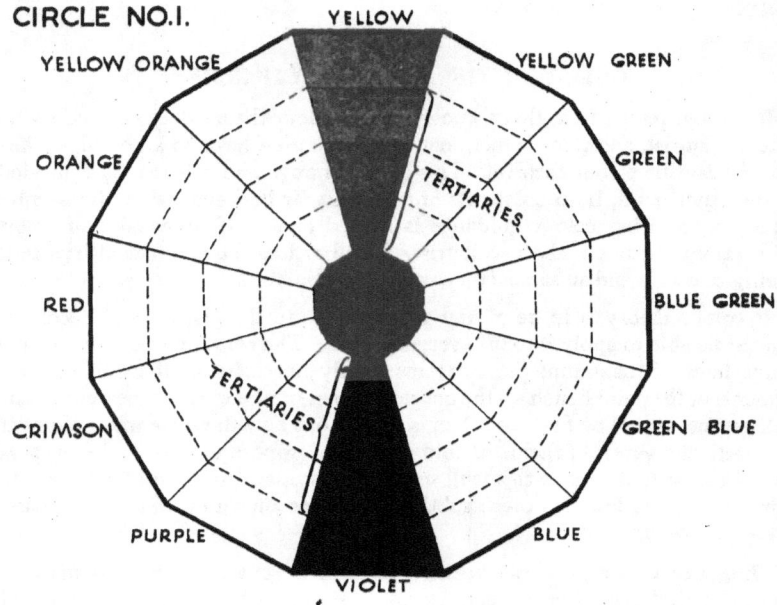
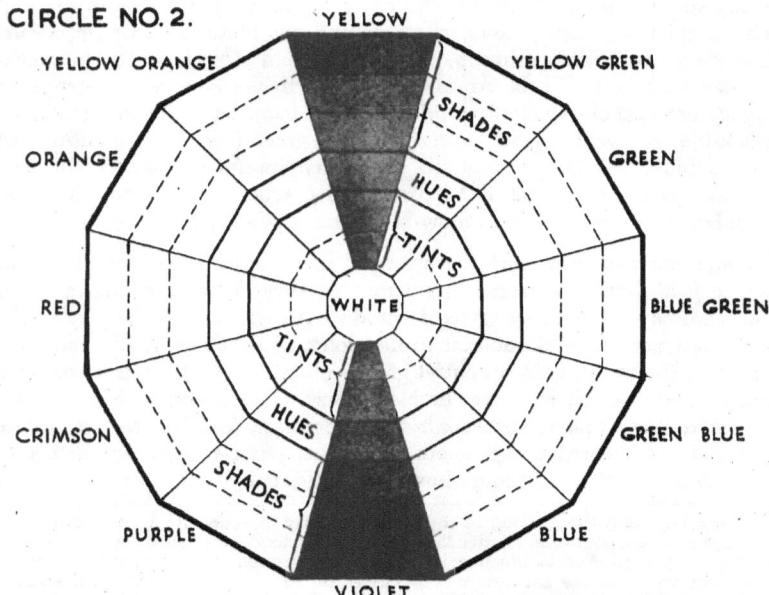

Fig. 191. How the colour circles are built up

Circle No. 1 shows a range of tertiaries and neutral grey obtained by mixing two complementary hues. Circle No. 2 shows how tints and shades may be arranged in relation to the parent hues

The yellow and violet represent the lightest and darkest colours in the circle and we now wish to find the colours which fall half-way in the natural *tone* order. Reference to the colour circle shows that these are red and blue-green. We therefore take the brightest red (vermilion) and mix a little with blue-green (adjusting the latter with yellow or blue as necessary) until a neutral grey is obtained as before; we now have a blue-green which is the true complementary to vermilion. When this is done, we have established four points in our circle which will enable us to gauge the correct tone order of the remaining colours. Orange and orange-yellow are next mixed from vermilion and mid chrome, making the steps between red and yellow as equal as can be judged by the eye; the opposite blues are then made and tested for true contrast by mixing them to produce neutral grey as before. Lastly yellow-green and green are made from lemon chrome and Antwerp blue and their opposites, purple and crimson, from crimson and ultramarine. This completes the twelve hues which should now appear equally spaced and in correct tone order. We will call this circle No. 1, to which we shall return presently.

Next take a small quantity of each of the twelve colours in turn and by adding white, make a series of equal steps (say three or four) graduating from full strength colour to a pale *tint*. Paint these out on prepared paper, letting each tint lie edge to edge. Then, by adding black similarly, make a series of *shades*, graduating from the pure colour in equal steps to the deepest shades possible without losing colour identity. One should now have twelve strips showing graduated steps ranging from the deepest *shade* to the lightest *tint* of each *hue*. When dry, cut out each strip into a long wedge shape and mount on a grey card to form colour circle No. 2; the *tints* should be in the centre and the *shades* on the outside. It will then be seen at once where the common pigments lie in the colour scale; they will be found among the *shades* near the periphery or outer edge of the circle — ochres, siennas and umbers among the dark yellows and oranges, the red oxides among the dark reds, etc. They will not be exact matches, of course — no single colour and black can match exactly the inherent quality of any individual pigment — but the approximations will be close enough to determine the position of our common pigments on the colour circle. (Incidentally, it is a very good plan to make similar mixtures of all the common pigments with black and white, in order to find their potential *tints* and *shades*. One will learn, for instance, that burnt turkey umber will produce a pinky *beige* and burnt sienna an attractive *peach* in their respective paler tints, while Italian ochre and black will produce a subtle *khaki-green* and so on.)

The chief value of colour circle No. 2, however, is that in addition to the normal hues arranged to show true pigment contrasts lying directly opposite, with harmonies lying adjacent or fairly close, we now have *tints* and *shades* of each colour in similar relationship. Moreover, we can just as readily find *discords* by selecting tints or shades out of their "natural order". A pale violet with a dark yellow provides an instance of maximum discord, while pale blue with dark orange (or brown) and pale purple with deep olive green are other obvious discords. The less obvious discords are those which lie adjacent or fairly close to each other — what would normally be harmonies in their natural tone order become discordant when the tone order is reversed. A few instances are — orange with pink; deep olive green with pale blue-green or blue; pale purple with crimson, etc.

Our circle No. 2 is obviously very useful, but even so it shows change in only two directions, i.e., change of *hue* (yellow to orange — red — purple and so on) and change of *tone* (from light to dark). We can now move in a third direction and show change of *purity*, i.e., from full colour to neutral grey, but we need a separate circle to show this and we therefore return to circle No. 1. We found in building up our colour circle that each pair of true contrasts produced neutral grey when mixed together; if we now take each pair in turn and make a series of inter-mixed hues showing the gradual transition from one to the other we shall discover a lovely range of subtle tertiary hues — just those greyed hues, in fact, that are of most use to us in interior decoration, as we shall see presently.

Take lemon chrome and violet as our first pair of contrasts and mix the two on a palette to obtain neutral grey. Then mix some of this grey with the yellow in varying amounts to produce, say, four equal steps, graduating evenly from yellow to grey; repeat this process with violet and grey. We now have a series of hues, passing from yellow, through grey, to violet in nine equal steps. These mixtures may now be painted side by side on prepared paper with a flat poster brush, the steps being carefully adjusted so that the transition from yellow to violet is made in correct tone order. These tone intervals will lessen as we progress from the vertical to the horizontal axis on the colour circle, where the transition from vermilion through grey to blue-green should be of *equal* tone value.

When the graduated strips are dry, cut into wedge shapes as before and mount in circle No. 1. We now have a good range of subtle greys of widely varying hues, but we must remember that this circle forms only *one* of the innumerable planes which go to the making of a "colour cylinder". Any *tints* or *shades* of these hues would occupy the same relative position in a higher or lower plane in the colour cylinder, according to their tone values, but since few people have time to prepare these different planes they have to be imagined. If the student can visualise colour three-dimensionally in this way, however, he will soon be able mentally to "place" any colour fairly accurately in an imaginary "colour solid".

It should be clearly understood that the preparation of these colour circles is intended (*a*) to demonstrate colour relationship, and (*b*) to arrange in a systematic manner the large number of colours arising from the intermixture of primaries and secondaries. It does not necessarily follow, in mixing colours for actual application on walls, that *pure colours* should be intermixed to produce tertiaries; it would be uneconomic, for instance, to mix a large quantity of a particular greyed hue from pure red, yellow and blue when in practice it may be possible to mix it more easily and cheaply from common pigments. In the studio, however, the designer will find it very convenient, when preparing his schemes, to mix all his tints from a limited range of pure colours, as previously suggested; such tints may then be matched on the job with ordinary materials.

COLOUR APPLICATION

All colour is modified by its environment or surroundings. Its effect can only be judged in relation to other adjacent colours in the scheme, the area occupied by it, and the amount and quality of illumination.

We have noted that when *true contrasts* are placed side by side they intensify each other without changing their hues. A small spot of one on a background of the other will glow with great brilliance, but when distributed in large amounts or in equal areas the effect is clashing and disturbing; this may be avoided by *reducing* the contrast, i.e., by adding a little of each colour to the other and producing what is sometimes called a "broken" colour.

Colours which are widely separated (but not truly opposite) on the circle tend to induce their contrasts in each other and therefore do not make good combinations; orange, for instance, tends to make purple appear bluer whilst purple makes the orange look slightly greenish. The effect of an *induced contrast* is clearly seen when a small patch of light neutral grey paper is placed in the centre of each of larger patches of say red, yellow and blue and viewed simultaneously; the grey will appear to incline towards blue-green, violet and orange respectively (see Plate VII).

It may be noted here that when we are looking at applied colours, we are, in effect, seeing coloured *reflected light* and any results of colour modification will therefore conform to the effects of *light* mixture and not to *pigmentary* mixture. For instance, if we paint bright yellow lines on an ultramarine ground and view from some distance away, the yellow will tend to appear *white*, due to the additive mixture of blue and yellow reflected light (whereas a mixture of blue and yellow *pigments* produces green). Similarly, if we look closely at scarlet spots on a bright green ground, each colour will appear quite intense and brilliant, but if we move away and view at some distance the green will mix optically with the scarlet and will incline towards yellow (due to the additive mixture of green and scarlet). Thus we see that the effect of juxtaposed colours at a distance may be quite different from that at close quarters (see Plate VII). The student should not be content to accept these statements but should test them out for himself.

In practice, of course, the decorator rarely uses colours of maximum purity except perhaps in very small areas. He certainly would not use an all-over pattern in complementary colours without first greying them off considerably; in fact, most of the decorator's palette is made up of greyed hues or pastel tints. Nevertheless, although pale tints will not show the effects of colour modification so noticeably as the examples quoted above, the *tendencies* will be the same. When contrasting tints of fairly equal tone value are intimately juxtaposed (as in sponge-stipple, spray-spatter or combed effects) they tend to neutralise each other when seen at a distance, due to visual intermixture; the resultant "grey", however, has a vibrant quality or liveliness that would be entirely lacking were the two tints actually mixed together.

PLATE VII

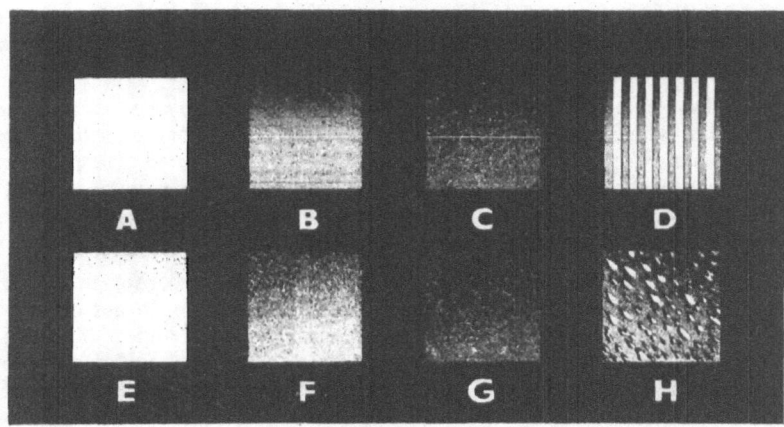

Colour mixing

Examples showing different results from physical and visual intermixture. Yellow and blue (*a* and *b*) mixed as paint produce green (*c*), but the same yellow and blue in fine lines (*d*) produce a greyish white when viewed at a distance. In the case of scarlet and green (*e* and *f*), the physical mixture (*g*) is similar in hue but darker and less vibrant than the optical mixture (*h*).

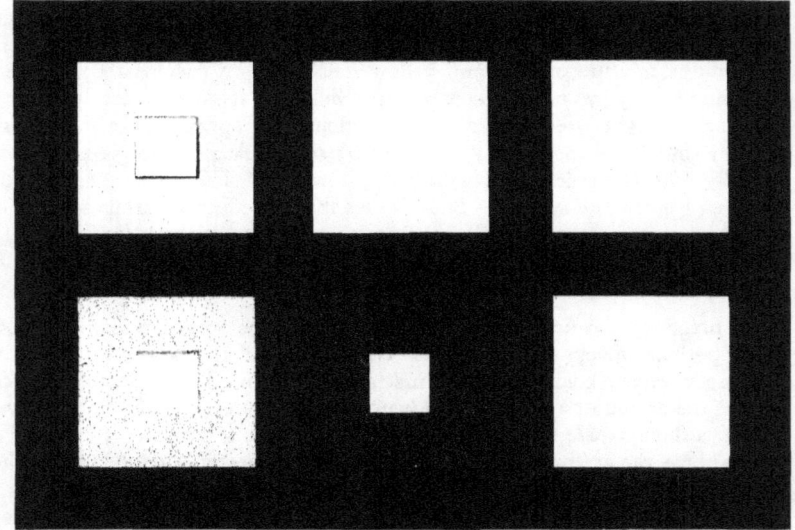

Colour modification

Note the influence of the background on the grey squares which tend towards the complementary hue of the surrounding colour. Thus, on red the grey appears greenish, while on green it inclines towards red, and so on.

Distribution and choice of colour

The art of applying colour lies in its satisfactory distribution. In general terms, the largest areas in a scheme should be occupied by the least insistent hues. In a domestic interior, for instance, ceiling and walls may be painted a fairly pale tint with woodwork to match, stronger tones being used in the furnishings; the deepest tones could be introduced in carpet or floor coverings, but the strongest and purest colours should be reserved for the smallest areas or focal points, such as flowers, pictures, cushions, and so forth.

Where there is dark furniture, as in some dining-rooms, the walls should not be too light, as this makes too great a contrast between walls and furniture; a deep cream, beige or peach would soften this contrast. Dark picture and dado rails, skirtings and architraves tend to "outline" a room and emphasize the wall subdivisions in a rather insistent manner; moreover, the picking out of such features in a colour different from the wall colour may attract more attention to such parts than is desirable.

We personally have a preference for woodwork being treated to match or closely harmonise with the walls unless it is specially desired to create a bright gay atmosphere, as in a nursery or in a kitchen, where a stimulating effect is desired; in such cases a note of contrast may be introduced. Choice of wall colour should always be *appropriate* to the type of room — restful in lounge and bedrooms, warm and cheerful in entrance hall and dining-room, light and cool in a warm room such as the kitchen. It is generally conceded that red is exciting and stimulating, that yellow and orange are both warm and cheerful, that green is pleasant and restful, that blue and grey are cool and tranquil and that purple, though rich and "regal", can also be depressing. Whilst such generalisations may be useful, much depends on the particular *quality* (i.e., purity and tone) of a colour and especially on the influence of other colours which may be in close juxtaposition. Green for instance *can* be pleasant enough, but it can also be very unpleasant in certain circumstances; green and yellow, for example, would be most inappropriate in ships' or aircraft interiors.

Light colours tend to make a room look bigger, whilst dark or strong colours have the opposite effect. Colours in the yellow to red range are of a forward, assertive nature, whilst the cooler greys, greens and blues are quiet and retiring, suggestive of distance. These characteristics may be usefully employed in the appropriate treatment of architectural features — warm advancing colours on projections, columns and pilasters, etc., with the quiet retiring hues for recesses, niches, alcoves and backgrounds. (See also "Colour" page 284.)

Whether or not panelling and enrichments should be picked out in colour is largely a matter of taste. In the case of "period" rooms it should be done in a manner appropriate to the period. In fairly small chambers it should be avoided if possible, since it may give undue emphasis to panels and mouldings and tend towards fussiness; if such mouldings or enrichments are painted uniformly with the wall or ceiling colour, or faintly glazed and wiped, the light and shade of the relief work will usually provide sufficient interest.

PAINTING AND DECORATING

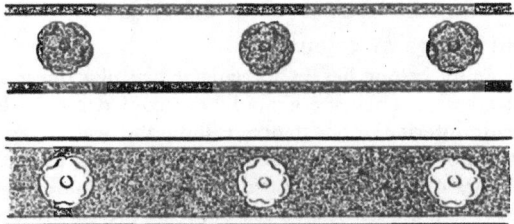

Dark colour applied on raised parts tends to read as a silhouette & hides the detail. When applied to the background, however, the relief ornament is enhanced.

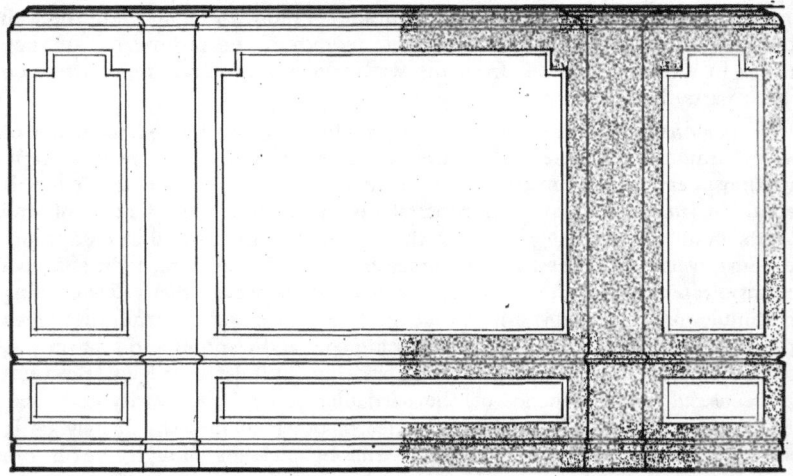

A panelled room usually has sufficient surface interest provided by light & shade of the relief mouldings; when stiles etc. are "picked out" in darker colour the "framing" effect may be unduly emphasised.

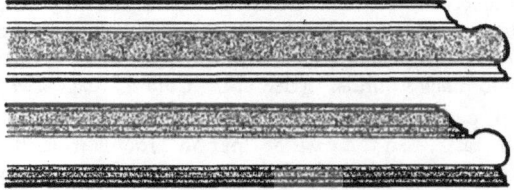

By applying dark colour to the recessed portions of cornices, etc., the natural light & shade is strengthened. Dark colour on the projections does the opposite.

Fig. 192

A large room or assembly hall is rather a different matter. Applied colour may be very desirable in order to avoid monotony, or to provide additional richness and emphasis to relief ornament and mouldings which might otherwise be lost because of height, or inadequate lighting. In picking out cornices, mouldings and enrichments, the colour should be applied in such a way that the relief contours are enhanced, since careless placing may easily result in *hiding* the modelling. For instance, if mouldings or relief ornament are picked out in a colour darker than the ground, the sense of relief is lost and the ornament will tend to appear, from a distance, as a flat painted silhouette. Reverse the position, however, and the ornament is at once enhanced, appearing as a light relief on a darker ground with the modelling now plainly visible (Fig. 192). When modelled relief and projections are thus painted *lighter* than the ground, with hollows and recesses *darker*, the colouring becomes complementary to the natural light and shade and the effect of relief is strengthened. The same thing happens when relief work is scumbled and wiped; the colour left in the hollows and interstices emphasises the higher parts that are wiped clean. (See also "Picking Out", page 360.)

Selective wall treatments

When the four walls of a room are painted a uniform colour, each wall is given equal interest. If we treat one or more walls in a different colour, we tend to give them a *special* interest which may or may not be justified. It is not enough to depart from the orthodox for the mere sake of novelty; walls should receive different colour treatment only for sound logical reasons. On the Continent where the vogue for selective wall treatment first appeared, walls continually lit by a brilliant sun were painted a dark tone to reduce glare, whilst the darkest wall, i.e., that containing the window, would be painted a light colour.

Rooms having panelled walls or other architectural features are not suitable for this sort of thing, of course, but on the other hand, there are those modern box-like rooms, devoid of cornice, picture and dado rail, etc., which simply ask for such treatment. In some cases the apparent height or shape of a room may be modified by careful placing and choice of colour. For instance, in a small bedroom the wall behind the bed could be a warm colour, say pink or peach, with the opposite wall in a pale blue to suggest distance, the remaining walls being treated with the ceiling in cream or off-white. In a long room, the two end walls may be treated in a forward colour such as a warm tan or a sunlight yellow, with the side walls in a retiring colour, e.g., pale blue or grey, the result being to minimise the effect of length. In the case of a long narrow corridor, one wall may be in a fairly strong decided hue and the opposite wall in a pale tint or cream; this tends to offset the "tunnel" effect. Again in a fairly lofty room the ceiling may be apparently lowered by treating it in colour, the walls being in cream or off-white; if the ceiling colour is too heavy or assertive, however, it is likely to appear oppressive. Black ceilings have been tried as a novelty, but such weight overhead is very disturbing and the result is far from happy; there is a sense of rightness in having weight on the floor and when this order is reversed the result is rather distracting. Blue is quite an appropriate colour for ceilings since we are used to seeing it overhead. A low room may have a coloured ceiling providing a very pale tint is used.

With selective wall treatments the attention or interest may be diverted to any desired part of the room simply by means of suitable colour. A wall may be selected as a background for a divan or a bedhead, or, in a dual-purpose room the dining-nook may be treated differently from the rest of the room; thus a "focal point" may be created at will. We have mentioned elsewhere (page 285) how pattern and texture in the form of paperhangings, may also be used in this way, in conjunction with paint and distemper.

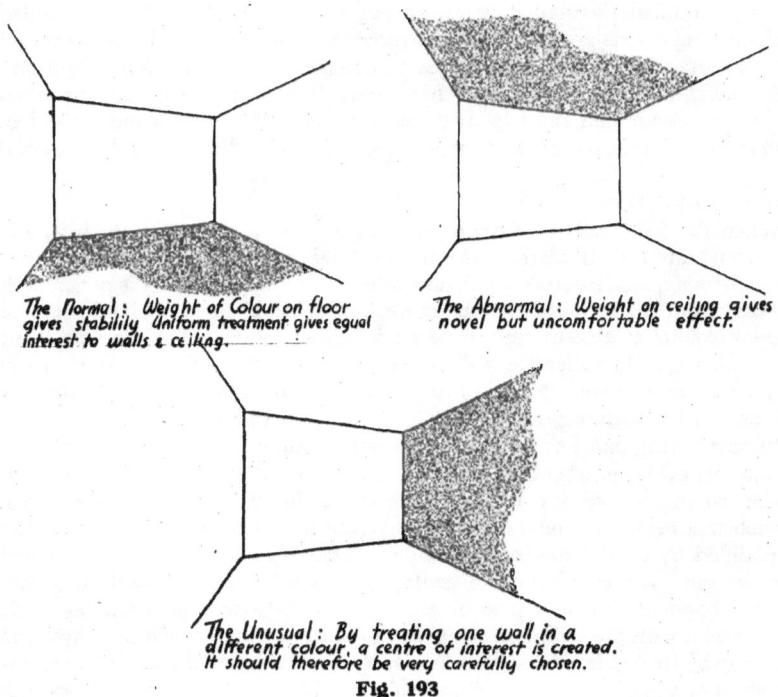

Fig. 193

When walls are treated in different colours it is generally desirable that they should have a decided change of *hue* in order to provide a clearly marked difference, for if there is only a slight variation in colour (as, for instance, cream and light stone) the effect may be totally cancelled out by the varying amount of daylight falling on each wall. The most satisfactory effect is secured when one wall is in a fairly decided colour such as pink, blue, primrose, rust, etc., and the adjacent wall in a neutral tint as, for example, cream, off-white, or a pale grey. When all four walls are evenly lit by means of concealed or diffused lighting, however, a more subtle colour change is then permissible between one wall and another.

In the schoolroom the decorator can employ these unorthodox schemes with every chance of success. Children respond to bright clean colour and desire it in large quantities. A sunlight yellow wall adjacent to cream or off-white walls, with ceiling in pale blue, the woodwork generally in a pale grey and doors in bright blue or signal red — such a scheme provides a stimulating and happy atmosphere for children to work and play in. The "blackboard" too may now provide a useful note of colour, for it has been proved that blue chalk on a yellow board gives greater legibility than white chalk on a blackboard. Adults may be afraid of colour but children simply revel in it.

It is good to note that factory owners are now realising the importance of colour in workshop and canteen. Clean wall tints of high light-reflective value induce high spirits and increase working efficiency. The colour of machinery need not be the usual depressing dark green or brown, since modern synthetic finishes and machine enamels in light colours stand up well to cleaning and hard wear. The "high lighting" of working parts might be used more in this country, as in America. For instance, the general framework of a machine may be in a pale grey or grey-green with dangerous moving parts, start and stop levers, etc., picked out in orange to make them clear yet not too distracting; any parts in shadow or difficult to see are made more visible when picked out in light buff; pulley guards and fences, etc., may be in a medium blue. Thus, machinery can be made good to look at, while increasing the safety factor and general efficiency. In any factory scheme it is highly important that all colours used as symbols should be consistent; signal red, for instance, should be reserved exclusively for all fire appliances, fire buckets, fire doors and escapes, etc., so that these are instantly visible in an emergency and confusion is avoided. Similarly, first-aid cabinets may be a standard bright green (for safety), and pipe lines, electric conduits, etc., may each have their distinctive identification colours as recommended by the British Standards Institution. Colour may thus be used functionally while adding to the general decorative effect.

Public buildings

Bright strong colour is very stimulating and exciting, but the eye quickly tires of it and seeks relief when over-stimulated. Neutral grey and greyed-hues are the most restful to the eyes. In places of entertainment, cafés, cocktail bars and similar places which are seen for comparatively short periods, we expect and enjoy more vigorous colour than we could tolerate in our home surroundings. Warm colours are generally preferred, with notes of sharp contrast introduced in the form of decorative motifs, drapery, seating or flooring. The principle of using paler or slightly greyed hues for the largest areas must still be observed, however, for large masses of strong "primary" colour tend to be overwhelming.

In Municipal or Civic Halls, more restrained and dignified colour is called for, but even here the ceiling may carry rich strong colour, especially if it is fairly high and has elaborately ornamental plasterwork. Deeply coffered (sunk) panels, for instance, may be painted vermilion, or an intense blue, relieved with gold and touches of contrasting colour, the supporting stiles, mouldings and lower walls being in more subdued tints and greyed hues. Such a ceiling seen from the ground will glow with an intense richness which has something of an heraldic quality about it.

In the Place of Worship, any rich colouring should generally be reserved for the focal point — the Chancel or Sanctuary — the rest being quiet and restrained; a scheme having warm dove grey or beige in the Nave, for instance, could have a fairly deep soft blue in the Chancel, relieved if desired with a gold powdering. The frontispiece shows a similar scheme applied to a modern Church interior.

Discordant colour

When the term *discord* is used, one instinctively thinks of music — unpleasant music, perhaps, for discords tend to jar; yet music, and life generally, would be unbalanced and incomplete without occasional discords. While subtle discords in music lend a note of piquancy which is pleasant to the ear, loud and prolonged discords are unbearable. In the same way, discordant colour can be violently unpleasant in large amounts, yet very pleasing and even beautiful when used with restraint and discrimination.

The important difference between aural and visual discords is that, whereas the musician uses discords intentionally and the result is instantly recognised by the hearer, the painter and decorator generally uses discords quite unwittingly and he may find the result pleasing or displeasing without knowing why. This suggests that our musical sense is more developed than our knowledge or appreciation of colour.

We have previously noted that discord is produced when the natural order of colour is reversed and in our Colour Circle No. 2 we have the means of finding such discords at will. We shall therefore know what to expect, for instance, when we make orange or green lighter than yellow; crimson or vermilion lighter than orange; blue lighter than green, etc., and use them adjacently. We shall know why pale mauve or lilac (pale violet) is the most difficult of all colours to use as the basis or background of any scheme, throwing as it does all colours darker than the ground out of their natural tone order. Nevertheless, many beautiful schemes (e.g., Persian wall paintings and manuscripts) are based on pale violet or purple backgrounds, whilst pale blue is also a common ground in oriental decoration; they often have touches of sienna, dark blue and crimson, etc., with a liberal use of grey, black, white and gold which, being neutral, pulls the whole scheme together. These schemes tend to appear somewhat bizarre at first, but their beauty grows as one becomes familiar with them. That is probably true of most schemes based on discords — they have an unusual and subtle quality which may appeal only to a person of cultured or refined taste.

Discordant colour is most unpleasant when used in large areas; for example, pale blue or green walls with brown dado or woodwork (brown being a dark orange). The brown tends to look hot and the walls look pale and washy. Yet a

PLATE VIII

[*Courtesy The Walpamur Co. Ltd.*

The Lounge
A restful scheme in green and russet brown

PLATE IX

(Courtesy The Walpamur Co. Ltd.

The Kitchen
A cheerful scheme in which the large "neutral" area of silver grey helps to balance the primrose, peach, pastel blue, and Tuscan red.

single note of brown, such as a sepia print on a pale blue wall, can look most satisfactory. The decorator need not therefore avoid discords, but he should try to recognise them and use them always with great caution.

The limited palette

We have noted that, in theory, any hue can be produced by intermixture of the three pigmentary primaries — red, yellow and blue — but that because of the darkening or neutralising effect of mixing pigments, the resultant hues are much less pure than pigments already available. It is this very neutralisation, however, that is responsible for the unified and harmonious result when a strictly limited palette is used.

If a complete mural or decorative painting, for instance, is carried out solely with (say) lemon chrome, vermilion and ultramarine, using white to lighten the tone and black to darken (though the latter is rarely necessary, since near-black is obtained by mixing all three primaries), the various hues obtained by intermixture are all *related* since they have something in common — a little of each other in their make-up. Such a palette is capable of producing a fairly bright range of hues, but by choosing three duller primaries such as yellow ochre, light red (or Venetian) and ultramarine, a more subdued and subtle colour range is produced, which, if pitched fairly light in tone, gives some lovely "pearly" or opalescent tints, well suited to large-scale murals where quiet and dignified colour is desired.

One is not obliged to use three colours, of course. Two-colour combinations such as Prussian blue and raw or burnt umber, ultramarine and burnt sienna, etc., produce a fine range of related greys when intermixed and reduced with white. A fine range of monochrome tints and shades too may be obtained from almost any of the common pigments when mixed with black and white. Pigments such as Prussian blue, Italian ochre, raw umber, Indian red and deep Brunswick green are each suitable for monochromatic murals, giving an effect similar to the familiar two-colour half-tone magazine illustrations, in which a single colour is overprinted with black.

Incidentally, when white is added to certain colours the resulting tint inclines towards blue. This is probably most noticeable with bright reds which, on reduction, tend towards purple or violet. A little chrome yellow is needed to correct this, or alternatively, tints may be made with cream instead of white.

Colour and lighting

It has already been pointed out in the section on *Light and Pigment* that the sensation of colour cannot exist without light and that pigments can only reflect their true colour when illumined by light which contains their colour. Thus, if red pigment is illumined by white or red light it will reflect red; if however, it is illumined only by blue-green light, there are no red rays to reflect and it will therefore appear black. For the same reason, violet seen under a strong yellow light and blue illuminated by amber or deep orange lighting would both appear black or near-black, since any coloured surface illuminated by a light of contrasting colour will absorb all rays and reflect none. These extremes are not normally encountered in practice, except perhaps in stage lighting, where the principle is sometimes used to produce the illusion of quick-change effects.

It will be seen then, that where coloured lighting is installed, as in modern cinemas, cafés and hotels, the colours for walls and furnishings require to be carefully chosen to avoid being negatived by the lighting. Such lighting normally contains a large proportion of white light, but nevertheless by reason of its colour content it will tend to neutralise any colours in the decorations in contrast to it. Thus a pale blue seen under amber lighting would tend towards russet or warm grey.

Ordinary electric light (*tungsten filament*) is rich in yellow and red rays (especially that from low wattage lamps) and we therefore find a corresponding deterioration in the purity of blue and violet tints in such light. Yellows are strengthened, though, curiously enough, they may appear *paler* if the surrounding colour is much debased by the same lighting. *Fluorescent* lighting is supplied in a variety of tints, each having different colour rendering properties; "warm white", for example, has a decided pinky tint, while "daylight" fluorescent is a cold white which is said to differ very slightly, if at all, from natural daylight. There appears to be no standard as yet, however, and some "daylights" are distinctly bluish (particularly towards the end of their useful life) and this, of course, affects adversely any warm colours in the scheme. It is very important to remember that, in addition to the neutralising effect which occurs when the illuminant is in contrast to the colour of the decorations, there is also bound to be a loss in lighting efficiency since some of the light rays are being absorbed instead of being reflected.

Sufficient has been said to show that in designing any interior colour scheme, the decorator and the lighting engineer must work in close collaboration and that, wherever possible, the decorator should try out all colours under the form of lighting to be used.

THE BRITISH COLOUR COUNCIL

This body was formed in 1930 with the object of promoting close co-operation between related industries using colour, and of standardising colour names. Hitherto, it has been impossible to order a colour by name with any certainty of getting the colour visualised, since there has been no accepted standard for names such as rose, beige, peach, apple green, etc. Moreover, it has often been impossible to obtain a good match in different materials such as vitreous enamel, tiles and plastics, etc. The Council has issued a Dictionary of Colour Standards for Interior Decoration, designed to ensure that such finishes, along with paints, carpets and furnishing fabrics, will in future be correlated.

By arranging exhibitions which demonstrate co-ordination of colour and design, the Council hope to arouse public interest in colour and to raise the general standard of taste. It is obviously in the decorator's interest, therefore, to follow the Council's activities as closely as possible.

THE IMPORTANCE OF COLOUR

COLOUR plays an important part in furnishing, and modern schemes provide a wealth of opportunity for originality. But balance must be maintained, or the effect may border upon the grotesque. Harmony can only be achieved by at least an elementary knowledge of colour values. The primary colours are Blue, Red, and Yellow, and the admixture of any two of these colours results in a secondary colour. Blue and red make purple. Blue and yellow give green. Red and yellow produce orange. By mixing any two of these the tertiary colours are obtained, and among these will be found, according to the preponderance of one or the other, the large number of beautiful shades so much in use to-day.

When a furnishing scheme appears to lack colour, the strong probability is that it lacks contrasting colour. The artist uses contrasting—or complementary—colours to emphasise the tones of a picture, and the making of a striking furnishing scheme also depends on a similar stratagem. To enhance blue, introduce orange. To strengthen red, use green. To augment yellow, purple may be relied upon. It will be apparent that certain secondary colours contrast with certain primary colours, and if this is borne in mind when designing any scheme, the result will be harmonious and pleasing. Black, also, the combination of all three primaries, must not be overlooked in its usefulness. It can be used advantageously with practically any colour, or with its contrast —white. If these two are mixed the result is grey, another delightful addition to any scheme. White can also be mixed with any colour according to the shade required. Here then are all the elements necessary, and from which any shade can be obtained.

The practical application of colour in Home Furnishing and Decoration is a fascinating study, and I commend it to my readers who have imagination and a balanced appreciation of colour values. A few suggestions here may help to stimulate ideas—some attractive colour schemes may be the result. As I have already said, black can be used most advantageously. With white it is most effective. Black and silver is another delightful combination, and so also is black and grey. Black and yellow are said to possess the strongest "attention value." Black and red—or orange—give the impression of a comfortable, warm atmosphere. Black and blue discreetly used can be employed for charming interior schemes, and black and green, if the right blue-green called Viridian is selected, are intensely pleasing.

To achieve one's ideal in any scheme, it is necessary to be able to visualise colour and to reject anything which is not in perfect harmony. The successful gardener must of necessity be ruthless at times to get the desired effect, and the interior decorator must be prepared to adopt the same principle. Having decided on the colours which are to be incorporated in any decorative scheme, it is imperative that all others which are not in complete harmony be eliminated. An immense amount of help in this connection is given by furnishing firms who specialise in colour schemes. The ideal which one has in mind may quite possibly be set out in the showrooms, and if it is not, all the material is there, so that within a short time the actual carpet, curtains, wallpaper and furniture can be assembled and the scheme becomes a practical reality instead of an "idea," thereby enabling one to judge whether the colour combination is as successful as was anticipated.

I always think it is a pity that greater use is not made of the service which is so willingly given by furnishing firms, such as Messrs. Oetzmann, particularly by those whose ideas are undecided, and who need help and guidance in the decoration or modernising of their rooms.

Facts Worth Remembering

It is an excellent plan to decorate and furnish any home with the thought in one's mind of the effect upon the senses of friends who may come on a visit—to make them feel entirely at their ease without knowing the reason. The visitor's mind will react favourably to pleasant surroundings, possibly without his taking note of any one thing in particular, and if this is accomplished, the originator of the decorative scheme will not have failed. Furnishing schemes have a direct effect on the senses, even apart altogether from the colour appeal. Take for instance one sense which would hardly be thought to enter into consideration in such a matter—touch. If, upon entering a hall, one walks upon hard linoleum, however beautiful it may be, the feeling of comfort is lacking. There is an instinctive command to walk warily—not to make too much noise—and consequently, however much time and thought may have been spent on the whole scheme, it fails in its first purpose—to make a pleasurable appeal.

A good carpet with a substantial underfelt beneath it, or a rug will instantly make that appeal to the feet, which have experienced the hard pavement outside, and may be tired. It is worth while to remember that the lower extremities are usually the first to register actual discomfort. Many people may prefer parquet floors, and indeed the style of decoration may call for this style of treatment. But parquet floors without good rugs are unyielding things, and though they are hygienic the feeling of comfort is not so complete as when one "walks on velvet."

Then again, there is the lighting of a room, when another sense comes into action, namely sight. Lighting must not be blatant or hard, but it should be well distributed. There should not be particularly bright lighting in the centre of the room, with all the rest in semi-darkness. So many varieties of illumination are available to-day to allow us to dispense with this reminder of the oil lamp on a table. Reflecting ceiling lights are quite satisfactory for a room which it is desired to be well lit, and give the nearest approach to daylight lighting, for it is not an easy matter to arrange a colour scheme which will be equally pleasing by daylight and by the older methods of artificial illumination. Modern lighting offers many possibilities, and a visit to the Lighting Service Bureau, Savoy Hill, W.C., followed by one to the electrical department of a house like Oetzmann's will prove to be the simplest and best method of coming to a clear decision on this matter. To state one's ideas, and to have them demonstrated as an actual fact, is more helpful than anything I can advocate.

The Hall

In the planning of colour schemes the hall is important, for here one receives the first impression of a home and of the character of its inhabitants. So much can be accomplished in a hall with just one or two well-chosen pieces of furniture and a definite scheme of decoration. Those who are artistic will probably have carefully selected pictures in the hall —those who revel in antiques will place one of their treasures in it—those who love the comforts of life will give the hall a restful atmosphere. I feel it is a place which should give a feeling of welcome to all who enter, and consequently it should be warm in its colour tones. Here is one colour scheme for the hall, in principal colourings of red, pale green and black. A thick pile carpet with patterning in red and green, light greenish-grey walls with two or three really good modern water-colours in the narrowest of black frames, and wide white mounts, a red lacquer chair, table, hall wardrobe and lamp. This pen picture of a hall surely suggests comfort, warmth, colour sense and a welcome.

I have advocated good modern water-colours as pictures in this hall with a very definite reason, because I feel that they are absolutely essential to the scheme. Heavy oil paintings for it would not be my choice—however valued they were—because something lighter in feeling is required. In ultra-modern decoration, pictures can be dispensed with altogether if desired, but in the hall outlined above they would certainly add to its interest. It may be that I have a liking for beautiful original pictures, and I cannot imagine anyone interested in colour who would not at any rate consider the inclusion of carefully selected and carefully placed works of art in most furnishing schemes.

The Dining-room

In imagination I will try to build up the room where hospitality is dispensed. A thick carpet with its main colourings of brown, gold and blue, cool grey walls panelled in oak, chintz curtains and pelmet picking up the gold and blue. Dark oak furniture and tall-back chairs having seats of gold-coloured material, and if space permits a brown hide settee and easy chairs with back cushions of the same gold material.

The mantelpiece, which could either tone with the walls or the furniture, should have blue tiles at the back and in the hearth. I think this room has possibilities, and when individual likes and dislikes are settled, it could be a dignified room with a very definite appeal to anyone's colour sense.

The Lounge

This is the room which is not only to give comfort, but to suggest it in its general scheme. Great strides have been made in comparatively recent years in making furniture really comfortable. The time has passed—not so very many years ago—when chairs and settees were so deliberately unrelenting that it must have been a pleasure to stand. To-day it is possible to revel in luxurious comfort on well-sprung furniture, for many armchairs have spiral springs in seats, backs and arms which give to the body with every movement, and loose cushions filled with beautifully soft down, so that one literally sinks into them to be encompassed about with resilience. The comfort of the lounge is therefore available, but the colour scheme of the room has to be determined. It must not be too heavy in tone, so I suggest here that the main colours should be camel, blue-green and beige.

The carpet could be camel with a green border, and the curtains mainly beige, with a pattern in green and touches of coral. The wallpaper a cool beige. The upholstered furniture would be covered with a fawn material, and would have its loose back cushions in green. Then with a writing-desk, a bookcase, a low tea-table, a floor standard lamp, and any other desired pieces—all in figured walnut—this room should be full of interest.

A scheme perhaps a little difficult to visualise, but with carefully chosen colours, one that could not be otherwise than charming.

The Bedroom

This must be a bright room, unless the aspect is very sunny, so let the walls be primrose yellow, and the carpet have a preponderance of that shade which green takes when the sun shines on it. The curtains should pick up both these colours. The furniture can be of figured walnut, with all its rich and wonderful tones, and if chosen in a dignified modern style the room would look delightful.

Now there enters the thought of contrast, so if the bedspread is primrose, a down quilt of soft powder blue is placed upon it. A bedroom easy chair is covered in material with a natural ground, but incorporating the same blue. A lamp on the bedside table, and the light over the dressing-table have touches of the same colour.

It will be seen that the whole scheme is yellow, sunny green, and powder blue—daring, but entirely beautiful.

The Bathroom

This can be made most attractive if the walls are painted or enamelled in pinky-beige or cream, with the ceiling treated in a lighter tint of the same hue, and the woodwork in apple green or pale coral. The furniture could tone with either the walls or woodwork. Colours in a bathroom should not be glaring, but subtle.

THE IMPORTANCE OF COLOUR

The Kitchen

Apart from the consideration that the kitchen must be well lighted, well ventilated, and well planned, it can also have its colour scheme. For the walls and ceiling washable papers, good enamel, paint, tiles and their substitutes are well employed where hygienic cleanliness must be thought of first. A dado of white tiles finishing with a row of blue tiles at the top, with white enamelled walls and ceiling, is refreshingly clean if the woodwork is painted blue.

Choose black and white or grey jaspe linoleum for the floor, and black and white, or blue and white check curtains for the window. A white enamelled china cupboard, with a blue and white dinner service will look particularly well. A dresser, should your kitchen boast one, may be made more practical by having the upper shelves fitted with glass doors, so that the china is not exposed to dust.

If wallpaper is chosen for the walls of a kitchen, choose a waterproof one with a matt surface, when stains can be removed with a damp cloth—a very necessary provision in a kitchen. Or a really good wallpaper can be effectively enamelled to any desired colour.

There are diverse opinions about ceilings in kitchens. Paint or enamel can be used, but however perfect the ventilation, steam will rise, and if a ceiling does not absorb it at all, there will be drips from it. Of course, ordinary whitewash, which seems to be the best coating for kitchen ceilings, on account of its absorbency, can be made into a blue or any other colour wash by the addition of suitable colouring.

New Rooms for Old

Generally after a period of years, the accumulation of oddments in a home tends to make it a place which retains many memories, but with all the artistic taste in the world it could not be transformed into a beautiful home unless drastic alterations and ruthless deletions were made. It is comparatively easy to decide on a colour scheme when everything is to be new, and the plain walls and bare boards can be covered according to the selected colourings, but the task is now to convert rooms which have almost become the storehouses of heirlooms, into rooms which have definite colour values.

The days of the "parlour" have gone by, but reminders of this Victorian atrocity are still to be found in many of to-day's drawing-rooms or lounges, largely because the hoarding instinct is difficult to eradicate in most people, especially where furniture is concerned.

I am imagining an everyday sort of drawing-room or lounge, and I trust none of my readers will think that I have been prying into their homes because of any apparent likeness which they may possibly notice. It is probably one of many thousands decidedly similar. This drawing-room has a good Wilton carpet, well covered with a conventional but nondescript design. The prevailing tones of it are rose, black and grey. There is also a fine black skin hearthrug. The walls are hung with a floral paper in

THE "SPRINGVALE"
A shaded decoration formed by 21 inch-wide papers hung horizontally. There are three different shaded papers, each graduated from its lower edge upward. Above these a paper without graduation is used, which can be repeated to continue the design to any height desired.

Reproduction by Courtesy of Arthur Sanderson & Sons, Ltd.

THE "SLOANE"

The horizontal bands of green "Sycamore" paper divide the walls in pleasing proportions and can be adapted to suit structural features. The natural colour Sycamore can be hung horizontally or vertically, space being allowed for the bands.

fawn shade, with pinks and greens. There is a three-piece suite—settee and two easy chairs—in a somewhat mournful blue and fawn tapestry covering, and in all probability with a geometrical design. They are delightfully resilient and comfortable, and the tapestry may possibly wear for ever, but it simply does not fit into any sort of colour scheme. A bookcase-cum-china-cabinet in mahogany graces one wall, a mahogany upright piano hides most of another, the tiled fireplace with quite a good mantelpiece occupies the third, and the bay window has orange artificial silk curtains. A couple of tub chairs, with nondescript tapestry seats, a dwarf tea-table, and a wall mirror, all in mahogany, complete my imaginary room.

To transform this room into one boasting some character means that drastic steps must be taken. The carpet is not the best foundation on which to build, but it is too good a carpet to be thrown away, so that with its rose, black and grey it must remain, while the curtains are altered to harmonise with it.

Selecting the rose as the colour upon which to consider possibilities, it is found that light green is its complementary. So the curtains become a soft shade of grey with a pattern in light green. Loose covers for the settee and easy chairs are secured in similar tones, and the seats of the tub chairs are made to correspond.

Antiquated vases are deliberately replaced with just one or two pieces which are also neutral, and the transformation is practically complete.

c

When refurnishing of any sort is decided upon, it is well to remember that conformation to a colour scheme costs no more than a hurried buying of certain pieces, and the joy of seeing the result of one's care in selection is ample reward for the forethought required.

Color Collaboration

The Power Is Yours

COLOR is the most important single factor in interior decoration. With color you create beauty, converting four bare walls to a room of charm and vibrant personality. With color you can determine a room's atmosphere, changing a dingy dullness to sunshine's glow; or a cold indifference to a welcoming warmth. With color you can establish optical illusions through emphasis or a planned neutrality. You can seemingly "push back" closely oppressing walls, or rectify any architectural oddities in the room. There is more sheer magic in your hands, with the knowledge of a controlled use of color, than in any bagful of the great Houdini's tricks—and it's yours for the reading. All you need to do is to grasp a few simple color fundamentals outlined for you here as they apply to decorating. With a keener appreciation of what you can do with color and what color means in your life, a whole new joy awaits you.

First Step—Know Your Colors

There are really no do's and don'ts as to what colors you may combine. It's how you combine them under given conditions that counts. There are really no do's and don'ts as to color restrictions for any given purpose, provided you understand what results to expect and work for that effect.

You don't have to belong to the "chosen few" with a special color intuition in order to use colors cleverly. *Color is an exact science,* but you must understand it, and know what to expect under varying conditions. For example, perhaps you were intrigued by a model room done in magenta, green, mauve and gold. You proceeded to copy it for your own room, only to experience disappointment. It wasn't that you couldn't use this combination of colors effectively in your home but that you needed to understand the necessity of applying them differently. The model room was

light and large; yours, smallish and dull. The mauve walls of the model room did not give enough light reflection in your duller room to seem cheerful. You needed, instead, to use the gold of that scheme in a soft light yellow tone for your walls. The rich magenta satin draperies and sofa of the model room were a magnificent accent in the larger, more formal setting, but became an overwhelming note when confined to the smaller area of your home. A softer tone and duller fabric, though of the same magenta color family, would have been charming in your smaller more informal home, whereas the magenta satin seemed garish. It all reduces to the formula of knowing colors and what they will do for you.

The Color Wheel

Artists and scientists have long referred to the spectrum (rainbow) as the source of all color. For white light (sunlight) is the source of all light rays and the rainbow is just sunlight split into its component light rays of violet, indigo, blue, green, yellow, orange and red which, when focused by our eyes, interpret color for us. A detailed scientific explanation,

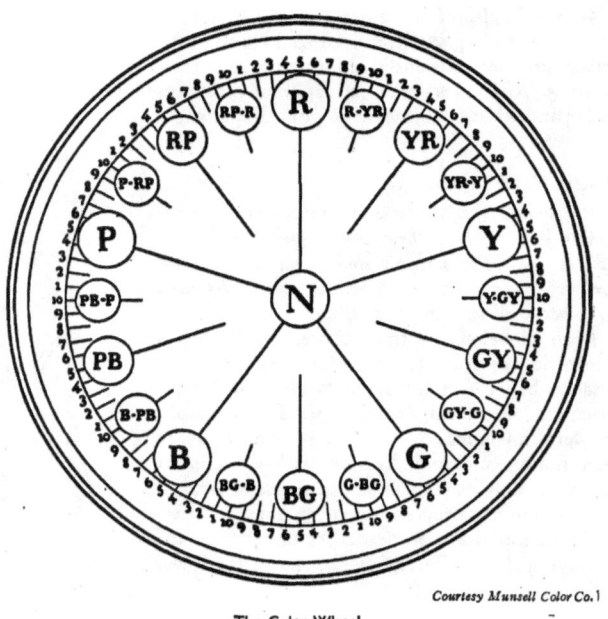

Courtesy Munsell Color Co.

The Color Wheel

however, of the phenomenon of color is too technical for our purposes here. For those of you, and I hope there are many, who wish to understand more of the scientific causes of color sensation, other texts are recommended in the reading list for this chapter. Sufficient, though, for our intention here to interpret color's practical application in decorating, is the provision that you start with the color wheel of the MUNSELL SYSTEM.

The MUNSELL SYSTEM is the one recommended by the United States Department of Agriculture, and used by the *Encyclopædia Britannica*, Walt Disney productions and many leading artists and decorators.

Study the color wheel carefully. You will note that there are *five Captains of color*, or principal hues, namely, RED, YELLOW, GREEN, BLUE AND PURPLE. Note that ORANGE (one of the rainbow hues, called yellow-red on this chart) has slipped to a second place. (Older color charts of other systems do not designate it this way but indicate RED, YELLOW, BLUE as primary colors; and ORANGE, GREEN, PURPLE as secondary colors.) Research, however, indicates that the new distribution of starting the color wheel with *five color captains* allocating ORANGE to an intermediary position, produces more perfect color blending.

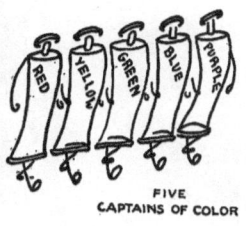

FIVE CAPTAINS OF COLOR

Next look for the *five Intermediary Hues* of YELLOW-RED, GREEN-YELLOW, BLUE-GREEN, PURPLE-BLUE, and RED-PURPLE. These *intermediary hues*, as they are called, result from the *combination of two adjacent* principal hues, GREEN-YELLOW being the combination of GREEN and YELLOW, *et cetera*.

Now locate on the chart the *ten Second Intermediary Hues* which result from combining adjacent intermediary hues. This extension, or color blending, can go on endlessly with an ever-increasing color range. For practical reasons here we stop at the one hundred hue mark which shows the *eighty special intermediary hues* on the chart by the numerals 1, 2, 3, 4, 5, 6, 7, 8, 9.

FIVE INTERMEDIARY HUES

Harmonious Colors

Hues which are adjacent on the chart are similar because they have a common basic color element. Because of this common color relationship they are said to be *harmonious*. For example, green, yellow-green, and yellow all have the common color *yellow*. Or blue, blue-green, and green all have *blue* as a basic color element. If you will get out a paint box and experiment you'll soon refresh your color memory in addition to having some fun.

Since kindergarten days you have probably known that, with a box of paints containing red, yellow, and blue you can try out various mixtures and derive any color in creation. In pigments, for instance,

>RED plus YELLOW—ORANGE
>RED plus BLUE —PURPLE
>BLUE plus YELLOW—GREEN

Then by taking the three new colors—orange, purple and green—and in turn mixing each with the original three—red, blue and yellow—a new set of colors come into being:

		Popularly called
RED plus PURPLE	—RED-PURPLE	—MULBERRY
RED plus ORANGE	—RED-ORANGE	—RUSSET
BLUE plus PURPLE	—BLUE-PURPLE	—PLUM
BLUE plus GREEN	—BLUE-GREEN	—SLATE
YELLOW plus ORANGE	—YELLOW-ORANGE	—FLAME
YELLOW plus GREEN	—YELLOW-GREEN	—CITRON

Now note that we did not list mixing RED with GREEN, nor BLUE with ORANGE, nor PURPLE with YELLOW because these combinations neutralize each other and turn the combination to neutral gray. Why? *Whereas red, yellow and blue by various combinations give us all colors in pigments, the three if blended together at the same time neutralize each other and form neutral gray.* Mixing red with green would be blending red with blue and yellow, the two colors which originally made the green, and so with the other combinations as noted. RED plus YELLOW plus BLUE—NEUTRAL GRAY.

Do not let this breakdown showing how paint colors are mixed confuse you because we start the color wheel with the *five captains of color.* The color wheel is arranged to show you how to classify colors and how to more easily develop interesting color combinations on a scientific basis. But this breakdown showing you how to mix colors from pigments is quite another phase of the color story.

To sum up pigment color derivation briefly, no colors, when in combination, will produce either red, yellow, or blue of the spectrum hues, yet from these three pigments—red, yellow and blue—you can mix any color (excepting white and black) that you desire.

Contrasting or Complementary Colors

Just as the colors that are close together on the color wheel are related and harmonious, those which are farthest apart, or on opposite sides of the color wheel, are unrelated,

for they have nothing in common. *These unrelated colors are called contrasting or complementary hues.* The greater the distance apart on the circle, the wider the contrast, until we come to those colors diametrically opposite, which are complete color contrasts such as blue and yellow-red. *Yet opposites attract.* Consulting the chart, you see that the color directly opposite another on the wheel is in each case that color's most perfect contrast, and is called its *complement*. Complementary colors blended together in light become white but in pigments they blend to neutral gray.

Applying Complementary Colors in Decorating

Complementary colors in pigment, when blended, gray or neutralize each other. This is one of the most important color facts to remember. Suppose you are working with a green paint for a wall color and it is too noisy and vibrant. You want to tone it down, or gray it, so to speak, but not lighten or darken your green tone. Add, then, some of that color's complement, the color opposite it on the chart, and your color will be softer and less stringent. In this instance with your green, if it is a green tending to blue-green, you note that a member of the red family is its complement. You have to learn to recognize colors and classify them nearest to a dominant tone of the chart.*

Although complementary colors neutralize each other in pigment mixtures, *they enhance each other when used side by side*, as with fabrics, each making the other more vibrant. This was true when you placed that warm gold chair next to your blue sofa. Remember this point in selecting adjacent colors in decorating. This added vibrancy is due, if you want the technical explanation for your own satisfaction, to what is called AFTER IMAGE. As an experiment, focus your attention for a minute on a strong color, such as red. Now shift your gaze to another object of a different color. As you do so, close your eyes for a second and in a flash you will see the shape of the red object at which you were just gazing, but this time, in your closed eyes, it will appear not as red but as red's complement, blue-green. Your eyes, "fatigued" with red, seek the relief and satisfaction of balance found in the complementary color. (More about this when we discuss how to develop different color schemes.) This demonstrates why complementary colors enhance each other when in juxtaposition. You can readily see that as you concentrate on red and then immediately switch to blue-green, the blue-

---

* For little cost you can procure a color wheel in colors at any leading Art Supply store. Be sure it corresponds to the Munsell System.

green will seem the stronger for the added image of blue-green already in your eye.

The Two Color Clans

Colors divide into two color clans. The rainbow red, red-yellow and their associate colors, indicative of sun, fire, and stimulating activity, belong to the WARM GROUP and are known as *warm colors*. The blues, blue-greens and violets, the colors of sky, water and mountain shadows are known as the COOL GROUP and each is known as a *cool color*. Literally this is so. If you were to take color's temperature with a thermopile (a highly sensitive thermometer) and place it in the different parts of the spectrum (as shown in light, of course) you would find that the red end registers warmer than the blue. *But pay special attention to* GREEN *and* RED-PURPLE, *for these in pure colors register relatively no more warmth than coolness; on the color wheel they mark the dividing line between the two color groups*. Refer again to the chart and draw the line dividing the circle this way. Also note that each warm color has a cool color for a complement and vice versa.

As you work with a color now you will always classify it as belonging either to the WARM or the COOL family. Certain greens and red-purples you will classify as being on the fence. Thus you will immediately know the personality of your color and what reaction to expect.

Warm Colors	*Cool Colors*
are	are
stimulating	restful
noisy	quiet
active	soothing
cheering	tranquil

Warm colors add spice and life to a room while cool colors are pleasantly refreshing. It is wise to use both freely, as we shall see as we go along.

WARM COLORS

Advancing and Receding Colors

WARM *colors are* ADVANCING *and focus objects to seem nearer*. COOL *colors are* RECEDING *and focus objects so that they are seemingly farther away from our eyes*. So, when we speak of advancing and receding colors it is no decorator's fancy but an actual physical fact as to the way color rays are registered by our eyes. *Actually red rays register behind the retina of the eye while blue rays (we speak of rays here as referring to color) register in front of the retina*. In making the compensating adjustment so that we see these various colored objects in sharp focus, the eye necessarily "pulls" red nearer to the eye than it actually is. Thus the chair in red seems nearer or more advancing. With blue the reverse occurs. Blue objects are necessarily "pushed back" for proper focus; so the blue chair seems farther away than the red one, even though they are of the same size and at the same distance from you.

PURPLE *and* YELLOW, on the other hand, focus normally. Our eyes make no special adjustment as we see these colors. These two colors, then, are known as *normal* colors because they are neither advancing nor receding.

      RED and RELATED COLORS —ADVANCING
      BLUE and RELATED COLORS—RECEDING
      PURPLE and YELLOW   —NORMAL

Can you not readily imagine what knowing just this one phase of color does for you in decorating? Whole new avenues of approach open before you when you realize that at your own direction in color choice you can determine whether a wall should "close in" to make a room seem more cozy; whether it should "shove back" to give more breathing space; or whether it should "stay put" since there is no special reason for any corrective treatment. This, of course, is but one of the many applications you will make of this knowledge.

Size Increasing and Size Diminishing Colors

Not only do WARM COLORS stimulate and advance, but by the same token they are *size increasing*. They make individual objects seem larger. WARM COLORS also tend to blend and unite objects. With COOL COLORS the action is reversed. While COOL COLORS give that wonderful sense of poise and restfulness, and while they tend to increase our vista, they likewise tend to make individual objects seem SMALLER, and to separate and break up groups.

      WARM COLORS—SIZE INCREASING
      COOL COLORS —SIZE DIMINISHING

RECAPITULATION

WARM COLORS	COOL COLORS
are	are
stimulating	restful
noisy	quiet
active	aloof
cheering	soothing

COOL COLORS

RECAPITULATION (*Continued*)

Advancing	*Receding*
Drawing objects closer	Pushing objects back
Size Increasing	*Size Diminishing*
Making the individual object larger	Making the individual object smaller
Tend to blend and unite groups.	Tend to separate and disintegrate groups.

*Slanting these facts to our practical application in decorating, you will use **warm colors** to:*

1. Bring life, added warmth and a feeling of glow to a color scheme. (You'll be grateful for warm colors on a cold night.)
2. Focus special attention on any object or wall by bringing it to closer view.
3. Give added significance to an object by seeming to increase its size.
4. Tone walls and floor to blend a room which seems at odds.

But by these very attributes, you must remember these same colors can work conversely if used too generously, causing irritation instead of creating a pleasant warmth; they may advance walls in a small room where the walls need to recede; or call especial attention to an object of ungainly proportions, such as that old chair you had upholstered as a tideover and which you certainly do not want to steal the show.

Cool Colors Will:

1. Bring an atmosphere of rest and relaxation to a room.
2. Extend range of vision, push back the walls of the too small room.
3. Reduce the size of an object. A sofa in soft green will not seem as large as if upholstered in coral.
4. Give a sense of separateness sometimes desired.

As a note of warning, complete coolness in a room is unpleasant. The room lacks cheer. A large proportion of cool colors makes the large barny room seem more barren, especially in a cool climate. A cool color in a light value, in particular, may not be strong enough to give sufficient emphasis. An entire room of cool colors tends to separate into the individual objects rather than seem a unified whole.

Color's Dimensions

To work with color still more effectively you need to know about the dimensions or measurements of color. Just as you, as an individual, are so tall, so wide and tip the scale at a specific weight, each color, so to speak, has individual measurements. These are called

HUE, VALUE, AND CHROMA

HUE is that singular characteristic which sets each color apart from its color fellows. HUE is a color's name or identification tag such as red, yellow, green, blue, *et cetera*. HUE also indicates a color's position on the color wheel (also called color circuit).

The hue of a color is not changed unless you add an entirely different hue to the original one. You may lighten a color with white, or darken it with black, making light blue, or deep blue, but it's still blue and known by that name. You may likewise make it weaker or more intense, but it is still blue.

VALUE: To "speak lightly" of a color is entirely correct, for this is the meaning of VALUE. The VALUE of a color is its degree of luminosity, or lightness and darkness in relation to white and black. *White* is the lightest light known and pure white is so light that you can see no color in it. *Pure black*, on the other hand, is the darkest of darks, so dark that no color can be distinguished in it either. Yet between these two extremes there are varying steps of light strength which range from black and then the darkest gray, just above black, to a barely perceptible gray which comes next to white. There are nine such gradations (or steps) easily visible to the eye, and color can be compared to these various intermediate levels of light strength ranging from black to white. Yellow, for instance, is a color which is usually light and is nearer to white than to black. Purple, on the other hand, is a darker color and nearer to black than to white.

Munsell Values	Description
1 and below	very dark
1–3	dark
4–6	medium
7–9	light

Colors of light value are more light-giving than colors of low value. Colors of low value are more light absorbing. A bottle-green, for example, for the walls of a dismal hall, wouldn't give the cheering light that yellow would.

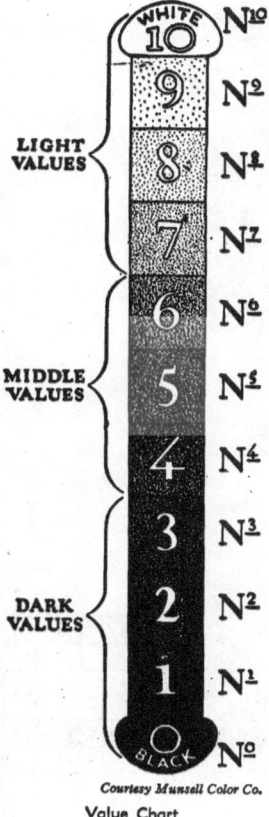

Courtesy Munsell Color Co.

Value Chart

Sharp contrasts in value influence each other when used together in decorating. If you place a white chair against a full-bodied colored background, the sharpness of the contrast makes the white seem whiter and the color seem darker by their very difference in value. A dark object, on the other hand, against a light value background makes the light background seem lighter. Use this fact to advantage when you want to emphasize a situation, and guard against too sharp contrasts when you don't. Value contrast is particularly important in the selection of wall papers and fabrics. (Each is treated more fully in its respective chapter.)

    TINT—A pure color lightened with white to raise its value.

    SHADE—A pure color darkened with black, or another darkening agent, to lower its value.
    Shell pink is a *tint* and maroon is a *shade*.

CHROMA is color's third dimension. Drop a dry sponge into a pail of water. When it becomes so saturated that it cannot possibly absorb another drop it is comparable to a color of full chroma, or full color strength. Two colors, for instance, may be of similar hue (both blue) and the same in value (that is, one is neither darker nor lighter than the other by comparison), yet both of these colors may appear entirely different because they are of different color strength. The one blue is a strong blue (very chromatic) and the other a weak, grayish blue (less chromatic). This difference in color strength is the difference in the amount of chroma present in each blue. Chroma can be measured scientifically showing the degree of a color's strength ranging from maximum chroma (full intensity) to neutral gray.

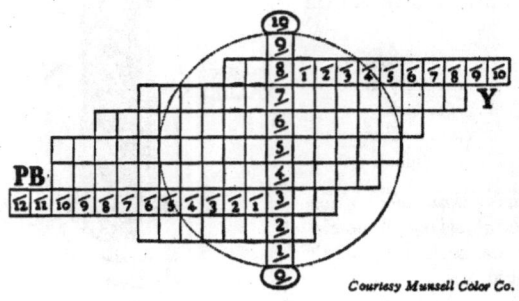

This Diagram shows how Yellow Reaches its Strongest Chroma at the Eighth Level of Value, whereas its Opposite Purple-blue Reaches its Strongest Chroma at the Third Level of Value.

Courtesy Munsell Color Co.

Munsell Steps (chroma)	Description
N to 1	very weak
2 to 4	weak
5 to 7	moderate
8 to 10	strong
11 to 13	very strong
14 and beyond	vivid

Putting this into practical application in decoration we find that *colors of strong chroma are difficult to live with in excessive amounts.* Keep them for your spot of zip, and for accessories.

Just as you found that marked contrasts in value intensified each other, you will find that strong contrasts in chroma react that same way. A light hue, for example, of moderate chroma, as sky blue, will appear weak and whitish when placed against a black background. The strong contrast in value of black overpowers the weaker hue and chroma of light blue. This same sky blue, however, will seem appreciably stronger in chroma if combined with white.

Any hue of strong chroma tends to induce its complementary color in a neutral. Red, for instance, when used with neutral gray makes the gray take on a greenish cast. If in your decorating you are using a neutral color as gray for the walls with a red rug or sofa, mix some red into the gray making it a warm gray for a more pleasing harmony. With blue or green mix the gray to be a cool gray.

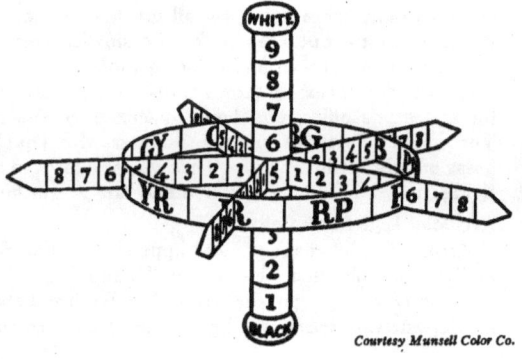

Diagram Shows Hue, Value and Chroma in Relation to One Another. Circular Band Represents the Hues in Proper Sequence. Upright Center Axis is Scale of Value. Paths Pointing Outward from Center Show Steps of Chroma Increasing in Strength as Indicated by Numerals.

Courtesy Munsell Color Co.

Light Reflection

Perhaps you have wondered at the appreciable difference a change of wall color makes in a room. The bedroom walls were a dull medium blue. When redecorating you switched to a light daffodil yellow. Sunlight flooded in. The reason is not because you associate yellow with sunshine, but because colors *absorb and reflect light in varying degrees.* Colors (in pigment) absorb a percentage of the natural or artificial light in the room and reflect the balance. White (there is no pure white in pigment) is the most nearly perfect and most closely approaches white light. It absorbs but 11 per cent of the light in the room, leaving the room up to 89 per cent light reflection, depending upon the prevailing conditions. The same room with ivory walls is still less light, and with silver gray becomes quite dark. The following chart gives you a working comparison.

This chart was compiled from the testing of paint colors of standard hues and all of the same texture.

	Per cent		Per cent
White	89	Buff	63
Ivory	82	Pale Green	59
Canary Yellow	77	Shell Pink	55
Cream	77	Bright Sage	52
Caen Stone	76	Silver Gray	46
Orchid	67	Olive Tan	43
Cream Gray	66	Forest Green	22
Ivory Tan	66	Cocoanut Brown	16
Sky Blue	65	Black	2

Light values of the same color are, of course, more light giving than darker values of that hue would be.

Walls, ceilings, floors, or any large color area have so much to "say" about the overall results in decorating that it is important to consult this chart. Why use shell pink walls in an already dark bedroom when ivory would add so much more more light? By all means use the shell pink if you want to, but keep it for the smaller areas such as draperies or bedspread and dressing table.

Or why use cocoanut brown walls (16 per cent reflection) for a doctor's office, and hope to encourage the patients? You might offset this extreme dullness with equally large areas of light, brilliant color. Then you would have a sophisticated room, no doubt, but it would not be soothing.

Artificial Light and Color

Artificial light changes color appreciably. For the effect of light on color see Chapter on "Lamp Light." Consult the charts giving you the marked difference between incandescent and fluorescent lighting in relation to color.

Basic Color Schemes—Which To Use and Why

The deft hand combines any colors with success, for it knows the right amount of what goes with what, and how to add that dash for color excitement. Yet even the experienced hand has developed its schemes according to one of the three basic possibilities:

The Three Basic Schemes:
> MONOCHROMATIC—variation of one color theme.
> ANALOGOUS—harmony of related colors.
> CONTRASTING OR COMPLEMENTARY—involving one or more pairs of complementary colors.

MONOCHROMATIC: The bluejay's coloring is an excellent example of a monochromatic color scheme. His feathers are *variations in chroma and value of one color, with the added possibilities of white, black or neutral gray.* This is the key to a whole room scheme and can be as sophisticated as it is subtle if worked cleverly. In a monochromatic scheme, which, of course, includes walls, floor, fabrics and all major accents in the room, you must rely on interesting textures in fabrics and strong value contrasts to relieve the monotony of everything being of one color concentration. This is of major importance or your room will be doomed from the start, for your eyes readily tire of one color sensation. They constantly crave new color interest. Marked contrasts in textures, as a nubby fabric and then a smooth one, and marked contrasts in value, as a light green, then a strong chromatic one much darker in comparison, stimulate interest and give your scheme vitality. To your monochromatic scheme add areas of white, black or neutral gray and the room becomes even more vibrant. But at its best a monochromatic scheme becomes surfeiting if lived with for long periods at a time. For this reason it is the least popular of all schemes and is best adapted to the odd bedroom, breakfast nook, bathroom, hallway—any room not too constantly frequented or where you stay for a long period at a time.

MONOCHROMATIC

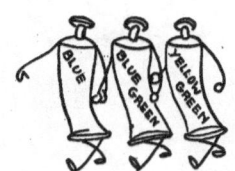
ANALOGOUS

COMPLEMENTARY

ANALOGOUS: Slipping into a smarter choice, second in popularity, is the analogous scheme, *the one of close harmony combining only related colors.* This means those in juxtaposition on the color wheel, such as blue-green, green, and yellow-green all sharing the common color factor, blue. You see an analogous color scheme in nature in a woodland scene in spring with the foliage a blending of the light yellow-green of the new buds and leaves, the deeper green

Circle Represents Color Wheel.

Analogous

Complementary

Split Complementary

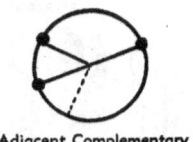

Adjacent Complementary

Triad

of developed leaves or fir trees to the blue-green of the spruce.

There is more "give" and color range in the analogous scheme than in the monochromatic and it holds your interest. It is particularly adaptable for special seasonal effects such as that achieved in a cooling room for a tropical home. Or it is used for a definite color sensation, as in a Modern room where textures of fabrics and graining of woods vie with color for importance.

The analogous scheme is well used in conjunction with a complementary or contrasting scheme (described later). Suppose your living room is developed in that ever-popular combination of rose, blue and gold (a scheme of contrasts), and your hall and dining room open directly from the living room so that you see all three rooms at the same time. Then an interesting and harmonious plan would be to expand the living room theme by using for the hall a monochromatic scheme of one of the living room colors (the rose, for instance) and developing an analogous scheme around the blue for the dining room. Which color you would use for the hall or dining room would, of course, depend upon the room itself, as you will know when you have completed the story of color and learned to analyze rooms at a glance.

CONTRASTING OR COMPLEMENTARY: The third and most popular choice of color schemes is the *combination of complementary colors from both the warm and cool color groups*, in a beautiful "harmony" such as you find in an old-fashioned flower garden. I use the word "harmony" advisedly, for although these colors are in direct contrast, they are pleasing in combination. This type of scheme may be built around one or more pairs of complements, adjacent complements, or triads as described below.

Complementary scheme uses any pair of hues opposite on the color circle, as red and blue-green.

Split Complementary Scheme consists of any one hue and the two hues to the right and left of its complement, red, blue, green.

Adjacent Complementary consists of a complementary pair and a third hue either to the right or left of either one of the pair. Red-yellow, blue and blue-purple.

Triadic scheme consists of any three colors equidistant on the color circuit. Red, yellow and blue.

White, black, or neutral gray may be added to any of these combinations from monochromatic to triadic without changing its classification.

There is no other color harmony that is as psychologically satisfying and good to live with as any one of these COMPLEMENTARY *schemes.* A complementary scheme, in its admixture of warmth and coolness, always combining colors from both color clans, brings color balance emotionally. The stimulation and excitement of the warm colors is relieved by relaxation and rest provided by the intervals of the cool colors. Physically it brings eye happiness, for your eyes soon fatigue when stimulated by only one color. It's like listening to one note on the piano until you crave a change. And decoratively your maneuver possibilities are greater with both warm and cool colors at your command. You may switch them in the scheme as the situation demands. Provide a predominance of warmth in the room where cheer is wanted, but make it more livable by adding cool color complements. Spice a cool serenity with warm complements to insure that necessary feeling of life. But combine the colors so that you have one thing or the other, NEVER JUST A FIFTY-FIFTY COLOR PROPOSITION WITH THE SAME AMOUNT OF BOTH WARM AND COOL COLORS IN THE SAME ROOM.

As you work with colors, you are not, of course, going to proceed with these diagrams in hand. With a little study you'll soon have them in your head! Once having analyzed color schemes and learned how to develop them, you will automatically combine the right colors for the desired effects.

Color Distribution

Fully as important as your selection of colors is their allocation. You must by now start to have the "feel" of color.

In art, equal areas of warm and cool colors, light and dark, strong and weak, are not only tiresome, they are not good color balance. This is due to the differences in hue characteristics, value, and chromatic strength. So in your decorating you can count on:

1. A lesser amount of warm color to counterbalance a greater area of coolness. For example, in a room decorated in rose, yellow and green, a considerably smaller area of rose and yellow (gold) will hold its own against a much larger area of the green.
2. A little dark to offset much light. A smaller amount of dark green balances a large amount of light yellow.

3. A small spot of brilliant coloring to balance a larger proportion of a muted tone, such as coral with soft moss green.

Color Rhythm

Do not introduce a brilliant tone in one spot alone. Be certain to repeat it elsewhere in the room even if only in the coloring of a picture, lamp base, the welting on a pair of cushions, or some accessory.

Color Linking

If a room is so separated from the other rooms of the house that it is seen as a unit alone, then the neighboring room schemes need not be considered. Rooms, however, often give one directly upon the other, such as an open hall connecting living room and dining room, or just the archway separating living room and dining room, practically making the two rooms one. These require COLOR LINKING for a pleasant color continuity.

You *link* one room to the next by employing a common color factor, sometimes by using the same scheme, but with different variations in pattern and fabrics; sometimes by repeating one color note throughout and adding different notes of emphasis in each room. In the latter case it might be plum, apricot, and green in the living room and apricot and blue in the second room, apricot being the linking color, as well as the blue, for there is blue in both plum and green.

Similar color in adjacent rooms does much to extend the vista in the small house, especially in using the same wall color. This avoids any abruptness such as one finds in the overworked color combination in a wine and blue dining room with its ubiquitous American Oriental rug, and a green, rust and gold living room. Each scheme screams at the other.

Color linking is not as limited in scope as you might at first believe. In fact it isn't limited at all; the two basic principles given above diversify in many directions. You might "lift" one of the colors from your living room theme and develop it into a monochromatic scheme for the adjoining dining alcove. Still another variation would be to again lift one of the major colors, as the link, and from it work an analogous scheme. Or when using the same color background, try a striped wallpaper for one room and a floral paper of the same colors for the next. The third room might be one of the plain colors of either design. These matching color scheme papers are now made by leading wallpaper companies. These themes and their variations go on and on, for even though you use the same colors in several rooms you can alter the proportions.

Color and Your Emotions

Live with colors that keep you happy. Color is a positive emotional force in your life. Scientists have proved that color so influences your nervous system that the colors you live with and wear have a definite bearing on keeping the corners of your mouth smilingly upward or dolefully down. Right now you can probably think of a favorite room that always gives you a color lift. Right now you can probably turn to a special hat or dress that gives you that springy, buoyant feeling because colorfully it does something for you.

Decorate with colors that you like. Never let a professional decorator assert his or her color preferences over yours either because you are too embarrassed to contradict, or because you are afraid that your preference isn't the fashionable thing. Regardless of the room, you can work out a scheme with your favorite colors once you know how to do it.

Color Preferences

Everyone has definite color preferences. Even your goldfish and hens cater to color!* RED is the favorite color of the great majority of women (incidentally of hens*) whereas BLUE is the preference of the average man (and the choice of fish*).

* By way of explanation and apology: Most animals are partly or completely color blind. Your poodle dog, for instance, doesn't care whether that bow you put on his neck is pink or otherwise, nor is that bull on the farm at all perturbed by your red dress. But, interestingly, bees are "strong" for yellow and blue. From a number of colored feeding dishes chickens seem to prefer red. Under a play of colored lights fish swim towards blue.

Women are conceded to be more sensitive to color than men. One man in every twenty is to some extent color blind, whereas only one out of two hundred women has defective color vision. Color's popularity chart for a mixed audience placed red first, blue a good second, with violet, green, orange and yellow considerably behind.

SHADES *and* TINTS *are preferred to strong rainbow hues when used in large amounts. But most people prefer the brightest tones as small accent areas.*

The fact that each member of your family has a different color favorite is no complication in effective decorating, for each one's particular room may be done to his or her taste while the general living rooms achieve a harmony agreeable to all.

Your Color Feelings

Unconsciously, over a long period of time, you have become accustomed to identifying different colors with your emotional reaction to these colors. "Feeling blue," "green with envy," "purple with rage," and "dark brown taste" are only everyday expressions which reflect an unconscious relating of mood to color. Upon further thought you may even discover that you have been employing that same color term (though generally a different shade or variation of that color is in your mind) for both happy and unhappy experiences.

CONCRETELY

Positive, happy reactions

YELLOW, characteristic of sun, cheer and lights. Most luminous of colors. Symbol of divine glory. Sacred color in China.

RED, the strongest color, is emblematic of vigor, life and courage. Positive, stimulating, and aggressive. Flag of the Crusader and the oldest color name in art.

BLUE, serene, passive, and steadfast. "Beautiful for spacious skys." Symbolic of truth, as "true blue." "Blue blood" in terms of good breeding.   Nonsensuous.   Expression of boundlessness and space.

GREEN, restful, refreshing, young life. More passive and not as reactionary as other colors. (Symbol of Baptism and Easter.)

PURPLE, dignified, rich. The color of royalty. It incorporates the vigor of red and the sincerity of blue. Healing.

WHITE, GRAY, BLACK, although theoretically not classified as colors, but as neutrals, also have emotional associations and reactions.

WHITE, graceful, delicate and airy. A positive color. Stands for purity, innocence, truth and peace.

Negative, unfavorable symbolism

"A streak of yellow" or "yellow dog" indicative of the coward. Usually a greenish yellow in color thought.

"I see red." Rage, danger, strife and anarchy.

"Blue from cold," or "I feel blue" when the corners of your mouth turn down.

"Green with envy." Freshness in terms of callow youth.

Purple is the sign of mourning. Violet is reticent and melancholy. Sign of advanced age.

"White as a sheet," ghostly. Sign of surrender in battle. Mourning color in China.

GRAY, a welcome neutral and fine foil for colors. Not as uncompromising as white or burdensome as black.

Gray signifies resignation and old age.

BLACK, full bodied, smart. Small amounts agreeable, especially if used as a background for brilliant coloring.

Black denotes deepest sorrow, gloom and foreboding.
Evil lurks in darkness.

These positive and negative associations should not, however, confuse you. As much as you like candy and continue to enjoy it, there is always the moment when its sweetness has no appeal. Irrespective of how much you are encouraged by red, or soothed by blue, there are times when red's strident note, especially in a large dose, gives you the jitters; or blue's excessive chill plunges your spirits to a new low. There's an old saying that blue homes make blue brides and crying babies. (Science has demonstrated that blue light retards the pulse rate and lowers blood pressure, whereas red light quickens it.) A greenish-yellow can literally upset you at the wrong moment—such is the power of color in your life.

Avoid many a jitter-producing moment by simply never using too much of any one color (especially in strong, intense tones) in any one room.

Personality of the House

In any event don't be afraid to use color and use it lavishly. If colorful, your house is a place where guests like to linger and you are *happy* to have them stay. Otherwise it is a drab nonentity because YOU HAVE BEEN A TIMID MOUSE WITHOUT THE COURAGE OF YOUR COLOR CONVICTIONS.

If your color problems have not been covered here, you will find the answers in subsequent chapters. Color, as it specifically applies to each phase of decorating, is developed further in each chapter.

www.ingramcontent.com/pod-product-compliance
Lightning Source LLC
Chambersburg PA
CBHW032001220426
43664CB00005B/95